W9-ATY-542

We <u>Have</u> Come A Long Way

40 2
POINTS 1 2 3 4 5
30 3
SEIKO
AVIS

We Have Come A Long Way

The Story of Women's Tennis

By Billie Jean King
with Cynthia Starr

A REGINA RYAN BOOK

McGRAW-HILL
BOOK COMPANY

New York St. Louis San Francisco Auckland Bogotá Hamburg London Madrid Mexico
Milan Montreal New Delhi Panama Paris São Paulo Singapore Sydney Toyko Toronto

Book Producer:
Regina Ryan Publishing Enterprises, Inc.

Editor: Regina Ryan
Design: Michaelis/Carpelis Design Associates, Inc.
Production Editor: Nan Jernigan
Administrative Editor: Maggie Higgins
Copy Editor: Renate Glaser
Proofreader: Pauline Piekarz
Picture Research: Wendy Talve Reingold
Sue Maynard
Indexer: Catherine Dorsey
Typesetting: Creative Graphics, Inc.
Printer: Horowitz/Rae

A REGINA RYAN BOOK

1 2 3 4 5 6 7 8 9 8 9 2 1 0 9 8

ISBN 0-07-034625-9

Library of Congress Cataloging-in-Publication Data

King, Billie Jean.
We have come a long way: the story of women's tennis / by Billie Jean King and Cynthia Starr.
p. cm.
"A Regina Ryan book."
Includes index.
ISBN 0-07-034625-9
1. Tennis–History. 2. Women tennis players.
I. Starr, Cynthia. II. Title.
GV992.K56 1988
796.342'088042–dc19 88–21816
CIP

Frontispiece, Chris Evert, foreground, and Mary Joe Fernandez, compete in Louis Armstrong Stadium during the 1986 U.S. Open at the USTA National Tennis Center. Slew Hester, USTA president from 1977 to 1979, was the driving force behind the open's move from the cramped grounds of Forest Hills to the National Tennis Center in 1978.

CONTENTS

ACKNOWLEDGMENTS

The authors and their producers thank the following individuals and institutions for their invaluable assistance in the production of *We Have Come a Long Way*: The people of Virginia Slims, who have made significant contributions to this book and to the game of women's tennis. Their enduring commitment to the game has gone a long way toward making women's tennis the great success it is today. Frank Van Rensselaer Phelps of King of Prussia, Pennsylvania, who shared the results of his own personal research into the early history of tennis in England and the United States; who provided access to hundreds of documents from his personal files; and who served as a worthy critic during the writing of this book. Julia S. Morris of Ann Arbor, Michigan, who researched hundreds of newspapers, magazines, and books; who served as an important critic; and who was there when we needed her, every step of a very long way. Sally Rousham of Loughborough, in Leicestershire, England, for her most professional research into the early history of women's tennis. Elizabeth Jochnick of West Hartford, Connecticut, who shared the results of her long and studious research into the life of Charlotte "Lottie" Dod. Patricia M. Barry of Staten Island, New York, who shared the fruits of her voluminous research into the life of Mary Ewing Outerbridge and her family.

The authors also thank the contributing researchers: Carrol Robertsen, Joe D. Morris, Connie Miller, Marie Thole, Carolyn Rehder, Beverly Morris, Katie Canty, Karen Garloch, Helen Russell, Marilyn August, Cindy Schmerler, and Robin Adair. We thank our translators, Ken Fisher of Xavier University and Marie Thole of Cincinnati. Special thanks to the following individuals: Alan Little of the Kenneth Ritchie Wimbledon Library and Valerie Warren of the Wimbledon Lawn Tennis Museum; Maureen Hanlon and Richard A. Remmert of the Women's International Tennis Association; Kacey Constable and Jan Armstrong of the International Tennis Hall of Fame; Lesley Poch of the Unites States Tennis Association; Charles L. Sachs of the Staten Island Historical Society; Tobi Smith and Carol Miller of the Santa Monica Heritage Museum; Szilvia E. Szmuk of the William Fischer Library at St. John's University; Nancy Bolger, Annalee Thurston, Ina Broeman, Vicki Berner, and Diane Desfor of Virginia Slims; Caryl Newhof of Smith College; Carla Stewart of Wellesley College; Caroline Rittenhouse of Bryn Mawr College; Jutta Field of Loyola University; Sargent Hill; Tim Gregg; Bonnie Hagerman of International Management Group; Phil de Picciotto of Advantage International; Mary Jo Schmees of Exec-Sec; Paul Deutschman and Maggie Higgins of Regina Ryan Publishing Enterprises, Inc.; Mary Witherell of *World Tennis*; Helen Russell and Ingrid Burkart of Domino's Pizza TeamTennis; Marianne Delhaye of the French Tennis Federation; G. Sanders of the German Tennis Federation; James Nicholls of Great Britain's Lawn Tennis Association; Greg Noble and Charlie Fry of *The Cincinnati Enquirer*; William A. Starr; Rose Laibson and Anne Wiemels. We thank the Kenneth Ritchie Wimbledon Library, the Ann Arbor Public Library, the Harlan Hatcher Graduate Library at the University of Michigan, the Public Library of Cincinnati and Hamilton County, and the Philadelphia Free Library.

We thank Margaret Osborne duPont, Louise Brough Clapp, Margaret Varner Bloss, Shirley Fry Irvin, Sarah Palfrey Danzig, Doris Hart, Gladys Heldman, and Ceci Martinez, who went beyond the call of duty in helping to ensure the completeness and accuracy of this book.

We thank the women players, past and present, who provided interviews: Kitty McKane Godfree, Pauline Betz Addie, Shirley Fry Irvin, Doris Hart, Sarah Palfrey Danzig, Ann Haydon Jones, Maria Bueno, Dorothy Bundy Cheney, Louise Brough Clapp, Margaret Osborne duPont, Margaret Varner Bloss, Darlene Hard, Margaret Smith Court, Angela Mortimer Barrett, Christine Truman Janes, Althea Gibson, Kay Stammers Bullitt, Thelma Coyne Long, Rosie Casals, Betty Stove, Evonne Goolagong Cawley, Wendy Turnbull, Nancy Richey, Olga Morozova, Stephanie DeFina Hagan, Valerie Ziegenfuss Bradshaw,

Pam Teeguarden, Cynthia Doerner, Peachy Kellmeyer, Ceci Martinez, Tracy Austin, Wendy White, Michelle Torres, Bonnie Gadusek, Terry Phelps, Carling Bassett Seguso, Manuela Maleeva, Peanut Louie, Zina Garrison, Lori McNeil, Rafaella Reggi, Susan Sloane, Martina Navratilova, Hana Mandlikova, Andrea Jaeger, Chris Evert, Pam Shriver, Helena Sukova, and Steffi Graf. Finally, we thank the following individuals for their interviews: Jimmy Evert, Lee Jackson, Merrett Stierheim, Pat Yeomans, Susy Jaeger Davis, Rex Bellamy, Brian Tobin, John Parsons, Rino Tommasi, Philippe Chatrier, Joseph F. Cullman 3d, Ellen Merlo, Pancho Gonzales, Jeff Austin, Pat Sloane, Bill Talbert, Sandra Haynie, Gary Addie, Allan and Mumsey Nemiroff, Bud Collins, Bob Kelleher, Conny Konzack, Pavel Slozil, Jerry Diamond, J. Howard (Bumpy) Frazer, Ron Woods, and Doug MacCurdy.

ILLUSTRATION CREDITS

Frontis.: Russ Adams Productions.

Ch. 1: 1, left, from *Tennis Origins and Mysteries,* Malcolm D. Whitman, The Derrydale Press, New York, 1932/William M. Fischer Lawn Tennis Collection, St. John's University, New York; center, Wimbledon Lawn Tennis Museum; right, Paul Thompson/William M. Fischer Lawn Tennis Collection, St. John's University, New York; 3, Isaac Almstaedt/Pat Barry; 4, top, Isaac Almstaedt/Staten Island Historical Society; bottom, Isaac Almstaedt/Pat Barry; 7, Wimbledon Museum; 8, from *Lottie Dod,* by Alan Little, Wimbledon Museum; 9, 10, Wimbledon Museum; 12, Smith College Archives; 13, USTA; 14, Hall of Fame, Newport, R.I.; 18, t. courtesy of Dorothy Bundy Cheney; b. Santa Monica Historical Museum; 21, Paul Thompson/William M. Fischer Lawn Tennis Collection, St. John's University, New York. ***Ch. 2:*** 23, 1. UPI/Bettmann Newsphotos; c. Photoworld/FPG; r. UPI/Bettmann Newsphotos; 25, t. l. The Granger Collection; t. r. UPI/Bettmann Newsphotos; b. The Bettmann Archive/BBC Hulton Picture Library; 27, from *Suzanne Lenglen* by Alan Little, Wimbledon Museum; 28, The Keystone Collection; 29, UPI/Bettmann Newsphotos; 30, t. Photoworld/FPG; b. Wimbledon Museum; 31, 32, UPI/Bettmann Newsphotos; 33, Edwin Leric; 35, Wimbledon Museum; 36, UPI/Bettmann Newsphotos; 37, t. Reuters/Bettmann Newsphotos; b. UPI/Bettmann Newsphotos; 38, 40, The Bettmann Archive; 41, Wimbledon Museum; 42, l. Topical Press Agency/USTA; r. Wimbledon Museum; 43, The Bettmann Archive; 44, AP/Wide World; 45, USTA; 46, t. Durant Collection/*Sports Illustrated,* photo by AP/Wide World; b. l. AP/Wide World; b. r. UPI/Bettmann Newsphotos; 48, 50, AP/Wide World; 51, The Bettmann Archive/BBC Hulton Picture Library. ***Ch. 3:*** 53, l. Sport and General/Wimbledon Museum; c. AP/Wide World; r. The Keystone Collection; 55, Leslie Gill, courtesy of Sarah Palfrey; 57, AP/Wide World; 59, courtesy of Margaret O. duPont; 61, Benn Schnall/USTA; 63, courtesy of Margaret O. duPont; 64, Reuters/Bettmann Newsphotos; 65, Black Star, New York; 66, 67, 68 AP/Wide World. ***Ch. 4:*** 73, l., r. Arthur Cole/LeRoye Productions; c. AP/Wide World; 75, l. The Press Association Ltd.; r. UPI/Bettmann Newsphotos; 77, UPI/Bettmann Newsphotos; 81, b. Arthur Cole/LeRoye Productions; t. Keystone Press/Wimbledon Museum; 82, The Press Association Ltd.; 84, AP/Wide World; 85, Photoworld/FPG; 86, 87, AP/Wide World; 89, l. UPI/Bettmann Newsphotos; r. Arthur Cole/LeRoye Productions; 90, The Keystone Collection/Wimbledon Museum; 94, Times Newspapers Ltd./Wimbledon Museum; 95, UPI/Bettmann Newsphotos. ***Ch. 5:*** 97, l., r. Arthur Cole/LeRoye Productions; c. Photoworld/FPG; 99, Photoworld/FPG; 101, Photoworld/FPG; 103, The Keystone Collection; 104, Wimbledon Museum; 105, D. R. Stuart, courtesy of Margaret O. duPont; 106, Arthur Cole/LeRoye Productions; 108, t. Russ Adams; b. l., r., 110, 111, Arthur Cole/LeRoye Productions; 112, Max Peter Haas/FPG; 113, Arthur Cole/LeRoye Productions; 114, AP/Wide World; 116, Arthur Cole/LeRoye Productions. ***Ch. 6:*** 119, l. Michael Cole; c. Russ Adams; r. Times Newspapers Ltd.; 122, AP/Wide World; 124, Walter Iooss/*SI*; 126, *Houston Post*; 129, t. Palm-Aire/Virginia Slims; b. l. The Keystone Collection; b. r. Russ Adams; 132, AP/Wide World; 133, 134, Times Newspapers Ltd.; 135, 137, 139, Russ Adams; 140, Gayle Burns; 143, courtesy of *World Tennis* Magazine. ***Ch. 7:*** 147, l. Michael Cole; c. Cheryl A. Traendly; r. Michael Cole; 149, UPI/Bettmann Newsphotos; 151, Russ Adams; 153, l. Paul Tople/*Akron Beacon Journal*; r. Michael Cole; 154, Melinda Phillips; 155, t., b. l. AP/Wide World; b. r. UPI/Bettmann Newsphotos; 157, 158, 159, Michael Cole; 160, AP/Wide World; 161, Russ Adams; 163, UPI/Bettmann Newsphotos; 165, Michael Cole; 167, Carol L. Newsom/Virginia Slims; 168, t. AP/Wide World; b. Carol L. Newsom; 169, Michael Cole; 170, Melinda Phillips. ***Ch. 8:*** 171, l. Carol L. Newsom/Virginia Slims; c. Times Newspapers Ltd.; r. Russ Adams; 172, Carol L. Newsom; 175, AP/Wide World; 176, Michael Cole; 177, Carol L. Newsom; 179, 180, 181, l. Michael Cole; r. Reuters/Bettmann Newsphotos; 182, Michael Cole; 184, Melinda Phillips; 185, 186, Carol L. Newsom/Virginia Slims; 188, Michael Baz; 189, Carol L. Newsom; 190, Melinda Phillips. ***Color Section:*** 1, l. Michael Cole; r. George Long/*SI*; 2, t. l., r., b. l. Russ Adams; b. r. Jerry Cooke/*SI*; 3, t., c. Michael Cole; b. Kevin Fitzgerald; 4, l. Russ Adams/Chris Morrow; r. Melchior DiGiacomo; 5, t. Russ Adams/*SI*; r. c. Walter Iooss/*SI*; b. Fred Mullane/*Time*; 6, l. Russ Adams/*SI*; r. Russ Adams; 7, t. Jacqueline Duvoisin/*SI*; b. Tommy Hindley; 8, t. Steve Powell/*SI*; b. Michael Cole; 9, t. Russ Adams/*SI*; b. Manny Millan/*SI*; 10, l. Russ Adams; r. Steve Powell/*SI*; 11, t. l. Melinda Phillips; t. r. James Drake/*SI*; b. Michael Cole; 12, Paul Zimmer; 13, l. Carol L. Newsom; r., 14, Russ Adams; 15, t. Manny Millan/*SI*; 15, b. Steve Powell/*SI*; 16, l. James Drake/*SI*; r. Russ Adams.

A NOTE TO THE READER

This is a book I have wanted to read ever since I was a child playing tennis on the public courts in Long Beach, California: the story of women's tennis. As a youngster I had difficulty finding any books about the sport I loved best. My library had only two, *How to Use Your Head in Tennis* by Bob Harmon, a teaching professional in Southern California, and *Tennis with Hart* by Doris Hart, the tennis star of the 1940s and 1950s. I wanted to read more—especially about history. It would have meant so much to me if I could have read about all the great women champions I admired so much.

In recent years libraries and stores have offered many books about women's tennis, but most have been autobiographical and instructional. The history books usually dealt with only the most famous female Wimbledon champions and typically devoted the majority of their pages to the men's game. None gave a detailed history of the modern era in women's tennis, a rich and dynamic period that began with the original Virginia Slims tour in 1970. I decided that if I wanted to see a complete history of women's tennis in print, I would have to do it myself.

When I began this project with my coauthor, Cynthia Starr, and my book producer, Regina Ryan, in the spring of 1985, we had several goals in mind. We wanted to document a fascinating story for posterity while many of the key personalities and players were still alive. We wanted to have the champions tell us, in their own words, how they saw themselves and their careers. Equally important, we wanted to tell the story of the enormous struggle for equality in women's tennis and to give credit where credit was due—not only to the players but also to the sponsors, promoters, media, and fans whose contributions are vital to the success of any entertainment package.

To achieve these goals, I recounted many of my own experiences during my long and occasionally turbulent playing career, which extended from 1959 through 1983. My coauthor, meanwhile, interviewed 80 individuals: current and former players, coaches, officials, and journalists. She and her team of researchers also read dozens of autobiographies and other tennis books, many of them old and out of print, and pored over thousands of periodicals and newspaper clippings. Together, with the help of our picture researchers, we examined thousands of photographs in search of those that would best illustrate the story of women's tennis.

Truth, we found, was often elusive. Memories frequently proved inadequate, and accounts of some historic events differed vastly. We did our utmost throughout to be accurate and fair.

Our main regret is that the book could not have included a section on every single person who helped further the game of women's tennis. To accomplish that task, we would have needed to write two books, not one.

Even so, we believe you have before you the most complete story of women's tennis ever told. It is a book for everyone—young and old, male and female—who loves tennis. It is also a book for anyone who enjoys reading about people who made a difference. We hope you draw inspiration and encouragement from the pages within.

Billie Jean King
May, 1988

Chapter 1

Early Times

1874-1914

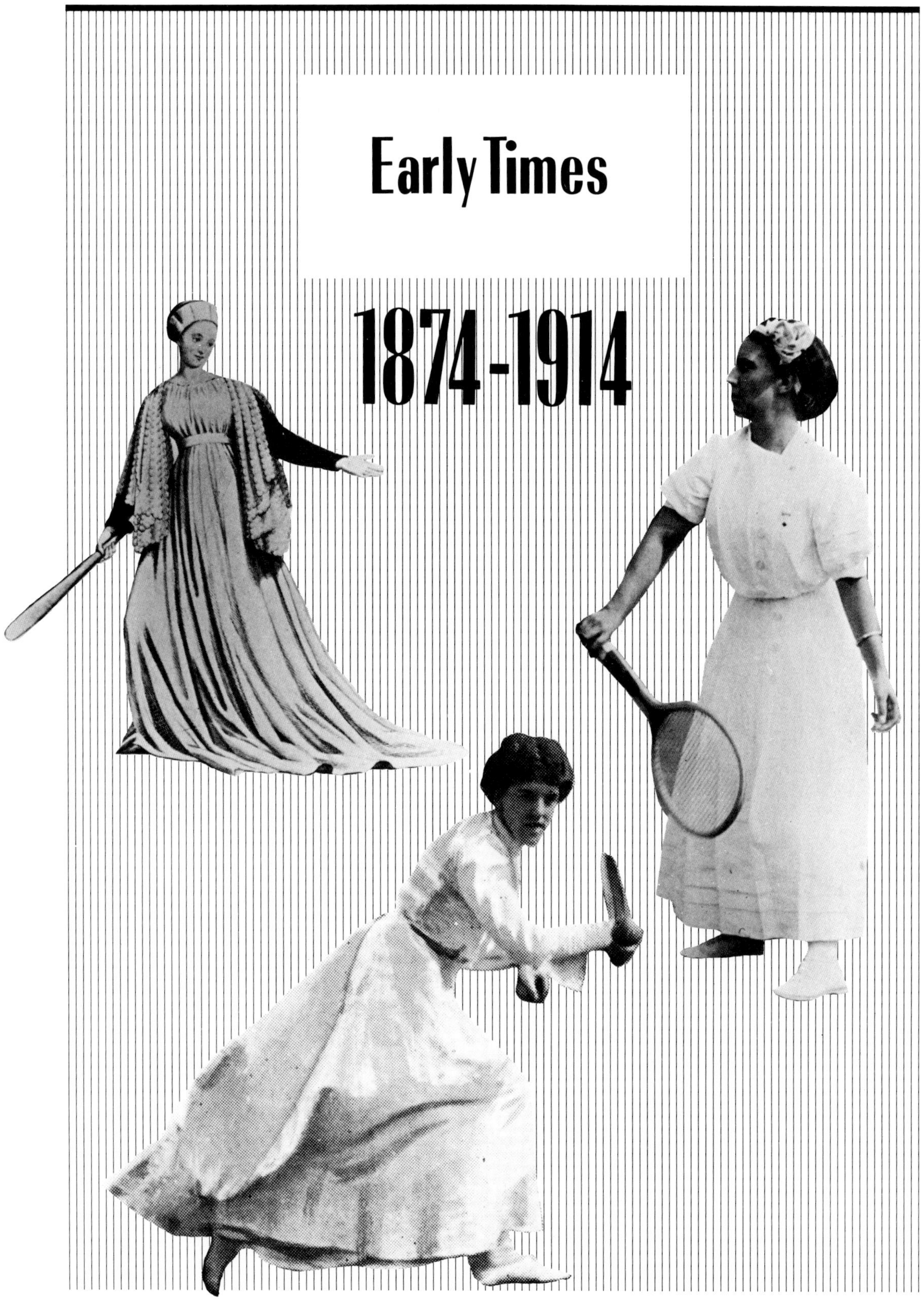

Early Times

They were there from the beginning. Tennis, from the start, was a game for women, too. The sport's female pioneers took the court in ground-length skirts, petticoats, and steel-boned corsets, with collars up to their chins and sleeves down to their wrists. They could not have run very quickly, and they could not have struck the ball hard with their heavy, loosely strung rackets. By today's standards, they were not good at all. Yet they are vitally important in the history of our game. They started a passionate love affair between women and tennis that has lasted for over one hundred years.

The first women to excel at tennis would have been amazed to see the great women players of today. Women's tennis at its highest levels is no longer played for pure enjoyment, with only a title and a silver cup at the end of the rainbow. Today's game is a major-league entertainment business played by highly focused professionals, who can compete and earn a large paycheck every week of the year if they so desire. No garden party, our sport has become a traveling extravaganza of athleticism enjoyed by millions of people around the world.

Nonetheless, if the dominant women players of the past could be united with the outstanding women players of the present, they would discover many parallels in their lives. Each generation of champions felt stress, ambition, and elation. Each experienced disappointment and defeat. Each had advantages that the preceding generation did not have. Each generation, in its own way, came a long way.

Overleaf, a young Frenchwoman, pictured at left in a sixteenth-century sketch, plays court tennis, an ancestor of tennis. Dorothea Lambert Chambers, center, was the greatest woman player from Great Britain before World War I. Hazel Hotchkiss Wightman won four United States championships between 1909 and 1919.

Exactly when a woman first picked up a racket is impossible to determine. Yet we do know that women appear to have played with rackets and balls from the time that such objects came into existence. For centuries women played court tennis, or real tennis, a net-and-racket sport played in an enclosed area. Court tennis, which is played only in isolated circles today, had its origins in twelfth-century France, where sportsmen first played *Jeu de Paume,* French for game of the hand. Court tennis was never as popular with women as tennis, because the racket was heavy and the leather balls, wrapped tightly around a core of wool or human hair, were extremely hard. (So hard, in fact, that King Charles VIII of France died after being hit on the head with one.) Still, some women did play court tennis, and quite skillfully at that.

The earliest known reference to a woman playing court tennis, dated 1427, describes Lady Margot, who came to Paris from Hainault, a town north of Paris, and "played better at hand-ball than any man had seen and played very strongly both forehanded and backhanded, very cleverly as any man could, and there were few men whom she did not beat, except the very best players."

Crude forms of lawn and racket games were in existence in England as early as 1793, and we can assume that women probably took part in them as well. By the 1860s men and women were playing croquet and the more strenuous sport of badminton together on the expansive lawns of the well-to-do. When Major Walter Clopton Wingfield patented the game of lawn tennis on February 23, 1874, a move that made it accessible to thousands of people, women took to it immediately.

Wingfield, a handsome man with a full, bushy beard, was a gentleman-at-arms in the court of Queen Victoria. He certainly intended for women to play his game, which he called *Sphairistike,* Greek for ball and stick. His *Book of the Game,* a rule book that accompanied his first equipment sets, shows a game of mixed doubles played on a court shaped like an hourglass. On his price list for equipment, he included not only "Full-sized Sphairistike Bats" but also "Ladies' Bats."

Major Wingfield's lawn tennis was far more suited to women than court tennis. The lighter balls made the game more enjoyable for women who were not naturally strong or athletic, and because tennis was originally so genteel, it was considered a proper pastime for a well-bred English lady. She could dress up for a garden party in all her Victorian ruffles and then bustle out onto the court just as she was. For her to join in a game of tennis with her friends was as natural, and as acceptable, as having afternoon tea.

Tennis spread rapidly, throughout the British Empire and to other parts of the world. It came to Scotland, Ireland, Bermuda, Australia, and South Africa; to Brazil and Argentina; and to Germany, France, Italy, and Sweden. It came to the United States, at least in part, through the enthusiasm of a young woman from Staten Island, New York.

Mary Ewing Outerbridge, who gave her occupation as "lady," was vacationing in Bermuda in January of 1874 or 1875 when she saw some British officers playing tennis. Mary was so taken with the game that she acquired a net, rackets, and balls from the British regimental supply and took the equipment home with her to New York. The following spring, as soon as the weather allowed, Mary asked for permission to set up a court in one corner of the Staten Island Cricket and Baseball Club.

Mary's younger sister, Laura C. Outerbridge, described the first game of tennis in a letter she wrote to the United States Lawn Tennis Association more than seventy years later, when she was ninety-five years old: "We laid out the course with white tapes, but soon changed to lime. No white line was used at the top of the net, and we made little colored wool tassels to mark the line, and the effect was very pretty. Miss Krebs, sister of the president of the cricket club, became an interested operator and coaxed us to give up the long dresses worn at the time, which touched the ground at the back. So we provided ourselves with flannel dresses to the tops of our boots."

Today we are not sure that the Outerbridge court was truly the first in America. Frederick Sears and James Dwight claimed an American first for their court, laid out on the property of William Appleton in Nahant, near Boston, at about the same time as the Outerbridge court. There is also evidence there was a tennis set in San Francisco as early as 1874.

Mary Outerbridge's brother Eugenius, who later provided the impetus for the founding of the United States National Lawn Tennis Association (USNLTA), wrote in his diary that the family's court was established in 1874, and his sister Laura also held firm to the 1874 date throughout her life. But the first known reference to the court, published in *Outing* magazine in 1887, put the date at 1875.

The debate over whether Mary Outerbridge's court was established in 1874 hinged on whether she could have secured one of Major Wingfield's tennis sets in Bermuda in January, shortly before the game was patented. For a long time, historians thought that she could have, and Mary was inducted into the International Tennis Hall of Fame in Newport, Rhode Island, in 1981 because she was believed to be the first. Now some historians assert that Mary must have purchased her tennis set in January of 1875.

Emma Janssen, an avid player at the Staten Island Cricket and Baseball Club, was said to have had so many suitors that her concentration on tennis was continually interrupted. Isaac Almstaedt, the club's official photographer, took the photograph around 1890.

I think we will never know who was first. Many men probably would be galled to think that tennis was first played in America by a woman. The debate, unless some historian discovers a long-lost piece of information, will have to remain unresolved, an interesting part of the lore of tennis.

In the end, it is probably irrelevant. The fact is that Mary Ewing Outerbridge was an enthusiastic young woman who introduced tennis to New York and helped Staten Island become one of the first prominent tennis cen-

The Staten Island Cricket and Baseball Club was a cradle of women's tennis in the United States. In the top photograph, young ladies pose for Almstaedt in 1887. Alice Austen, top row far right, was to become a famous amateur photographer. In the photograph below, also by Almstaedt, men and women play mixed doubles at the club.

ters in the United States.

For poor Mary, those happy days on the courts of the Staten Island Cricket Club were all too short. She spent her young adulthood caring for the children of her brother Emelius, whose wife had died prematurely. Mary herself did not live to hear the controversy over who set up the first court. In 1886, following three years of illness, she died of kidney disease at the age of thirty-four.

In 1982 a golfer looking for lost balls in an abandoned cemetery adjacent to his Staten Island home found Mary's grave in disrepair. Three years later the United States Tennis Association provided a grant of $1,250 for perpetual care of her grave.

For women, joining the garden party scene was the easiest part of their trek through tennis history. The more difficult second step—to the competitive arena—was blocked for several years by society's views of women and propriety. The thought of wives or daughters competing (and perspiring!) while spectators looked on was more than most gentlemen of the time could bear. The first secretary of England's Lawn Tennis Association, Herbert Chipp, went so far as to call these female athletic pursuits "unalloyed heathenism." No doubt, many men of that era were brought up to think the same thing.

Fortunately, there were some progressive-minded men around, including one we now know only as Mr. Hora. In 1879 Mr. Hora proposed that a ladies' singles tournament be staged by the All England Croquet and Lawn Tennis Club (the words Croquet and Lawn Tennis were later reversed), an increasingly powerful tennis organization based in the town of Wimbledon. Two years earlier, the club had begun a gentlemen's championship. Sadly for the ladies, Mr. Hora's brainstorm met with strong opposition, and his proposal was swiftly struck down during a meeting of the All England Club Committee. "At present," the minutes read, "it is not desirable to have a ladies tennis cup for lady members of the club under any circumstances." The committee did finally adopt a ladies' championship five years later, in 1884, but only after it learned that the London Athletic Club was about to take the step first. Much credit for the committee's belated move went to another forward-thinking man, Henry Jones, cofounder of the All England Croquet Club in 1868 and the inspiration behind the club's addition of tennis courts several years later.

In America competitive tennis for women progressed no more quickly. Although the first United States men's championship was held in 1881, a women's event was not begun until 1887, three years after the inaugural ladies' championship at Wimbledon.

The Irish and the Bermudians, less inhibited than their English counterparts, were the ones to get tournament play for women under way. Although the Dublin aristocracy was deeply influenced by the Victorian principles of the time (Dublin's female players were credited with discovering that white clothing was an excellent means of concealing perspiration), the Irish were not as appalled by the sight of sweaty women as the English.

Dublin's historic, if unheralded, women's tournament was played in 1876 in conjunction with the Irish Championships for men; it had a draw of two, and the record shows that a Miss W. Casey easily defeated a Miss Vance for the title. The Bermudian tournament, also played in 1876, had four entries, and the winner was Mary G. Gray, one of the first women to play tennis in Bermuda.

In Ireland the 1877 women's championships had a draw of only three. The Irish Championships were not held the year after that, but in 1879, when they were revived, the women's draw attracted a record field of eight. Because of the size of the draw, historians recognize this as the first important tournament in women's tennis.

Still, while the men's edition of that championship was played on beautiful grass courts laid out for the occasion on the lawns of Fitzwilliam Square, in the heart of Dublin, the women's matches were played in the heart of obscurity. Male members of the sponsoring Fitzwilliam Club, apparently struck by a case of English prudishness, decided that the Fitzwilliam courts were too public for women. Thus, the ladies' event was relegated to more private grounds. If this slight irritated the women, it did not discourage their participation. May Langrishe, a skillful fourteen-year-old who later competed at Wimbledon, won the championship.

Meanwhile, in England and the United States, women were making inroads into the game. In the early 1880s in England, women began competing in several small tournaments that had sprung up in cities like Edgbaston, Cheltenham, Bath, and Exmouth. In the eastern part of the United States, women were playing at one-third of the forty organized clubs in existence, and they had established a few clubs and tournaments of their own.

By 1884 the debate was raging among tennis aficionados in London and New York as to whether, during a game of mixed doubles, the gentleman should serve his hardest to the lady. While some believed that a man should serve more gently to the female partner than to the male, others argued that this deprived the male server of a rightful chance to win the point. Clearly, the ladies were becoming so proficient that they were formidable opponents, capable of returning soft, gentlemanly serves with considerable force and direction.

By this time women had even risen to the heights of the umpire's chair. The London sports periodical *Pastime* noted in 1884 that one Blanche Williams was asked, in a "daring experiment by the referee," to umpire an important championship match. She performed "in such an effective manner that many of those zealous young men who love to 'sit up aloft' must have felt particularly small."

The proliferation of tournaments enabled the best of the women to become seasoned and skillful competitors, and in the early 1880s, England's Maud Watson emerged as the first woman to dominate her peers. Intense and unflappable, she won the first two ladies' singles championships ever held at Wimbledon, in 1884 and 1885. She also won fifty-four consecutive matches over a five-year period.

Maud Watson was a pretty young woman, with dark curly hair, a longish nose, intent and expressive eyes, and a small mouth. The youngest of three children, she grew up in Berkswell, a small village near Coventry, where her father, the Reverend Henry William Watson, was rector. Her father was also a prominent mathematician. Maud honed her game on the rectory grounds with her older siblings, Lilian and Erskine, and frequently practiced with the male mathematics students who visited her father. Maud reportedly had an even temper, excellent concentration, and a solid forehand and backhand. She often rushed the net, and, unlike many of her female contemporaries, she served overhand instead of underhand. She was a favorite mixed doubles partner among the top male players of the day; she and William Renshaw, a seven-time Wimbledon champion, frequently teamed up, making a formidable pair.

Today the winner of the annual tournament at Maud Watson's tennis club, the Edgbaston Priory Club in Birmingham, is awarded the Maud Watson trophy. Maud won the same silver cup here in the 1880s, and it is more than just a beautiful antique. It is a link to the past, a link to the first great champion of women's tennis. The players love the trophy. I loved winning it in the early 1980s, even though I was allowed to hold it for only a moment. The cup reminded me of what Maud Watson's tennis world must have been like: small, social, and relaxed, like a garden party. People walked or rode their bicycles to the courts. During the matches, they stood around with parasols or sat down and had tea. I could hear them saying "jolly good shot" and "jolly good try" to the runner-up. It was a much slower game in every way.

Maud Watson was nineteen years old in 1884 when she entered the first ladies' singles at Wimbledon as the heavy favorite. She had not lost a match in three years and had recently won the Irish Championship by beating May Langrishe, the defending champion, in the final.

The first ladies' field at Wimbledon consisted of thirteen players and offered an elegant first prize: a silver flower basket, valued at twenty guineas. Second prize was a silver-and-glass hand mirror and a silver brush, worth ten guineas. The ladies' prizes, though pretty, were not equal to those awarded to

Maud Watson, seated, won the first two ladies' singles championships at Wimbledon. She is shown here in 1884 with Ernest Renshaw, also seated, and with her sister, Lilian, and Herbert Lawford. Renshaw and Lawford were top players of the day.

the men. The gentlemen's champion, in addition to winning an expensive prize, also had the honor of temporarily possessing a handsome and valuable silver challenge trophy, a trophy owned by the All England Club and passed along from winner to winner, beginning with the first Wimbledon in 1877.

The 1884 Wimbledon was played at the All England Club's original site on Worple Road. The Centre Court, which could seat at least 2,500, had permanently covered stands for the first time. Major Wingfield's hourglass court had long since been abandoned in favor of the conventional rectangular court; the height of the net, which had been dropping steadily over the years from its original height of five feet at the posts, was three feet six inches at the posts, just as it is today. Spectators were formally dressed, the men in suits and hats, the women in long, pastel dresses. The ladies' singles event—it is called the "ladies' " singles to this day—was held during the second week of July, the week after the gentlemen's singles, along with another new event, the gentlemen's doubles. Despite rainy, blustery weather during the week, tennis enthusiasts found the ladies well worth watching.

Maud Watson, who wielded a handmade wooden racket with an oblong head, provoked much discussion as she ran about the court in her ankle-length white dress, driving and volleying with expertise. Could she, some wondered, beat a good male player? It was a question asked of many top women over the years. One observer there said Maud could defeat one-third of the gentlemen entered in the championship that year, but another argued that "the worst of them" could give her a 30-love lead in every game and still win.

Maud easily beat her first-round opponent, losing only two games to Mrs. A. Tyrwhitt-Drake, who held her racket halfway up the handle, a bizarre style even then. In the semifinals, Maud came from behind to defeat a very determined Blanche Bingley, 3–6, 6–4, 6–2, and then encountered a surprisingly difficult challenge from her own twenty-six-year-old sister, Lilian Watson. Playing before an enthusiastic crowd of between 400 and 500 spectators, Lilian hit numerous outright winners and frequent passing shots when Maud rushed up to the net. But the more talented Maud prevailed, 6–8, 6–3, 6–3, and became the undisputed women's champion of Great Britain, a title she had already earned by reputation.

Maud became Number 1 in Britain in 1884 and remained Number 1 throughout 1885, a year in which she lost only one set. Like all the champions who followed her, Maud had an extra spark, an extra measure of physical ability and mental strength that placed her ahead of her peers. Yet she undeniably had few serious challengers in Britain at that time. The largest known field for a ladies' singles event had consisted of twenty-five players.

Her competitors, however, were rapidly improving, spurred on by the high visibility of the first women's tournament at Wimbledon, and in 1885 Maud began to meet more skillful opponents. In the final of the Irish Championships, she had to labor to defeat Irishwoman Louise Martin in three sets as 3,000 spectators looked on.

Another of Maud's challengers was Charlotte "Lottie" Dod, the thirteen-year-old

''Little Wonder.'' In their first meeting, at the Northern Championships at Manchester, England, Maud barely managed to defeat the strong and athletic Lottie in two difficult sets.

In 1885 at Wimbledon, its second year of women's tennis, the women were again treated unequally. They still had no handsome challenge trophy, and while the defending men's champion was allowed to sit out and play only the ''challenge round,'' a match against the winner of all the preliminary rounds, Maud Watson, the defending ladies' champion, was required to play through each round of the competition. This was common practice at most women's tournaments. *Pastime,* always quick to defend members of ''the fair sex,'' commented: ''Evidently, 'women's rights' will require advocating in lawn-tennis, as elsewhere!''

Maud retained her Wimbledon title that year with a victory over Blanche Bingley, despite suffering from a sudden attack of rheumatism.

In 1886, at a tournament in Bath, Maud's winning streak was ended by the fast-rising newcomer Charlotte Dod. The reign of tennis's first queen was over. Maud lost at the 1886 Wimbledon as well, this time to the much improved Blanche Bingley, who went on to win five additional Wimbledon titles as Mrs. George W. Hillyard. The 1886 match was of historical note because, for the first time, the defending ladies' champion was not required to play a match until the challenge round, and because the women were finally presented with their own challenge trophy. By thus elevating the status of the women's championship, the All England Club Committee showed it was taking the women's event seriously.

The All England Club could not have produced a more distinctive or beautiful challenge trophy than the silver salver, partially overlaid with gold. The word salver, or serving tray, derives from the French noun *salve,* a tray for presenting food to the king, and from the Spanish verb *salva,* to taste food to detect poison. The heavy salver, which was made by Elkington & Co. of Birmingham, England, is nearly nineteen inches in diameter. (The exact weight is a secret known only to the All England Club, which will not reveal it for security reasons.)

The salver is inscribed with the names of the winners from 1884 until the present. The interior of the plate has been filled entirely, and the names of recent champions appear on the exterior. The salver is ornately decorated with mythological figures. The central figure is Temperance, seated, with a lamp in her right hand. Depicted at the base of the salver are Venus, Jupiter, Mercury, and a water goddess. Embossed around the rim are Minerva and figures representing the seven liberal arts: astronomy, geometry, arithmetic, music, rhetoric, logic, and grammar.

Maud Watson remained competitive for a few years after losing the 1886 Wimbledon championship, although a wrist injury hampered her play. She quit competition altogether in 1889, after she nearly drowned in a swimming accident, but she never lost her love of tennis and frequently attended Wimbledon and other tournaments as a spectator. She died in 1946, at the age of eighty-one.

Charlotte ''Lottie'' Dod drew a crowd from the time she was fourteen. She was allowed to wear a shorter-than-normal tennis dress as a child, but not as an adult.

Once Maud Watson had passed her prime, the top position in women's tennis swung back and forth between her former rivals, Blanche Bingley Hillyard and Charlotte Dod. Between them, they captured eleven singles titles at Wimbledon between 1886 and 1900.

The history books invariably refer to Charlotte as Lottie Dod, the singsong name she used as a little girl, but in one of the few documented interviews with this great sportswoman, she said, "Pray do not call me Lottie. My name is Charlotte and I hate to be called Lottie in public." Therefore, I am going to refer to her as Charlotte, because that is what she would have wished.

Charlotte and Blanche had similar backgrounds. They came from English upper-class families, they grew up playing tennis in their backyards, and they had the luxury of being able to devote their lives to sport.

There was one major difference between them, however. Whereas Blanche never tired of the game, Charlotte, the superior athlete, mastered tennis quickly, then gave it up and went on to win national recognition in other sports. Blanche, who won her sixth and last Wimbledon title fourteen years after she won her first, is remembered for her longevity in the game and for her tireless devotion to it. Her career at Wimbledon, which began in 1884 and ended in 1913, spanned more years than that of any other player in the history of the game. She played her first match at Wimbledon at age twenty and her last at forty-nine. She was thirty-six when she won her final singles title in 1900, and she remains the second-oldest winner of the ladies' singles in Wimbledon history. (The oldest was Charlotte Cooper Sterry, who won the 1907 championship at thirty-seven.) Blanche married Commander George Hillyard, who was equally smitten with tennis; he was secretary of the All England Club from 1907 to 1924.

Despite her remarkable record, Blanche was far from being a finished player. She had an excellent forehand, which she could place with accuracy, but she had a weak backhand, an average overhead serve, and no volley. "Her backhand is ugly but sure, while her lobbing is remarkably safe," *Outing* magazine reported in 1901. Blanche herself was never one to boast about her abilities. "I am well aware that my own style of play is in most respects not such as I should hold up as a model," she once wrote.

Blanche Bingley Hillyard did not have classic strokes, but her perseverance and zest for competition brought her six Wimbledon singles titles.

Other players, including Louise Martin of Ireland, had much better form than Blanche, but whereas Louise often fell apart because of nervousness, Blanche steadily ground out victory after victory. As Charlotte Cooper Sterry once said of Blanche, "Certainly no keener player ever stepped on a tennis court." Then, as now, players had to believe in themselves to win.

Blanche's success fluctuated with the presence and absence of Charlotte Dod, her equal in mental toughness and her superior in skill. "I know that when I am within a point or two of losing a game," Charlotte once said, "I *do* feel very determined and remember that I must keep a strict command over myself."

Blanche played Charlotte many times but

defeated her only once, in Charlotte's first year of competitive singles. In the 1887 Wimbledon final, Charlotte routed Blanche, 6–2, 6–0, to become the youngest champion to this day at fifteen years and 285 days. Charlotte played Blanche again in the 1888 final and this time won, 6–3, 6–3.

In 1889, with Charlotte yachting off the coast of Scotland, Blanche won her second Wimbledon, beating Irishwoman Lena Rice in a memorable final. Blanche, who had nearly lost to Lena in the Irish Championships the month before, was beset by an uncharacteristic case of nerves.

Lena won the first set, 6–4, and held double match point at 5–3, 40–15, in the second set. Then Blanche did something that would be unthinkable today. "In my despair," she later wrote, "I said to Mr. Chipp, who was umpiring the match, 'What *can* I do?' His grim answer was, 'Play better, I should think.' I then fully realized that I had not been playing my best game, and that to win I must hit harder. This I did . . . and I snatched this game from the fire—although Miss Rice was three times within a stroke of the match—and I eventually won the set at 8–6." Blanche won the final set, 6–4, and claimed herself "most lucky to win at all."

The following year, Lena Rice became the first, and last, Irishwoman ever to win Wimbledon. She is among the tournament's forgotten champions, most likely because the 1890 women's Wimbledon was among the most forgettable. Only four players entered, and several of the best women were absent. Maud Watson was no longer playing competitively, Blanche Hillyard chose not to compete, and Charlotte Dod was off experimenting with golf. Despite the growth of the women's game, it still had its low points, and this was one of them. Tennis was but one of many activities enjoyed by the upper classes before the turn of the century. Furthermore, the stakes were not yet high enough to entice accomplished players to enter every major event. But the lull of 1890 was short-lived, for Charlotte Dod returned to tennis the next year.

Charlotte, who won five Wimbledons before she permanently retired from competitive tennis in 1893 at twenty-one, was the first great woman athlete in tennis. She lost only five singles matches during her entire career, and she won her Wimbledon titles with the loss of only one set.

In 1901 Charlotte Cooper Sterry became the first player to win the Wimbledon triple crown. Her daughter, Gwen Sterry, played for the British Wightman Cup team in 1927.

She was five feet six, tall for those days, and strong. She had a sweet, round face that masked her fierce determination to excel at everything she did. She was a woman of supreme versatility. She could sing and play the piano, and she was so gifted in athletics that after dominating British tennis, she mastered golf, field hockey, and archery. She won the British national golf championship for women at Troon, Scotland, in 1904; the same year she was co-medalist in qualifying for the United States women's amateur golf championship before losing in the first round. She captured the silver medal for archery in the 1908 London Olympic Games and twice played for England in field hockey competition against Ireland. The *Guinness Book of World Records* lists her as the most versatile sportswoman of all time.

Charlotte Dod was more than a champion: she was a progressive thinker with whom I feel a kinship. She was, first and foremost, a strong advocate of exercise for women, and she set an example with her approach to sports. "She uses her shoulders with a freedom we have not noticed in any other lady," wrote one observer. Charlotte herself said: "Ladies should learn to run and run their hardest, too, not merely stride."

She had "good muscular biceps," which obviously did not bother her one bit. "I have heard that tennis tends to develop the figure unequally, that the arm and shoulder grow out of proportion," Charlotte once said. "But I have never found it so."

In 1888 Charlotte played in tennis's first battle of the sexes. Following a tournament in Exmouth, where she won the mixed doubles title with Wimbledon champion Ernest Renshaw (the twin brother of William), she was pitted against Ernest in a rare exhibition match. Charlotte, never afraid to display her athleticism and ambition, relished such a challenge. As an enthusiastic crowd looked on, Ernest gave her a 30–love lead in every game and barely won, 2–6, 7–5, 7–5.

Charlotte Dod, the fourth and youngest child of a wealthy cotton broker, grew up in Edgeworth House, a large stone house with many chimneys and gables, in Bebington, Cheshire, a four-hour drive from London. Edgeworth had two tennis courts, one grass and the other crushed stone. At age nine Charlotte was playing tennis with her older siblings. She developed a powerful forehand drive and solid backhand, an excellent volley, a fine overhead smash, and an underhand serve that she used throughout her career.

The underhand serve, a remnant of the more genteel garden-party scene, was still widely used in the 1880s and 1890s. Charlotte, whose serve was deep, hard, and well placed, declared that the overhead serve was no more effective against good players than the underhand and was simply an unnecessary exertion.

She was undoubtedly correct, because women could not possibly have hit strong overhead serves. Women were smaller in those days, and their rackets were cumbersome, having evolved into much heavier models than the ones originally patented by Major Wingfield. These "modern" wooden rackets weighed as much as fourteen and a half ounces and had no leather grips. Compared with the graphite rackets of the 1980s, which weighed as little as eleven ounces, those relics must have felt like lead. Besides, how could a woman have executed an effective overhead serve while wearing a tight-fitting dress and corset? I put on one of those outfits for a television special and I could hardly breathe.

As a child, Charlotte was allowed to wear slightly shorter dresses than her rivals and to dress without the steel-boned corsets that were in fashion, a decided advantage. But as she grew older, she, too, was forced to wear ankle-length dresses and corsets. Charlotte, like the other women, adjusted to the clothing restrictions, because many years later she said, "I don't think our old-fashioned dresses were as much of a handicap as people now suppose . . . I remember Mrs. Hillyard telling me that she persuaded Ernest Renshaw to play her one day dressed up in one of her skirts, and it made no difference to his form. But of course it would be shorter on him." In fact, the dress was so short on Ernest that his long pants showed underneath. Unlike a woman, he was never in any danger of tripping over his petticoats.

Charlotte abandoned her tournament career after winning three successive Wimbledon titles; she was ready for new challenges. "The great joy of games," she once said, "is the hard work entailed in learning them."

Charlotte lived in London during her later years and was a frequent visitor at Wimbledon. She died in a nursing home on the southern coast of England on June 27, 1960, at age eighty-eight. She was said to have died while listening to the Wimbledon championships on her radio. Edgeworth House, her childhood home, is today a cozy little hotel, with four guest rooms and a fine restaurant.

With Charlotte Dod running her hardest and setting an example for others to follow, the women were on their way. Charlotte Cooper arrived just in time to replace Charlotte Dod as Blanche Hillyard's chief rival, and soon the game was leaping forward again. In 1900 Charlotte Cooper became the first woman to win an Olympic gold medal in women's sin-

Smith, Bryn Mawr, and Wellesley

Tennis was the first outdoor sport to gain popularity at the eastern women's colleges before the turn of the century. The game was introduced at Smith College in 1881, and soon courts were covering lawns all over the upper campus. In order to preserve the lawns, students marked out the boundaries with tape instead of lime, fastening down the tape with hairpins. When the first tournament was held at Smith in 1882, the "entry fee" was two hairpins.

At Wellesley College, a tennis association was organized in 1885, and tennis was included (along with a potato race and a three-legged race) in the first campus field day in 1899. Tennis instruction was first offered by Wellesley's department of hygiene and physical training in 1906.

In 1892, Bryn Mawr College held the first intercollegiate tennis invitational contest for women, which may have been the first intercollegiate contest for women in any sport. Wellesley, Vassar, and Smith turned down invitations to compete, but Radcliffe sent three representatives. The winner was Radcliffe's Sarah S. Whittelsey, the daughter of a USNLTA official. Sarah is believed to have been the first woman author of a tennis book. She and an unknown coauthor, possibly her father, wrote *A Manual of Lawn Tennis,* published in 1894.

Elizabeth "Tip" Lawrence, a member of Smith College's class of 1883, poses against a photographer's backdrop. The lines on Smith's early grass courts were not much smoother than those shown here.

gles. When she won her fourth of five Wimbledons in 1901, she had to defeat six opponents, more than any previous ladies' champion. The days of the four-woman draws were over. The days of British dominance in women's tennis would soon be over, too.

After Great Britain, women's tennis developed most quickly in the United States. The game made strong inroads among upper-class women in the East, particularly on Staten Island, where the Outerbridge family had introduced the game, and in Philadelphia, a city that boasted several private athletic clubs before the turn of the century. Women's tennis also thrived in Boston, Pittsburgh, Atlanta, Cincinnati, New Orleans, and Chicago, and in the West.

Not all of the tennis was played at private clubs; public courts appeared in Manhattan, Brooklyn, Philadelphia, and Boston in the 1880s, and private courts sprang up on many a home lawn. Ellen and Grace Roosevelt, two early champions and first cousins of Franklin D. Roosevelt, the future President of the United States, played on a private court with lines gouged into the earth. "There was never any doubt if a ball was out," Grace Roosevelt Clark said many years later. "As soon as it struck a sideline it was dead." Ellen Hansell, the first national women's tennis champion, played on a court with a clothesline for a net.

Despite the growing interest in tennis among women, the USNLTA ignored women for many years. The United States championships, inaugurated at Newport Casino, Rhode Island, in 1881, were for men only. I sometimes wonder whether Mary Ewing Outerbridge tried to persuade her brother Eugenius, one of the USNLTA founders, to stage a women's championship along with the men's.

Several years later, a handful of Philadelphia women took the matter of a women's championship into their own hands. These pioneers included four accomplished players, known as the "Big Four," from the Belmont Cricket Club: Bertha "Birdie" Townsend, Margarette Ballard, Louise Allderdice, and Ellen "Nellie" Hansell. They played with squared-off rackets, served with a sidearm motion, and hit wristy ground strokes with plenty of slice. All were close friends; when Ellen married Louise's brother, Taylor Allderdice, in 1890, Louise, Bertha, and Margarette served as bridesmaids.

The "Big Four" of Philadelphia's Belmont Cricket Club were, from left, Bertha Townsend, Margarette Ballard, Louise Allderdice, and Ellen Hansell.

As members of the Belmont Club, which was not among the most exclusive in Philadelphia, the Big Four were part of the upper class but not necessarily the Philadelphia elite. Ellen Hansell, daughter of an upholstery manufacturer, later recalled that the cost of special tennis shoes and annual $10 dues "surely hurt" her father's pocketbook. To keep expenses to a minimum, Ellen walked a mile and a half to the club instead of paying the five-cent horsecar fare.

With the backing of these enthusiastic women, a forerunner of the women's national championships was held in 1886 on the velvety green lawns of the Philadelphia Cricket Club, in the exclusive neighborhood of Wissahickon Heights. The tournament was staged by the Chestnut Hill Tennis Club, which rented the courts from the cricket club.

The new tournament had three events: women's singles, women's doubles, and mixed doubles. Only five women entered the singles competition, but fourteen entered the doubles events. All were members of Philadelphia's upper class. The singles winner was seventeen-year-old Birdie Townsend, a bold, if sometimes inconsistent, shotmaker and the best of the Belmont Cricket Club's Big Four.

The 1886 tournament was so successful that a year later a challenge trophy honoring "the female champion of the United States" was offered by proprietors of the Wissahickon Inn, whose grounds were adjacent to those of the Philadelphia Cricket Club. The trophy, valued at $35, was a statue of a woman tennis player holding a small serving tray. It was to remain in the hands of the winner for one year and become the permanent prize of anyone who won it three times. There was a string attached, however. The Wissahickon Inn would retract the cup should the tournament move to another site. It was a shrewd move on the part of the inn's proprietors, who in essence became the first sponsors of women's tennis. Tournament visitors naturally needed a place to stay, and the Wissahickon Inn, which is today the Chestnut Hill Academy, was clearly the most convenient place.

The 1887 tournament at Wissahickon—the first official United States championship for women—was historic, but only in retrospect.

The USNLTA did not recognize the tournament as a national championship until 1889. That year, presumably, the USNLTA retroactively granted national status to the 1887 and 1888 championships.

A death in the family prevented Bertha Townsend from vying for the title in 1887, and the championship went to her friend, seventeen-year-old Ellen Hansell. Ellen, who was awarded a pretty silver belt buckle in addition to the Wissahickon Cup, had been one of seven women, again all upper-class Philadelphians, entered in the singles.

That first United States championship was a highly social affair, with guests arriving by horse and carriage from the wealthy parts of Philadelphia. Men and women alike relished the entertainment. In a memoir written in 1931 for the USLTA (the association had dropped the "National" from its name), Ellen Hansell Allderdice described the gallery as "a loving, openly prejudiced crowd" that stood within two feet of the sidelines, "calling out hurrahs of applause," and making suggestions like "run to the net" or "place it at her left."

Ellen was surely one of the favorites. Anemic as a child, she had grown into a healthy and attractive young woman, who was considered tall at five feet eight. She wore a corset and a plaid gingham dress, and her long blonde hair was wound and piled neatly under a red felt hat. When forced to retrieve a particularly difficult shot, Ellen grabbed her bustling skirt with her free hand and ran as hard as she could.

Marion Jones of Santa Monica, California, daughter of a United States senator, was the first California woman to win the national singles championship and the first American woman to play at Wimbledon.

In 1888 players from cities other than Philadelphia entered for the first time, hoping to take the prized Wissahickon Cup. Among the contestants were Adeline King Robinson of Staten Island, who had won more tournaments than any American woman until that time, and the Roosevelt sisters of Poughkeepsie, New York.

The tournament's broader geographic base did not make it any less exclusive, however, or any less social. The results of the matches were taken seriously enough to be reported in the major newspapers of Philadelphia and New York, but they were reported in much the same manner as dances and receptions. As Helena Hellwig, the 1894 champion, said, "Are not [tennis] tournaments social events as well?" Helena also said, "Tennis is purely an amateur sport, which fact alone would bar out all undesirable persons."

Helena herself was a member of New York's privileged social class. She attended private schools, married well, became affiliated with the New York Council of Girl Scouts and the Women's Republican Club, and later served as president of the Daughters of the American Revolution.

Eleonora Sears of Boston, national champion in 1907, was another member of the social elite. Her father, Frederick Sears (who may have played on the first tennis court in America), was heir to a shipping fortune, and her mother, Eleonora Coolidge, was the great-granddaughter of Thomas Jefferson.

Nevertheless, Eleonora and other early champions might have taken issue with Helena's belief that tennis was strictly a social pastime. Eleonora was a highly competitive woman, who won more than 240 trophies in a number of different sports, including golf, field hockey, horse racing, swimming, and distance walking. She enjoyed playing football and baseball, too.

Ellen and Grace Roosevelt took their tennis just as seriously. The sisters, among the first to develop strict training habits, watched what they ate and went to bed early. According to Ellen Hansell Allderdice, their father "coached and treated them as if they were a pair of show ponies."

While many of the less ambitious women chuckled at the Roosevelts, they could not argue with the results. In 1890 Ellen won the women's championship at the Philadelphia Cricket Club and teamed with Grace to win the second national women's doubles championship officially sanctioned by the USNLTA.

It was no accident that the 1890 tournament attracted 1,000 spectators a day. People in America were beginning to admire the healthy, athletic woman, the "new woman," as she was called. This new woman of the 1890s was typified by the "Gibson Girl," in a series of drawings by Charles Gibson in *Life* magazine. The Gibson Girl was simply dressed and frequently shown engaging in tennis, golf, or bicycling.

Attention was also being focused on women politically. The year 1890 marked the dawn of a vigorous women's movement in America, which culminated with the right to vote after World War I. Feminism was not so strong again until the 1960s.

In women's tennis, the increased stakes and exposure led to the first documented feud, which was perhaps more accurately described by *The New York Times* as a "tempest in a teapot." The brouhaha involved Ellen Roosevelt and a future national champion named Mabel Cahill, a fine player in her late twenties who had recently come to the United States from Ireland. Ellen and Mabel met in the second round of the championships, which were played in oppressive heat. Mabel, who hit the ball harder than any of the other women, split the first two sets with Ellen but then suffered a cramp in her foot. She had been accustomed to far cooler temperatures in Ireland and had made the mistake of wearing a heavy blue dress that went well with her black hair and blue eyes. Unfortunately, it was not practical.

Although Ellen gave her opponent two opportunities to rest her cramping foot during the match, Mabel eventually was forced to retire. By one account, Ellen offered to complete the match later, but the tournament committee said no. By another account, it was Ellen who ungraciously insisted that Mabel forfeit. In any event, Ellen went on to win the tournament, and Mabel, seeking revenge, joined the Far-and-Near Club of Hastings-on-Hudson, New York, in order to challenge Ellen, the defending champion, in the Hudson River Valley Association's annual tournament. 'Local tennis fans eagerly awaited the match between the two best women of the day. But Ellen, apparently taken aback (and quite possibly outraged) by Mabel's boldness, refused to be challenged. In a move that raised eyebrows within tennis circles, she defaulted, allowing Mabel to win the title virtually uncontested.

Mabel eventually got her rematch with Ellen, in the challenge round of the 1891 national championships at the Philadelphia Cricket Club. The rules of the tournament were by that time identical to those of the men's national championships at Newport. The tournament was divided into an all-comers' championship, a single-elimination event for all players except the defending champion, and a subsequent challenge round, in which the all-comers' winner played the defending champion for the title. In 1891, for the first time, the USNLTA required the women to play the best-of-five sets in the all-comers' final and challenge round. Mabel fought her way through the all-comers' tournament and then beat Ellen in four sets. Mabel retained her title in 1892 with a victory over Elisabeth Moore of Brooklyn in the first five-set match ever played by women for the national championship.

Five-set matches were common among women between 1891 and 1901, as most women's tournaments in America adopted the best-of-five format for the final rounds. The women must have been very fit to play five sets while wearing long dresses and corsets.

One of the hardiest was Juliette Atkinson of Brooklyn. Juliette, the first three-time winner of the United States singles championship, holds the distinction of never having lost a five-set match. Her victory over Marion Jones in 1898, by the score of 6–3, 5–7, 6–4, 2–6, 7–5, remains the longest women's singles final played in the nationals.

Five-set matches for women became an issue within the all-male USNLTA after Elisabeth Moore, the first American woman to win four national singles titles, played two of them in two days in 1901. Elisabeth outlasted Marion Jones in the final of the all-comers' tournament, 4–6, 1–6, 9–7, 9–7, 6–3. In the challenge round the next day, she defeated Myrtle McAteer, the defending champion, 6–4, 3–6, 7–5, 2–6, 6–2. Elisabeth was still standing after playing 105 games of singles in forty-eight hours (although she defaulted her doubles match that was to follow), but the men within the USNLTA no doubt were alarmed. While most men and women regarded tennis as a healthy and beneficial form of exercise, some believed that too much strenuous exercise of any sort could be dangerous. The condition of Marion Jones, who was in acute physical distress by the end of her five-set match in the all-comers' final, helped bolster the more conservative opinion. Lyle Mahan, one of the top American men players at the time, was among those who—"for the good of lawn tennis"—called for an end to five-set matches for women.

In the winter of 1902, without consulting any of the leading women, the USNLTA shortened the women's finals and challenge rounds to the best-of-three sets, the format still in use today. Elisabeth Moore was among the women who criticized the USNLTA's patronizing and secretive decision. "I do not think any such change should have been made without first canvassing the wishes of the women players," Elisabeth wrote in a letter to the USNLTA's official publication, *Lawn Tennis*. "I venture to say that if this were done today, a very large majority would be found to be against the change. Lawn tennis is a game not alone of skill but of endurance as well, and I fail to see why such a radical change should be made to satisfy a few players who do not take the time or have not the inclination to get themselves in proper condition for playing."

Eleven years later Carrie Neely, a high-caliber player from Chicago, requested a return to the best-of-five format, but she had few sympathizers. In a poll of ten women by *American Lawn Tennis* magazine, nine said they preferred playing best-of-three. The issue went no further.

Elisabeth Moore herself fainted on the court while playing Marion Jones in the challenge round in 1902, but only because she was ill. Marion had won the first set, 6–1, and was leading in the second, 1–0, when Elisabeth collapsed and was carried off by friends. Marion offered to continue the match the next day, but Elisabeth, still unwell, forfeited.

Elisabeth Moore came back to win her third national title in 1903; she captured her fourth and last championship in 1905. The year between Elisabeth's final two championships is the one best remembered, though, for it marked the arrival of a sensational new champion—the best woman player yet to come from the United States.

The eastern women who had dominated the national championships did not know what to make of seventeen-year-old May Sutton, soon to become famous as Wimbledon's first foreign champion. May, of Pasadena, California, came from the less inhibited and more adventurous West, where women avoided some of the traditional social constraints and won voting privileges long before their eastern sisters.

Unlike her eastern counterparts, May dressed for the game, not the show. Her dresses hung just above her ankles, and the sleeves of her oversize shirts (some thought they belonged to her father) were pushed up to the elbows to allow her freedom of movement. Although most women were wearing only loose-fitting corsets at that time, it is questionable whether May, at 160 pounds, wore any kind of corset at all.

May did not look like the former champions and she did not play like them, either. Instead of slicing the ball on her forehand side with an open racket face, May pounded it, imparting topspin with a racket face that was slightly closed. Her backhand, however, was a defensive shot, her overhead serve only average. But in 1904 the East Coast women could do nothing to overcome that forehand, which kicked off the ground in a manner they had never seen.

In addition to shorter skirts and a topspin forehand, May had something else that was new to American tennis: a fierceness that was reflected in her unsmiling eyes and square jaw. Her bitter rivalry with another California player, Hazel Hotchkiss, made the "feud" between Ellen Roosevelt and Mabel Cahill look like a fireside chat. Shortly before her death in 1974, Hazel recalled that before their matches, May refused to warm up in the standard and courteous fashion. Instead of hitting the ball directly to Hazel, May would slam it out of Hazel's reach. "She was very hard for me to play against because she was not ladylike," Hazel said in an interview with *American Heritage* magazine in 1974. "She was rude, she was unsportsmanlike, and it upset me."

May usually beat Hazel. On the two occasions when Hazel won, in 1910 and 1911, May stalked off the court and did her best to avoid shaking Hazel's hand.

Hazel might have won a third time, had May's gamesmanship not interfered. Having lost the first set but won the second, Hazel was eagerly awaiting the start of the third, when she realized that May was stalling. Apparently tired, May told the umpire she would not continue until she had had some tea and crumpets. Twenty minutes later, her energy restored, May came back to win the final set and the match.

Hazel Hotchkiss was capable of challenging May while other women were not, because she did not stay in the backcourt and allow May to dominate the match with her forehand. Hazel was the first American woman to attack the net consistently in singles, and she scored many points against May by hitting to her weaker backhand and then rushing in to the net to put the ball away.

The eastern women were not prepared to play this attacking style of tennis when May arrived in 1904, and she won the national tournament with the loss of only ten games in five matches. She whipped Elisabeth Moore in the challenge round, 6–1, 6–2, and was apparently so unimpressed by the level of competition that she did not return to the nationals until seventeen years later.

May Godfray Sutton was born in Plymouth, England, the daughter of a British naval officer and the youngest of seven children.

The Sutton family moved from Plymouth to Pasadena when May was six. They eventually settled on a ten-acre ranch, where they built a clay tennis court. The oldest Sutton sister, Adele, had played tennis in England, and the four other sisters—Ethel, Florence, Violet, and May—developed an even keener interest in the game.

Because May was such a chubby little girl, her older sisters refused to play tennis with her. Angered, May shook her fist and said, "Someday I'll beat you all." It was a vow she kept.

May learned her "California drive," as Elisabeth Moore called it, on the family's clay court, which allowed for higher, truer bounces than the slick lawns of the grass courts in the East. Thus May's topspin forehand was born.

The four Sutton sisters began dominating southern California tennis in the late 1890s and accounted for every singles title in the Southern California Championships between 1899 and 1915. Their unrivaled skill gave rise to the saying, "It takes a Sutton to beat a Sutton."

After running away with the national title in 1904, May decided she wanted to move on to Wimbledon, the most prestigious tournament of all. Only one other American woman, Marion Jones of Santa Monica, California, had played at Wimbledon, but an ever-increasing number of foreign entries was making Wimbledon a truly international event.

Friends of the Sutton family helped raise the money May needed to make the costly trip, and at age eighteen she set off alone on the 6,000-mile journey. She was not alone once she arrived, however. She had written to Blanche Hillyard, the former Wimbledon champion, and had arranged to stay at her home. Blanche's first impression of May was that she would be too slow to contend for the Wimbledon title because of her heavy build. But after losing to May in a practice match, Blanche changed her mind.

At Wimbledon in 1905, May created an immediate stir, not only with her booming forehand but also with her attire. Dorothea

Douglass, the two-time defending champion, later wrote, "One of our players was so horrified that she made Miss Sutton let down her skirt a bit before playing on the Centre Court!"

May advanced to the challenge round without the loss of a set, yet she found the British women generally much better than the Americans—not surprising, because women's tennis in England had a ten-year head start.

Awaiting May Sutton in the challenge round was Dorothea Douglass, destined to become the greatest British woman player before World War I. Dorothea, who later married Robert Lambert Chambers and became known as Dorothea Lambert Chambers, won more than 200 titles during her career and was unbeaten in five different years. She won seven Wimbledon singles titles between 1903 and 1914, a record that was not broken until twenty-four years later, when Helen Wills won her eighth. Dorothea won two of her Wimbledon titles after the birth of her first child, and she won two more after the birth of her second. She was the last mother to win at Wimbledon until Evonne Goolagong Cawley triumphed in 1980.

Dorothea was one of the first women to command attention not only for her success but also for her grace and style. Tall and slender, she hit hard and accurately from the baseline, had excellent anticipation, and

Californian May Sutton, physically strong and mentally tough, brought a new look to tennis: She pushed up her sleeves, shortened her skirts, and whacked the ball with all her might.

moved easily around the court. A correspondent for the magazine *The Queen* wrote in 1903, "To see her playing in a hard match would suffice to convince anybody of the attractiveness of lawn tennis and its supreme suitability to ladies who have the requisite physical skill and endurance."

Dorothea Douglass was born eight years before May Sutton, in Ealing, Middlesex. Her father was an Anglican vicar, and young Dorothea spent many happy hours batting tennis balls against the vicarage wall. Even then, she had an audience: a row of her favorite dolls and stuffed animals.

She began competing in tournaments at seventeen and made her debut at Wimbledon in 1900, when she was twenty-one. Within the year she was the fourth-best woman in England.

When Dorothea won her first Wimbledon title in 1903, some questioned her stature, because several of the best players, including Charlotte Cooper (then Mrs. Sterry) and defending champion Muriel Robb, had not entered. A year later, however, Dorothea soundly defeated Charlotte in the challenge round, 6–0, 6–3, and established herself clearly as the best in England. Thus, the stage was set for a wonderful showdown in 1905, when Dorothea met May Sutton on Centre Court for the championship of Wimbledon.

It was a tribute to Dorothea that she played at all. She had suffered a sprained right wrist several months earlier during the South of France Championships at Nice and had not competed since. Originally, Dorothea had planned to bypass Wimbledon altogether. "But when this little American girl was winning round after round and beating all our players," she wrote many years later, "I thought it was up to me anyway to defend and not allow her to win the title by walking over without a match in the challenge round."

The match generated interest throughout London, and 4,000 spectators jammed the stands. Dorothea put up a good fight, but she was not strong enough to cope with May's deep and penetrating shots, which brought the crowd to its feet. May won the match, 6–3, 6–4, and the first overseas champion of Wimbledon was crowned. "Miss Sutton is a phenomenon," Dorothea said afterward.

Dorothea Lambert Chambers won seven Wimbledon singles titles, a feat that would be surpassed only by Helen Wills and Martina Navratilova.

May Sutton returned to Wimbledon to defend her title in 1906, again playing before a packed stadium. But this time Dorothea, now Mrs. Lambert Chambers, was the victor. The score was 6–3, 9–7. In 1907, the result was reversed again, with May defeating Dorothea in the challenge round, 6–1, 6–4.

It is worth noting that in each of the three meetings, the defending champion lost. In theory, the defending champion had the "advantage" of sitting out during the all-comers' tournament and then playing only one match, against the all-comers' champion. In fact, the champion had the distinct disadvantage of having to walk out on Centre Court before thousands of people without benefit of any tune-up matches, especially when the opposition was formidable. As Dorothea later wrote: "I always felt that my opponent must be playing at the top of her form to have reached the challenge round, and that she must have got so used to the court and the crowds to feel quite at home there, while I was only making my debut of the year." This sentiment, almost universal among players, led to the abolition of the challenge round at the women's United States championships in 1919 and at Wimbledon in 1922.

For many years after winning the 1907 Wimbledon title, May Sutton confined most of her tournament play to California, where players like Hazel Hotchkiss, Mary K. Browne, and Elizabeth Ryan provided ample challenge. May had proved herself to be one of the two best players in the world, and continuing to make the point would have been a time-consuming and expensive luxury.

In 1912 May married Thomas C. Bundy, the national men's doubles champion, and eventually had four children. She named her third child and only daughter Dorothy May, a name that evoked memories of the brief but wonderful rivalry of the early 1900s.

In the 1920s, May returned to Wimbledon and the nationals and did remarkably well against women many years her junior. She reached the semifinals of the national championships at ages thirty-six and thirty-seven, and in 1929, at age forty-four, she reached the quarterfinals at Wimbledon.

Her daughter, nicknamed "Dodo" and later known as Dorothy Bundy Cheney, ranked among the best American women players in the 1930s and 1940s, and in 1938 became the first American woman to win the Australian championship. Both May and Dodo continued to compete as older adults and once reached the final of a mother-daughter tournament in La Jolla, California, when May was eighty years old.

Hazel Hotchkiss Wightman rarely defeated May Sutton Bundy, but her fame and contributions to the game far outdistanced those of her California rival. Hazel Wightman's name is woven into the tapestry of women's tennis like a shining golden thread that stretched from the 1900s through the 1920s, 1930s, 1940s, 1950s, and 1960s. Champion, patron, coach, and founder of the famed Wightman Cup team championships, she devoted her life to teaching, encouraging, sheltering, and enlightening aspiring young tennis stars. In a statistic not recognized by the record books, "Mrs. Wightie" will be remembered as the most beloved tennis figure of all time.

Mrs. Wightman was the ultimate amateur; she never earned a penny from the game. She valued sportsmanship above all, and she was outspoken when she found women lacking in it.

Hazel Hotchkiss Wightman, born in Healdsburg, California, grew up in Berkeley, the only daughter in a family with five children. Three months younger than May Sutton, Hazel became interested in tennis at the relatively advanced age of sixteen, as she watched a match between May and another of the Sutton sisters. Hazel became *more* interested when she saw the rapid-fire volleying of a men's doubles match.

Hazel began playing tennis with her brothers on Berkeley's only court at that time, on the University of California campus. Because girls were not allowed on the court after 8:00 A.M., Hazel arrived daily at 6:00. She soon established herself as the best woman player in northern California, and inevitably her matches with May, the best woman in southern California, generated widespread interest. One of their meetings, an exhibition match arranged by the Pacific Lawn Tennis Association in 1910, drew 3,000 spectators and several "moving-picture photographers."

With May at home in California, Hazel won three successive national triple crowns at the Philadelphia Cricket Club. From 1909 through 1911, she won the singles, doubles, and mixed doubles championships, a feat since equaled only by Mary K. Browne and Alice Marble: In the years that followed, Hazel married George W. Wightman of Boston and began raising a family of five children. She won her fourth and last national singles title in 1919.

The on-court achievements, however, were just so many small baubles in the crown of the "Queen Mother of Tennis," as she came to be known. In 1919 she urged tennis officials to stage an international team championship for women along the lines of the men's Davis Cup, initiated in 1900. Hazel wanted the championship to include Great Britain, the United States, France, and all other nations with prominent women players. One of her major objectives was to bring the spectacular Frenchwoman Suzanne Lenglen to America.

Hazel backed up her idea with her pocketbook. She walked into a Boston jewelry store, N. G. Wood, and plunked down $300 for a tall, slender, silver cup. "I wasn't very crazy about it, but that was the most appropriate thing they had, and I'm a purchaser, not a shopper," Hazel told *The Boston Globe* many years later. "I gave it to the USLTA with the idea that a competition would be started."

Unfortunately, tennis was not yet ready for a female version of the Davis Cup. For four years the trophy sat. Then, in 1923, USLTA officials decided they should do something special to celebrate the opening of the new tennis stadium at the West Side Tennis Club in Forest Hills, New York. Several British players were in town for the nationals, and the USLTA officials thought a team match between the British and American women would be appropriate. Finally, Mrs. Wightie's trophy was put to use. Inscribed on the trophy are the words "Ladies International Lawn Tennis Challenge Trophy," but it is known by its unofficial name, the Wightman Cup.

The annual team match, played alternately in the United States and England, helped generate tremendous interest in the women's game. It was most popular in Britain, where for years it preceded Wimbledon. The Queen of England honored Mrs. Wightman in 1973 by making her a Commander of the British Empire.

In 1940 Mrs. Wightman was divorced from her husband and moved to a new home in Chestnut Hill, Massachusetts, not far from the Longwood Cricket Club. The Longwood club had a rich tradition in tennis. In 1898 it had established the first important New England tournaments for women, and in 1935 it became the site of the men's and women's national doubles championships. (The doubles championships remained at Longwood through 1941, were moved to the West Side Tennis Club in 1942, and were again played at Longwood from 1946 through 1967.)

At Longwood, Hazel conducted clinics and numerous tournaments. During tournament weeks her three-story home became a kind of sorority house for aspiring young girls and women from all over the world. Guests slept everywhere, from the basement to the solarium, coexisting peacefully with Mrs. Wightie's cats, which came and went as they pleased through the open windows.

Mrs. Wightie rose at dawn. She would whip up batches of brownies and chocolate-chip cookies for her guests and to satisfy her own sweet tooth. Then she headed for the washing machine. "She did all the laundry for us," recalled Doris Hart, a Wimbledon and United States champion in the 1950s. "She didn't want us to mess with her machine. It wasn't like the machines today. It had one of those ringers. It was always going."

Shirley Fry, another champion, recalled that Mrs. Wightman washed the dishes herself, too, "because during the war she had learned to save soap, and no one else could do it right." She shook out just the necessary amount of flakes from a little basket.

Following an evening meal at a large table, Hazel played bridge or poker with her guests. Women who went out for the evening signed

Mary K. Browne, left, won three successive American triple crowns between 1912 and 1914. She won the national doubles in 1913 and 1914 with Louise Riddell Williams, right.

out and in on a blackboard. There was no curfew, but Hazel watched over her girls with the eye of a hawk, or perhaps the eye of a mother hen. "Shirley!" she would say, narrowing in on a too-casual teenager. "Stand up straight!"

Mary K. Browne, a Californian and volleyer in the mold of Hazel Hotchkiss, was the last American woman to win the United States championship before World War I. Mary K., also known as "Brownie," followed a career parallel to that of Hazel. She was not as good as Hazel or May Sutton, but the adventurous spirit that led her east brought her three successive triple crowns at the national championships between 1912 and 1914.

Brownie remained active in tennis after World War I, but she focused much of her attention on golf. In 1924 she performed one of the most remarkable feats in the history of American sports: she reached the semifinals of the national women's tennis championships and three weeks later made the final of the United States women's amateur golf tournament.

The years before the war were restless times for women. Women's organizations were flourishing in the United States and Canada. In England, as in the United States, suffragettes were demanding the right to vote, and, to make themselves heard, some members of the British movement set fires on private properties. Twice the suffragettes invaded Wimbledon in an effort to burn down the grandstands. One woman was caught and jailed for two months. Among the incriminating evidence was a notice left behind: "No peace until women have the vote."

On the tennis courts, meanwhile, stars were emerging throughout Europe. Marguerite Broquedis of France won the gold medal for women's singles at the 1912 Olympic Games in Stockholm, and she won the French championships three successive times. Dora Koring of Germany won the silver medal at Stockholm, and Molla Bjurstedt of Norway won the bronze. Tennis was also flourishing in the eastern European countries of Russia, Czechoslovakia, and Hungary.

But at the Wimbledon championships of 1914 an era was rapidly coming to an end. On June 28, in the middle of the Wimbledon Fortnight, Archduke Francis Ferdinand of Austria-Hungary was assassinated in Sarajevo, Yugoslavia, an event that set off World War I.

For a few short weeks, all seemed well enough. Dorothea Lambert Chambers won her seventh Wimbledon singles title with a marvelous victory over Ethel Larcombe. In the women's doubles, Elizabeth Ryan, a wealthy Californian living in England, won the first of her nineteen Wimbledon doubles titles.

Elizabeth, whose record number of Wimbledon titles stood until I surpassed it in 1979, then proceeded to St. Petersburg for the Russian championships, which were held in July. She and Heinrich Kleinschroth, the German men's champion, had been invited to compete, and they enjoyed royal treatment from the Russians: at courtside they were given tennis balls on a silver platter. Unaware that war was looming, they traveled to Moscow for another tournament; when they finally departed, apparently in late July, they were on the last train to leave Russia for Germany. Elizabeth, in turn, boarded the last train from Berlin to Belgium. It was the beginning of August 1914. War broke out one day later.

For four years, Wimbledon and other important European tournaments were abandoned. Women everywhere went to work, among them Maud Watson, Charlotte Dod, and Mary K. Browne. When championship tennis resumed in 1919, the game changed forever.

Chapter 2

The Incomparable Years

1915-1940

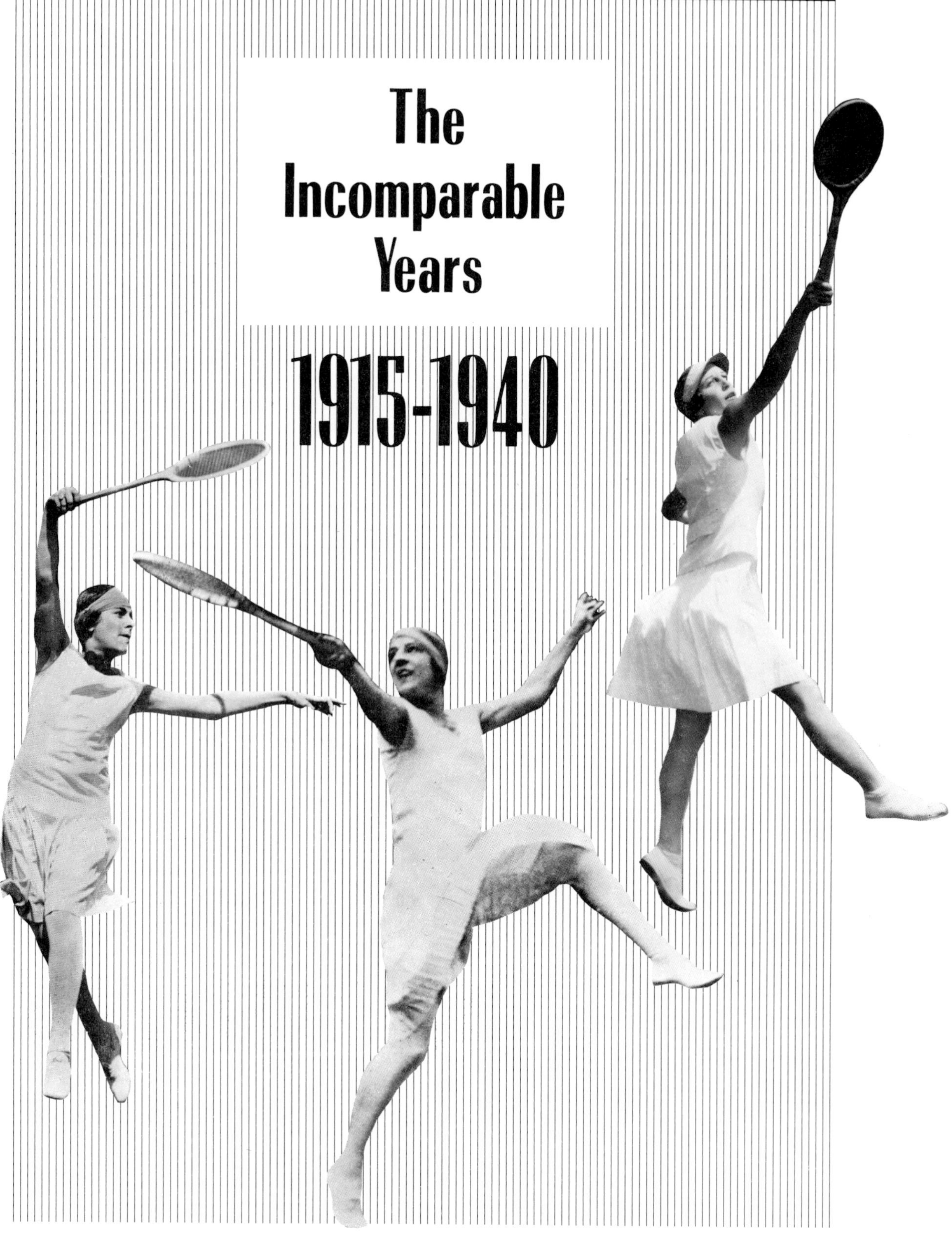

The new woman who came to Wimbledon after World War I was unlike any that tennis had ever seen. Suzanne Lenglen did not merely dominate the game after the war, she revolutionized it. Her tennis skirts hung to midcalf, not to her ankles, and she did not wear a corset. She was unshackled, free, and she ran and leaped as hard and high as she pleased. Her glorious, balletic style captivated galleries everywhere she went.

With her lovely tennis dresses, designed for both practicality and show, the Frenchwoman single-handedly shattered the old rules governing women's attire and brought new glamour into the game. She set new standards, too, for athleticism, excellence, and training. During her prime in the mid-1920s, no one could win more than a few games from her. Suzanne, who won both the Wimbledon and French championships six times, showed how good a woman could become if she devoted her life to tennis.

Suzanne was a genius who played with a beauty of movement that was approached in later years only by Maria Bueno in the 1960s and Evonne Goolagong in the 1970s. Writers groped for metaphors that would do justice to this "Diana of Tennis." "She reminds you of the movement of fire over prairie grass," one of them wrote. To the less poetic, she was simply incomparable.

Suzanne's grace derived from her marvelous leaping ability, the flexibility of her joints, and her flair for the dramatic. World tennis champion Bill Tilden, not one of her fans, said her acrobatics were unnecessary. Elizabeth Ryan, her friend and doubles partner, agreed. "She had a stride a foot and a half longer than any known woman who ever ran, but all those crazy leaps she used to take were done after she hit the ball."

If Suzanne was, in Elizabeth's words, "a poser," few seemed to care. Suzanne was the first superstar of tennis, the first woman to generate as much interest as the leading men players of the 1920s, Tilden included. Theatrical, controversial, and if not beautiful, certainly glamorous—she often repaired her makeup between sets—she was the first champion whose personality and actions away from the court drew as much interest as her unparalleled play.

At Wimbledon, fans came by the thousands to see Suzanne, forming long lines that were called the "Leng-len Trail a'Winding," a play on the words of a popular World War I song. Wimbledon officials had no choice but to abandon the Worple Road site for larger grounds. The new Wimbledon, situated on Church Road and opened in 1922 by King George V, featured a twelve-sided stadium with seating for 14,000 spectators. Other tournaments also gained financially from Suzanne's presence, and the issue of professionalism versus amateurism was inevitably born. Suzanne was one of the first of many who over the years criticized the injustice of a system that used amateur players to reap huge profits. She asked rhetorically, "If we amateurs are to contribute a life's work to learning to play for nothing, why isn't there an amateur gallery which can look on for nothing?" Not that Suzanne went away empty-handed. She was treated like a princess during her amateur years; she dressed expensively and lived well.

Fame was becoming to Suzanne, but it turned her into a prima donna. One day at Wimbledon, when she found Elizabeth Ryan's clothes in a dressing cubicle she had previously selected for herself, Suzanne threw every piece of clothing out the window. On another occasion, during a tournament on the Riviera, she lost her temper after a close call went against her and threw down her racket. When she was called for a foot fault on the next point, she scolded the linesman, who was deaf and could not hear her. Suzanne, undaunted, scribbled out her protest on a piece of paper. The linesman, deeply insulted, walked off the court.

Despite her outward display of arrogance and vanity, Suzanne was not a supremely confident champion. She was invincible not because she was a mentally tough competitor day in and day out, but because she was so much better than her female peers. Close matches were sheer torture for her. She suffered from acute nervousness, and at times the strain of competition made her physically ill. She proved that she could win close matches, but every brush with defeat left her

Overleaf, a gallery of international stars made the 1920s and 1930s among the most memorable in the history of women's tennis. The contenders included, counterclockwise from left, Lili de Alvarez of Spain, a three-time Wimbledon finalist; Frenchwoman Suzanne Lenglen, winner of six Wimbledon and six French championships; and American Helen Wills, winner of eight Wimbledon and seven United States titles.

Frenchwoman Suzanne Lenglen, with her graceful leaps and dashes, brought dance to tennis. She floated over the court like a ballerina, or perhaps a bird, her feet scarcely seeming to touch the ground. She enchanted audiences with her athleticism and occasionally shocked them with her revealing attire. In bottom photograph, she wears a lucky gold bangle on her left arm.

physically and emotionally drained. It came to the point that promoters scheduled her matches with the addendum, "if her health permits." Indeed, small-boned and frail, Suzanne never enjoyed robust health.

She defaulted in the middle of some tournaments and once quit during the middle of a match—the one time in her seven-year, postwar career when defeat appeared certain. Competition took a great toll on Suzanne, and I think it is no coincidence that in photographs taken during the 1920s she looks many years older than she actually was. Her father once said, "Glory is often worth the price one pays for it." Surely Suzanne paid that price. When she turned professional in 1926 she told her friends, "At last, after fifteen years of torture I can enjoy my tennis!"

Although Suzanne was unique in personality and style, she symbolized the women champions who made the 1920s and 1930s among the most colorful and romantic decades in the history of our game. The players who vied against Suzanne and those who followed her were profoundly influenced by the standards she set. They copied her fashions, improved their tennis, fought bitterly on the court (and sometimes off), all under an international spotlight that Suzanne helped create.

Suzanne Rachel Flore Lenglen was born May 24, 1899, in the village of Compiègne in northern France. Her parents also had a winter home in Nice, on the Riviera. Suzanne's father, Charles, became interested in tennis as he watched many of the world's great players who flocked to the Riviera to practice and to compete in the many tournaments held in Monte Carlo, Cannes, and Nice from December until May. Charles himself learned to play, and he gave the eleven-year-old Suzanne a toy racket. To his delight, he found she used it quite skillfully. He soon began coaching her.

Although Suzanne played with a natural grace, she developed into a champion through calculation and exhaustive work. Her father, whom she called Papa, taught her in the style of the great men players because he thought they were better and more interesting than the women, who labored in their long dresses from the baseline. Although not a great player himself, Charles became an astute coach and an innovator in the area of training. He made Suzanne swim, jump rope, and run hurdles, and he made her practice, practice, practice.

Mary K. Browne, who toured professionally with Suzanne in 1926, was amazed to discover the methods that led to Suzanne's success. Suzanne, she said, was "a product of intelligent coaching, persistent practice, and keen observation." Mary also said she learned more from Suzanne on their four-month tour than she had "in all the twenty years before." Mary believed that May Sutton was equal to Suzanne in natural ability, "but like the rest of us, May did not have the same quality of coaching and systematic training in technique."

Compared with today's methods, training was only in its infant stages. Suzanne drank wine or brandy before and during her matches, had inconsistent eating habits, and smoked cigarettes. Once, when asked whether she drank before she played, Suzanne replied, "Nothing is so fine for the nerve, for the strength, for the morale. A little wine tones up the system just right. One cannot always be serious. There must be some sparkle, too." Molla Bjurstedt Mallory and Helen Jacobs also smoked. Helen Wills had a list of foods she avoided before matches but did not follow a strict diet. Mary K. Browne said that a tennis player "would be foolish to take up weight lifting, which tends to bind the muscles," but she recommended jumping rope, fencing, running, and dancing the Charleston, which she called "excellent exercise and riotous fun combined—the best kind of training."

Suzanne could hit the ball hard when she wanted to but usually did not. Her game was based on control; she won her points on placements and her opponents' errors. She could hit every shot with precision, including the difficult backhand down the line, and she came to the net whenever she had an opening. "Suzanne has only one weakness," Mary K. Browne said. "She is not a man. If she were a man, I would back her to defeat Tilden."

Suzanne's targets were the zones two feet

inside the sidelines and three feet inside the baseline. Strategy and technique were so thoroughly ingrained that when she began a match, the right shots came instinctively. Said Suzanne: "I just throw dignity to the winds and think of nothing but the game."

For Suzanne, working under Papa was not easy; he was satisfied only with perfection. Her best, if it fell short of perfection, was insufficient. When Suzanne practiced badly Charles punished her by giving her bread without jam. Sometimes he did worse; his voice full of scorn, he berated her on the court in front of others. He was known to criticize her even when she won. He thought she should win all of her matches, 6–0, 6–0. She played with his standing order seared into her consciousness: *"Tu Gagneras!"* You will win!

"I was a hard taskmaster," Charles Lenglen admitted, "and although my advice was always well intentioned, my criticisms were at times severe, and occasionally intemperate!"

Despite his rigorous and cruel methods, Suzanne loved her Papa dearly and depended on him for inspiration during her matches. When she seemed to falter during competition, he tossed her brandy-soaked sugar cubes. Some people said she could not win without him.

Suzanne was fifteen when she scored her first major triumph: she won the women's singles title at the 1914 World Hard Court Championship in Saint-Cloud, France. After war broke out later that year, tennis went on almost as before in the United States. But in Europe it continued only in isolated pockets like the south of France. On the Riviera, an oasis of peace and safety for wounded soldiers and for the rich, Suzanne perfected her game.

When tournament play resumed in Europe in 1919, Suzanne, then twenty years old, was more than ready. Conversely, the world was ready for Suzanne. People were eager to turn away from the tragedies of World War I, and sporting events were natural avenues of relief. Sports also provided an outlet for nationalistic emotions generated by a war that left many disputes still unresolved. Suzanne did not represent only herself when she played

Suzanne learned the game from her father, Charles, pictured here. Charles was a hard taskmaster, who denied her jam on her bread if she did not play well.

tennis; she stood for the pride of France.

Suzanne's emergence coincided with an international focus on women. Women had performed admirably during the war, and their contributions served to heighten their status and visibility in the years that followed. In America, women were on the threshold of winning the right to vote. In England, women could become lawyers for the first time.

Within this historical context, Suzanne became the talk not only of London but also of the rest of Europe as she swept through the all-comers' singles draw at Wimbledon and reached the challenge round against seven-time champion Dorothea Lambert Chambers, then forty years old. Eight thousand spectators, including King George V, Queen Mary, and Princess Mary, saw what proved to be a turning point in tennis history. The match was more than Lenglen versus Chambers: it was the new era versus the old, and in the minds of some, it was France versus England. Ultimately, it became one of the longest and most memorable in the lore of the women's game. Suzanne, wearing a skirt to midcalf, a blouse with short sleeves, and a hat that hid her eyes, won the first set, 10–8. Dorothea, fighting gamely in her traditional long skirt and long sleeves, won the second set, 6–4. Suzanne then called to her Papa for some brandy cubes.

The liquor settled her, and she took a 4–1 lead in the final set. Dorothea then rallied to reach double match point at 6–5, 40–15. Suzanne saved the first match point with a desperate return that trickled off the wood of her racket and dropped over the net. She saved the second match point when Dorothea hit a drop shot into the net. Inspired, Suzanne went on to win, 10–8, 4–6, 9–7. France had its greatest heroine since Joan of Arc.

When Suzanne returned to Wimbledon in 1920, she no longer wore a simple skirt and blouse but the fabulous creations of French couturier Jean Patou. Her new outfits, sleeveless, delicately pleated silk dresses, were a sensational—and controversial—break from tradition. Clingy and filmy, like those of a ballerina, they did much to accentuate Suzanne's figure and grace. Suzanne added further dash to her appearance by wearing a brightly colored cardigan, a matching turban (or *bandeau*) clasped with a diamond pin, and white stockings, each twisted into place above the knee with a small French coin. Over all, even on the hottest days, she wore a fur.

Thus did Suzanne bring fashion to tennis. The Lenglen bandeau, which became the rage among women all over Europe, was as common a sight at Wimbledon as tennis balls. In the years between the wars other women players set their own styles, bringing to the courts the eyeshade, pleated trousers, shorter skirts, bare legs, and, finally, shorts. Many of the changes created a stir; without exception, they were noted and discussed by the public and the press.

The parade of fashions contributed greatly to the popularity of women's tennis. In 1923 people began betting on the color of the bandeau Suzanne would wear during her next match. Spectators always wondered what the women would do next. In this sense the women were more interesting than the men, whose lone clothing innovation, the transition from long pants to shorts, would not begin until the 1930s.

The gloriously garbed Suzanne, meanwhile, was a walking advertisement for couturier Patou. She was probably violating the rules of amateur tennis, but then again, amateur rules were never strictly enforced with Suzanne. A typical scene allegedly went like this: A tournament promoter, knowing that Suzanne's presence guaranteed a large crowd, made a personal wager with Charles Lenglen that his daughter would not show. "I will bet you one thousand francs that she *does* show," Charles countered. When Suzanne arrived at the tournament, Charles pocketed the money.

In 1920 Suzanne won two Olympic gold medals at Antwerp and retained her Wimbledon singles crown with ease. In the Wimbledon challenge round she met Dorothea Lambert Chambers, who had scored lopsided victories over two outstanding players, Molla Mallory and Elizabeth Ryan, in earlier rounds. Against Suzanne, Dorothea could win only three games.

Suzanne triumphed at Wimbledon again in 1921 and, having won every set she had played during a two-year period, decided she was ready for a new challenge. She wanted to win the United States title and become the undisputed champion of the world. To reach that goal she would have to prove herself

Though not a beauty, Suzanne Lenglen was internationally renowned for her glamour and style.

against the best player in America: Molla Mallory, whom she had easily beaten at the World Hard Court Championships that spring. Beating her in America, Suzanne reasoned, would not be difficult.

Molla, christened Anna Margrethe Bjurstedt, was born in Norway. She was an active child who was reportedly "invincible" in snowball fights. She took up tennis, competed throughout Europe, and won the Norwegian national championship eight times. When she visited America in 1914, she liked it so much that she stayed, settling permanently in New York City.

Molla played tennis throughout the war. She won the United States championship four times in a row between 1915 and 1918 and captured the title a fifth time in 1920, the last year the women's nationals were held at the Philadelphia Cricket Club. Ultimately, Molla won eight United States championships, more than any woman in history.

Molla, a thunderous backcourt player, hit the ball on the rise, before it had reached the top of its bounce, and aimed it low over the net and toward the lines. Helen Jacobs said that she had never seen a woman hit harder than Molla. Molla probably would have agreed. "I find that the girls generally do not hit the ball as hard as they should," she once said. "I believe in always hitting the ball with all my might, but there seems to be a disposition to 'just get it over' in many girls whom I have played. I do not call this tennis."

Molla's philosophy of tennis bordered on the dogmatic. "I do not know a single girl who can play the net game," she once said. Throughout her career she believed women should concentrate on passing shots instead of volleys. With regard to training, Molla was more flexible. Not only did she smoke, but she also went dancing, even on nights before her matches. In one important respect she was much like Suzanne. She hated to lose. She was a relentless competitor and an intimidating one. The "fighting Norsewoman," they called her. She was solidly built and had bronzed, leathery skin. Former USLTA president Robert (Bob) Kelleher, who served as a ball boy during Molla's era, remembered Molla as "a nice lady," but added, "She looked and acted tough when she was on the court hitting tennis balls. She walked around in a manner that said you'd better look out or she'd deck you. She was an indomitable scrambler and runner. She was a fighter."

Molla Mallory accepts the Wissahickon Cup—with a friend inside—from Joseph Jennings, chairman of the National Tennis Committee. The victory, Molla's third in the national championships, gave her permanent possession of the cup.

In August of 1921 Suzanne Lenglen began her eight-day journey to the United States, where she was to compete in the American championships and then play a series of exhibitions for the benefit of war-devastated France. Although her father had opposed the trip because she had been ill, Suzanne insisted. She made the trip accompanied by her mother and Albert de Joannis, vice-president of the French Tennis Federation.

While Suzanne was still en route, the USLTA made the fateful draw. Those were the days before seeding—the deliberate spacing of the best players throughout the draw—and officials drew Suzanne's and Molla's names so close together that the two champions were on course to meet in the second round. Suzanne's first-round opponent was Eleanor Goss, another of the top Americans. When Eleanor withdrew from the tournament, reportedly because of illness, some people speculated that the USLTA had asked her to in order to force Suzanne into a showdown with the defending champion in her very first match.

The confrontation between Suzanne and Molla generated enormous publicity and drew a sellout crowd of 8,000 to the West Side Tennis Club at Forest Hills. Although Suzanne had expressed some reservations about her health shortly after her arrival, she looked well and appeared to be supremely confident when she walked into the large horseshoe stadium.

From the beginning, however, she played tentatively and was not herself. Perhaps she sensed that, for the first time in her life, she was not the darling of the crowd. Molla, advised by her friend Bill Tilden to "hit the cover off the ball," attacked with a vengeance. The British sportswriter A. Wallis Myers wrote that Molla "was like a tigress finally let loose in a pen with her victim." Suzanne was trailing, 0–2, love–40, in the first set, when she began to cough. She looked up toward her mother in the stands, but it did no good. Suzanne needed her Papa—and probably some of his brandy-soaked sugar cubes. This was the age of Prohibition, however, and the USLTA had reneged on its initial promise that she would be allowed to have her spirits at courtside.

Molla Mallory, known for her hard and accurate ground strokes, won eight United States women's singles titles, more than any other player in history.

Suzanne Lenglen, having defaulted in the middle of her match with Molla Mallory, is assisted off the court by Albert de Joannis of the French Tennis Federation, left, and referee Joseph Jennings.

Molla won the first set, 6–2, and Suzanne continued to cough. She served the first game of the second set and fell behind, love–30. Then she double-faulted, something she reportedly did only half a dozen times during her career. She did not play another point. Suzanne had learned many things from her Papa, but she had never learned how to lose. She approached the umpire's chair, shaking her head. She was ill and could not go on. Then she walked off the court, weeping and coughing. Many in the crowd hissed.

Molla Mallory went on to win the United States title with a victory over Mary K. Browne in the final. Suzanne, still ailing, canceled her exhibition tour for the benefit of devastated France and went home.

For months afterward the debate raged in France and the United States: Was Suzanne really ill or had she simply "coughed and quit"? The USLTA said Suzanne had feigned illness. There were reports, denied by Suzanne and others, that she was seen dancing the night of her defeat. Suzanne was quoted as saying, "I thought I could stay the course but I just couldn't. My chest felt like nothing on earth; I could scarcely breathe; I wonder I went on for nine games. In France my parents would not have allowed me to play at all." Suzanne also admitted that she had underestimated Molla Mallory.

Although the French Tennis Federation exonerated Suzanne, accepting her testimony (and a doctor's) that she had been ill, Albert de Joannis, who had accompanied Suzanne to the United States, quit his post as vice-president in protest of the federation's conclusion. Suzanne was "perfectly fit" when she met Molla at Forest Hills, de Joannis said. "She was defeated by a player who on that date showed a better brand of tennis."

Although Suzanne Lenglen never returned to the United States as an amateur, she got her revenge against Molla Mallory. In 1922, at the beautiful new Wimbledon, Suzanne breezed through the tournament and played Molla in the final. Thriving before an adoring crowd of 14,000, Suzanne won, 6–2, 6–0, in twenty-six minutes.

Afterward, she reportedly told her opponent, "Now, Mrs. Mallory, I have proved to you today what I could have done to you in New York last year." To which Molla reportedly replied, "Mlle. Lenglen, you have done to me today what I did to you in New York last year; you have beaten me."

The two women played for the last time that summer in Nice, with Suzanne the victor, 6–0, 6–0. (Her Papa must have been pleased.)

While most spectators in the stands at the West Side Tennis Club were trying to decide what had happened to Suzanne Lenglen in 1921, one young fan watched the proceedings with an entirely different viewpoint. Helen Wills, the newly crowned national junior champion, was enthralled by the skill of the two women. She wrote in her autobiography, *Fifteen-Thirty,* that after seeing them, "I knew the goal for which I hoped to aim, the kind of tennis I wanted to play." At fifteen, Helen was closer to playing that kind of tennis than she realized. Two years later she was champion of the United States.

Helen Wills, who won many of her titles as Helen Wills Moody, became the American counterpart of Suzanne Lenglen. She was a unique and multifaceted individual: a celebrity, a prima donna, and a card-carrying socialite. She was an excellent student who earned her Phi Beta Kappa key while attending the University of California, and she was an artist whose work was shown in major galleries (though the extent of her talent was subject to debate). Above all, she was a perfectionist. "I know that I would hate life," she wrote, "if I were deprived of trying, hunting, working for some objective within which there lies the beauty of perfection."

The sturdily built Helen Wills was not as quick or agile as the sylphlike Suzanne Lenglen, but her strokes were more powerful.

During the heart of her career, Helen *was* perfect. From 1927 until 1933 she won every set she played and at least 158 successive matches. She won eight singles titles at Wimbledon, a record that stood unmatched for forty-nine years. She won seven United States singles titles, a feat surpassed only by Molla Mallory, and four French singles titles. That is nineteen major singles titles in all. Had she been ambitious enough, Helen could have won more. Illness or injury kept her out of the major tournaments in 1926 and in 1934, but she willingly passed up many others. She won her last Wimbledon in 1938 after a two-year absence from the tournament, and she did not play at Forest Hills after 1933.

Unlike the versatile Suzanne, Helen was a backcourt player. She had a powerful forehand, a deep, crosscourt backhand, and a hard, sliced serve. Her weakest strokes were her volleys, which she seldom used in singles, and her passing shots, which she almost always hit crosscourt. She moved well from side to side but had difficulty running forward and backward. Some said that compared with Lenglen she seemed immobile. Hazel Wightman, her frequent doubles partner, encouraged her with the cry, "Run, Helen!"

Helen made up for her lack of speed with her anticipation and consistency. She nearly always arrived at the ball on time and rarely missed. Only a few players in history erred as seldom as Helen Wills.

In 1930 Mary K. Browne said that to beat Helen, a player needed a serve as strong as Helen's, a penetrating backhand and forehand drive, and a "concentrated, consistent" net attack. Happily for Helen, she had no rival who could play such a game.

Helen was strong and fit, the result of practicing with men nearly every day, year-round. Some said Helen practiced for hours, the way players do today, but Helen said she never played more than two sets a day. She believed in conserving energy, even during her matches. When balls were hit beyond her reach, she refrained from chasing them, standing flat-footed as they landed.

Helen Wills, idolized by young and old, signs autographs for a cluster of society girls during a tournament at Easthampton, New York.

America's answer to the chic Suzanne was the wholesome, lovely, and stylish Helen Wills.

As a young woman, Helen Wills captivated America with her beautiful, chiseled features, gray-blue eyes, porcelain complexion, and wholesome athleticism. One male sportswriter asked her the secret of her lovely skin. "Soap and water," Helen replied.

Her answer to the Lenglen bandeau was the Wills eyeshade, a white visor she wore to keep the sun out of her eyes. Although visors were common in California at that time, Helen was the one who made them famous.

The eyeshade did more than protect Helen from the sun; it concealed her emotions and heightened the aura of mystery surrounding her. She was by all accounts an unusual woman, introverted and detached. On the court, she rarely smiled or showed emotion. She ignored her opponents during competition and took no notice of the crowd. Grantland Rice, the famous American sportswriter, nicknamed her "Little Miss Poker Face" early in her career. She was still called "Miss Poker Face" long after the "Little" was dropped. "The secret of mirth," she once said, "is to keep it secret."

Helen was a mystery away from the court as well. At Wimbledon she refused to ride with any other player in the limousine to and from her hotel. Kitty McKane Godfree, Wimbledon champion in 1924 and 1926, recalled that "Helen was a very private person, and she didn't really make friends very much. But she was always polite and pleasant."

For a while Helen's remoteness attracted people to her even more. They wanted to know what she was really like and what she was thinking. But try as they might, they never penetrated her privacy. She revealed herself only through her actions, never through her words.

Helen fell out of favor with the public and the journalists who covered tennis in later years, when she became too regal, too remote, and too successful. She then earned other nicknames, "Queen Helen" and "the Imperial Helen." Indeed, she looked like a queen as she walked onto the court with her head held high, her red cardigan and the red trim on her rackets contrasting brilliantly with her white dress and visor.

One might argue that her indifference to her audiences stemmed from her absolute concentration. In her autobiography she wrote, "I had one thought and that was to put the ball across the net. I was simply myself, too deeply concentrated on the game for any extraneous thought."

Helen remained aloof when demolishing the easiest of foes. Her refusal to acknowledge the fans who cheered her, even after her matches, gave them the impression that she thought herself above them.

Helen's outward hauteur possibly was a mask for the insecurities within her. Hazel Wightman, who knew her as well as anyone in tennis did, once said, "Helen was really an unconfident and awkward girl—you have no idea how awkward . . . I thought of Helen as an honestly shy person who was bewildered by how difficult it was to please most people."

Helen Newington Wills, a physician's daughter, spent her childhood in Berkeley, California. She learned to swim and ride her own horse and, at age thirteen, she received a tennis racket from her father, Clarence. A year later, in 1920, her father gave her a membership in the prestigious Berkeley Tennis Club, where William "Pop" Fuller was the teaching professional.

That same year Hazel Wightman, while making her annual pilgrimage to the West Coast, spotted Helen. Hazel spent six weeks working with Helen on her quickness and her volleys. A year later, the fifteen-year-old with the two long dark braids down her back won the United States junior championship.

In 1922 Helen competed in the women's

The young Helen Wills, already in perfect form, is shown wearing her trademark as a teenager, a middy blouse. The eyeshade would endure, but the blouse—and the stockings—would not.

national championships for the first time and reached the final, where she lost to Molla Mallory. The following year seventeen-year-old Helen surprised the experts by beating Molla, then thirty-one, for her first of three successive United States titles.

While Helen dominated American tennis, Suzanne Lenglen maintained a parallel reign at Wimbledon. For three years, the two champions played at top form but never met.

They had a chance to meet in 1924, when Helen made her first trip to Wimbledon, but the unpredictable happened. Suzanne, who had skipped the French championships because she was ill with jaundice, entered Wimbledon overweight, out of shape, and out of practice. Some people who remembered her Forest Hills fiasco three years earlier speculated that her health worsened as she saw Helen Wills march easily through the other side of the draw toward the final.

Suzanne had an enormous struggle in the quarterfinals against her doubles partner, Elizabeth Ryan, barely managing to win in three sets. Afterward, she was a nervous wreck. Her doctors immediately declared her unfit to continue, and she withdrew from the tournament. Suzanne fueled the rumors that she was afraid of Helen when she went shop-

KITTY GODFREE

"During the war, women had to do all kinds of jobs and therefore had to wear the necessary or suitable clothing. Sometimes they wore slacks or trousers, and all that business of not showing an ankle became a thing of the past. After the war, women could do almost anything.

"A lot of us made our own tennis dresses. White piqué was very popular. It was beautifully white and it washed and laundered well. We didn't go in for silk.

"We had to play in white stockings because of the Royal Box. Queen Mary came frequently to Wimbledon. She was a great patron, a Victorian lady, and no one wanted to do anything that she might not care for.

"I don't think we noticed the stockings because we always wore them, you see. Except at the seaside. The suspender belt was tight around the waist, because you had to make sure things weren't slipping or going to fall off.

"But then there was a young player from South Africa, a girl, who came over to play. Just as she was ready to go on the court, one of the committee members noticed that she wasn't wearing stockings. And he said, 'Oh, Miss Tapscott, I'm afraid you'll have to wear stockings. You're not allowed not to.' And she said, 'Well, I'm awfully sorry, I haven't got any stockings. We never wear them in South Africa.' So he said, 'Well, you'll have to go on then.' So she did.

"Well, nobody said anything. I don't think anybody noticed because her legs were brown. And she looked perfectly all right. She was young. And as soon as we all heard that, we all discarded our stockings and our suspender belts. That's how things happen, isn't it? Very relieved we all were. We had been so used to them we didn't really notice them. Until we gave them up. And then we thought, 'This is rather nice.' It's funny isn't it, about the old days.

"And then, inch by inch, the dresses came up shorter and shorter, until the last one I played in was probably just knee length.

"The [British] Lawn Tennis Association had strict rules about one's amateur status, as it was called. You weren't allowed to report for a newspaper on a tournament in which you were playing. In other words, you couldn't really make any money out of it. You could write an article on lawn tennis just generally speaking.

"The prize voucher that I won at Wimbledon in 1924 was for five guineas at Mappin & Webb, one of our famous jewelry shops. We always called them prize vouchers. I would save up a lot of vouchers in order to get something nice. I think I got a nice watch on one occasion, and a dressing-table set with brushes, comb, and a mirror. And then I thought, well, I'm not keen on jewelry really; it doesn't suit me. What I really want to get, I said to myself, is a motor car. I saved up as much as eighty pounds, which was worth a lot of money in those days, and I bought a diamond ring.

"Later, a friend of mine, an Irishman, invited me to stay with his family during the Irish Championships, and he said: 'If I take your diamond ring and sell it to a friend of mine, who is a jeweler in Dublin, we can take the money and go to a car dealer and buy a second-hand car. That's how you can get your motor car.' So I bought a little two-seater sports car, bright green, and it had a little thing on the front of the bonnet. Then it was easier to get around to tournaments, because I could get in the car and go, instead of lugging my bag by tube or bus.

"I didn't talk about it, but there was really no reason why one shouldn't do that actually. You see, I didn't buy food or clothes or pay the rent or anything of that sort. I merely bought a luxury. So they really couldn't say that I wasn't an amateur, could they?"

Kitty McKane Godfree, a two-time Wimbledon champion, trained by bicycling, skipping rope, playing badminton, and playing tennis against men.

ping the day after her default and later watched the women's final from the stands.

Elizabeth Ryan, who might have had a chance to win Wimbledon that year had Suzanne withdrawn earlier in the event, was the best player of her era who never won a major singles title. In the 1926 United States championships two years later, she would have match points in the final against Molla Mallory and lose. Yet she was never beaten during her seven-year doubles partnership with Suzanne.

Of course, more than bad luck conspired to frustrate Elizabeth. She was overweight, and she did not have classic ground strokes. She was known as "Miss Chop and Drop" because of her severely chopped forehand and her nasty drop shots. To hit the chop, she carried her backswing high in the air and slashed down and under the ball. This motion imparted so much spin to the ball that it bounced low and to the side. Even the best players found it a terrible nuisance. "I liked least the idea of meeting Elizabeth Ryan," wrote Helen Wills. Unfortunately for Elizabeth, if her timing was off, the chop had a tendency to fly out of the court.

At the 1924 Wimbledon, Kathleen "Kitty" McKane was the biggest beneficiary of Suzanne's withdrawal. She advanced by default into the final, where she met Helen Wills.

Kitty McKane, later to become Kitty Godfree, was a player in the mold of Suzanne. Although she had not enjoyed the advantages of lessons and year-round play that Suzanne had, she was a beautiful athlete and a capable volleyer. Her game, one critic said, was characterized by "speed, speed, speed." Kitty was also a fighter. Helen Wills said that Kitty was 25 percent better on Centre Court than anywhere else.

The 1924 final between Kitty and Helen was a classic. Kitty remembered it well more than sixty years later: "Helen started off playing very well, hammering the ball. I lost the first set, 6–4. I was well down in the second set, 1–4, when I remember saying to myself, 'You're losing this match quite easily, so you *must* try doing something else. Change the tactics.' I proceeded to do that, which meant that I began going all out for my shots instead of just returning them and hoping that Helen would make a mistake, which she practically never did. And luckily, I suppose it was desperation, it began to come off. I gradually began to creep up, and I won the set, 6–4. Well then, the final set was a ding-dong battle. I think Helen was slightly rattled, and I was of course full of confidence."

Helen later said that during this match she lost her confidence for the only time in her career. The partisan crowd, which was hoping to see its first English woman champion since before the war, unsettled her. Kitty won the final set, 6–4.

Then, Kitty remembered, a strange thing happened. "Helen said 'Thank you very much' to me, 'Thank you very much' to the umpire, and then said to the umpire, 'What were the games in that set?' And I thought, now that's extraordinary, because you don't play a final set without knowing what the games are in the end. I think because she was concentrating so hard she did not realize that it was over."

Helen went to the locker room and cried bitterly. It was the only time she ever cried over a match. It was also the only time she ever lost a singles match at Wimbledon.

A year later Suzanne Lenglen reached the zenith of her career. She won the French championships with the loss of only four games and Wimbledon with the loss of five. Her victories at Wimbledon included a 6–0, 6–0 thrashing of Kitty Godfree, the defending champion. Suzanne's biggest challenger, nineteen-year-old Helen Wills, was not entered in either event. The USLTA did not sponsor an international team that year, and thus Helen did not travel abroad.

While Suzanne was no doubt glad to avoid the blossoming young American, Helen Wills was eager to take on Suzanne. In the winter of 1926 Helen decided she could wait no longer. She begged her parents to allow her to travel to the Riviera, where Suzanne was competing. When Clarence and Catherine Wills finally consented, Helen took a semester off from her studies at the University of California.

Although Helen made the trip ostensibly to study art, everyone on the Riviera knew her real purpose: to compare the art of Suzanne's tennis with her own. The boldness of Helen's challenge—"cheeky," Lenglen called it—gave the impending clash the drama of a prizefight. A crowd of sportswriters greeted Helen upon her arrival in Paris and then in Cannes, and reporters came from as far away as Norway and South America to cover a match that was not even a certainty. Helen wrote: "No tennis game deserved the attention that this one was getting." That may have been true, but in the Roaring Twenties, an era of excesses, sports stars, and spare time, the public could not resist the idea of a showdown between the two glamorous champions.

The match did not take place immediately. Like two boxers jockeying for position, Suzanne and Helen competed simultaneously but in separate tournaments. Helen later wrote that she did not want to play Suzanne in Nice, where Suzanne would be on her home court. Critics speculated that Suzanne would play Helen only under conditions to her liking.

Finally, in mid-February, both women entered a tournament at the Carlton Club in Cannes. The Carlton Club, which consisted of six courts adjacent to a narrow, dirty street, seemed an unlikely setting for the historic confrontation. But Suzanne had warm feelings for the place because it was owned and

Suzanne Lenglen and Helen Wills met only once in their storied careers, at Cannes, France, in 1926. This aerial view shows the scene at the Carlton Club, where fans packed the stands and watched from neighboring rooftops.

run by some of her close friends.

The anticipation grew as Helen and Suzanne advanced easily through the draw. By the time they had reached the final, the event no longer resembled an amateur tennis tournament. An American motion picture company reportedly offered $100,000 for the rights to film the proceedings; promoters generated 800,000 francs from ticket sales, fabulous sums in the 1920s.

On February 16, 1926, a crowd of 4,000 jammed the bleachers, most of which were erected especially for this match. Those who could not get a seat watched from hotel windows and rooftops, showing their enthusiasm by waving handkerchiefs and flags. Others peered out from the branches of eucalyptus trees. Men standing outside the fences used periscopes. Several members of royal families were present: the former King Manuel of Portugal, the former Grand Duke Michael of Russia, Prince George of Greece, and the Rajah of Pudukota.

The buildup that preceded Suzanne's match with Helen seems to me remarkably similar to the one that preceded my battle of the sexes with Bobby Riggs in 1973—unnatural and unreal.

Not surprisingly, the tension showed in Suzanne's game and in her behavior. She played without her usual daring, staying rooted in the backcourt for most of the match. She took frequent sips of brandy to calm her nerves, and when the crowd cheered noisily,

Top, Suzanne and Helen pose before their famous showdown at Cannes. Bottom, they shake hands, thinking the match is over. The man in the foreground is trying to hold back the photographers: The match was not over after all!

during points and after, Suzanne unsuccessfully begged them to be quiet.

Helen, too, looked nervous at the beginning, and with good reason: she was not as complete a player as Suzanne. Helen hit virtually all of her backhands crosscourt, and Suzanne quickly became grooved to the returns. Furthermore, Helen, who preferred hard-hitting opponents, was confused by the pace of Suzanne's slow drives. Helen lost the first set, 6–3.

She found her rhythm in the second set and was leading, 4–3, 30–15, when a controversial call upset her. On that crucial point, Suzanne hit a drive that appeared inches wide of the line, and Helen made no attempt to return it. When Helen realized the ball had been called good, she made a rare demonstration of emotion.

''What did you call that?'' she asked the linesman.

''Inside,'' he replied.

Helen threw up her hands in despair. She was so rattled that she lost the game. Had she won it for a 5–3 lead, the outcome at Cannes might have been different. Tennis critics doubted that Suzanne had the strength to survive a third set.

After her reprieve, Suzanne reached double match point at 6–5, 40–15, whereupon another controversy broke out. When Helen hit a crosscourt forehand close to the line, a male voice bellowed, ''Out!'' The two women went to the net and shook hands; photographers and spectators rushed onto the court, and the umpire (George Hillyard, husband of Blanche Bingley) awarded Suzanne the match. Suddenly, one of the linesmen came forward and told Hillyard that a spectator had called the ball out, but it had really been in. Suzanne, who thought her ordeal was over, was not the winner after all.

Summoning all her courage, and without a word of protest, Suzanne returned to the court. The moments that followed were among the proudest of her career. She lost her second match point and the game to fall even with Helen at 6–all, but she did not lose her composure. The woman plagued by nerves held firm and pulled out the set, 8–6, with a placement that Helen could not reach.

Suzanne then collapsed on a bench and wept. Photographers pressed around her; well-wishers emerged carrying flower arrangements six feet high. Helen, after watching the scene in awe, left the court with a handsome young man she had met on the Riviera, Frederick Moody, whom she would marry three years later. "There will be other tennis matches," she told newsmen. "Other years are coming."

Suzanne was led into the small clubhouse. When she saw what was inside—thousands of francs from the ticket sales—she became hysterical. Was she laughing because much of the money would be hers, or was she crying because she was to get so little? One cannot discount the possibility that the club owners paid her well for allowing them to stage the match. But Ted Tinling, a friend who umpired many of her matches on the Riviera, believed that was not the case. "It has often occurred to me that the sight of the piles of money, when she was making so much for everybody else and so little for herself, may have unconsciously set off her hysterics," he said. I myself feel sure that neither Suzanne nor Helen received a fair share. Most of the proceeds undoubtedly vanished into private pockets.

Later that day Suzanne and Helen played against each other in the doubles final. Although Suzanne and her partner, Julie "Diddie" Vlasto, defeated Helen and Helene Contostavlos, Helen dominated the match—slamming shot after shot directly at Suzanne—while Suzanne played "in a collapsing state" and fainted after the final point. Thus many onlookers became convinced that if the two women were to meet again, Helen would probably win.

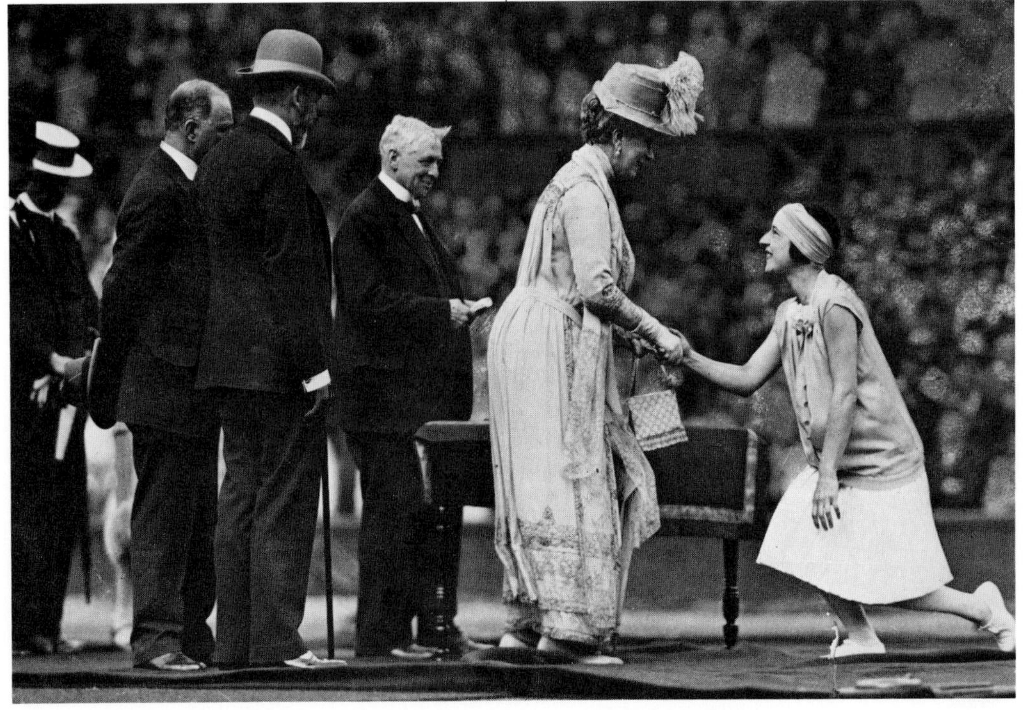

Suzanne is shown receiving her commemorative medal from Queen Mary, as King George V looks on, during Wimbledon's Jubilee ceremony in 1926.

The tennis world eagerly awaited a rematch, but the two champions never played each other again. Helen Wills was stricken with appendicitis early in the French championships that spring and underwent surgery. In her absence, Suzanne won her sixth and last French singles title.

Suzanne then proceeded to Wimbledon, which was celebrating its fiftieth anniversary in 1926. The "Jubilee Championships" should have marked a festive occasion for Suzanne. All of the past Wimbledon singles champions were to be honored on Centre Court and presented with medals by the King and Queen. Furthermore, with Helen still recuperating from appendicitis, Suzanne was highly favored to win her seventh title and to equal the record set by Dorothea Lambert Chambers. Sadly, instead of showcasing her greatness, the tournament brought a tumultuous and unhappy end to one of the greatest of amateur careers.

Suzanne's woes began almost immediately. After the Jubilee ceremony on the opening day of the tournament, Suzanne and Elizabeth Ryan, who had been undefeated in six years at Wimbledon, lost a one-set exhibition. They were not to play in the Wimbledon doubles event that year because the French Tennis Federation had forced Suzanne, against her wishes, to play with countrywoman Diddie Vlasto instead of her lifelong partner. To make matters worse, the draw pitted Suzanne and Diddie against Elizabeth and Mary K. Browne in the first round.

Suzanne, who had recently developed a sore arm, looked shaky in her first-round singles match the second day of the tournament. What followed was a complicated series of events that has been told and retold so many different ways over the years that it is difficult, if not impossible, to know what really happened. By one account, Suzanne, reportedly not feeling well, left the grounds without being aware of a late scheduling change that called for her to play a 2 P.M. singles match in addition to her 4:30 doubles match against Elizabeth and Mary. Suzanne reportedly learned of the change the next day, but only after she had made a 12 P.M. doctor's appointment. By another account, however, Suzanne knew the schedule before she left the club and was very much opposed to it.

Historians agree that F. R. Burrow, the strong-willed tournament referee, did not believe in giving anyone special treatment. If Suzanne *did* leave the club unaware of a scheduling change, Burrow almost certainly made no attempt to inform her of it—even though he knew that Queen Mary would be in attendance. Suzanne claimed she sent a message via a friend informing Burrow that she would not arrive in time for the singles match. Burrow maintained that he never received it.

Suzanne arrived late for her first match, only to discover that Queen Mary had been sitting in front of an empty court for thirty minutes. When the officials scolded Suzanne, she went into a frenzy, declaring she would not play her matches in the order scheduled and then retreating to her dressing area, where she was heard sobbing hysterically. "Everyone seemed to be telling me what a naughty girl I was," Suzanne said later. "Of course, I was upset; of course, I cried and talked excitedly and told them to scratch me from the competition since, after all, I was merely an ordinary competitor."

The officials chose not to default Suzanne, perhaps reasoning that a default would hurt them at the gate. Suzanne, however, played only two more matches in the tournament. The Wimbledon crowd, believing she had snubbed Queen Mary, had turned against her, which was more than Suzanne could bear. Complaining of illness and a sore shoulder, she withdrew. Kitty McKane Godfree, who had won Wimbledon after Suzanne defaulted in 1924, won the championship on this occasion as well.

Suzanne never played at Wimbledon again. She said good-bye to the tournament, a sad and broken woman. "My health?" she said, "It gets worse and worse. I have no peace." A few days later she added, "You must remember that I am only a girl, not a medieval warrior who thrives on disturbance. . . . Truly, I tell you, I have been a most miserable girl the last few days."

The "miserable girl" left behind a glowing record. In a span of eight years, she won six singles titles, six doubles titles with Elizabeth Ryan, and three mixed doubles titles. In singles matches she was 32–0, in sets 64–2, and in games 405–99. Her record of five successive singles titles was unequaled for sixty-one years.

A month after Wimbledon, Suzanne accepted a $50,000 offer to turn professional from the American entrepreneur Charles C. Pyle. Strictly speaking, Suzanne was not the first woman tennis professional; May Sutton's sisters, Violet and Florence, had been teaching professionals in California for several years. But Suzanne was the first woman to agree to accept payment for *playing* the game. The second woman to sign with Pyle was Mary K. Browne, who had been ranked sixth in the United States in 1925. Four men also signed: Vincent Richards, who would have been ranked first in the United States in 1926; Howard Kinsey, the United States doubles champion; Paul Feret, a leading French player; and Harvey Snodgrass, a former top American player who had become a teaching professional. For four months Lenglen and her troupe toured the United States, Canada, Cuba, and Mexico.

Suzanne was widely criticized within the tennis community and in France for her decision to turn professional. The All England Club revoked her honorary membership. One British publication, *Lawn Tennis and Badminton,* went so far as to say her retirement was good for the game, because "her unbridled temperament was always making for difficulties." At the same time, Suzanne was supported by many members of the press, particularly in the United States, where professional golf and football were gaining rapidly in popularity.

Mary K. Browne, an amateur for twenty years, said she had felt "contaminated" just

An international lineup of stars poses before a 1920s Wimbledon. From left are Elizabeth Ryan, Suzanne Lenglen, Diddie Vlasto, Dorothea Lambert Chambers, Joan Fry, Lili de Alvarez, and Kitty Godfree.

thinking about Pyle's offer, which she said was for something less than the published figure of $30,000. But Mary was practical enough not to feel contaminated for too long. "There were many things to consider," she wrote at the time. "The money was one. I am still Miss Browne and therefore obliged to take a husbandly view of opportunities."

Suzanne had no difficulty making the decision. Her family's fortune had withered away, she was in need of money, and she had no wish to continue filling promoters' pockets at the expense of her own. She once described the act of turning professional as "an escape from bondage and slavery." In an article that appeared in her tour's program, Suzanne wrote, "In the twelve years I have been champion I have earned literally millions of francs for tennis and have paid thousands of francs in entrance fees to be allowed to do so. . . . I have worked as hard at my career as any man or woman has worked at any career. And in my whole lifetime I have not earned $5,000—not one cent of that by my specialty, my life study—tennis. . . . I am twenty-seven and not wealthy—should I embark on any other career and leave the one for which I have what people call genius? Or should I smile at the prospect of actual poverty and continue to earn a fortune—for whom?"

Although Suzanne may not have been entirely candid about the amount of money she gained from tennis, she probably earned only a small fraction of what she was worth to the tournaments she supported.

Suzanne's criticism of tennis went beyond self-serving arguments. She saw how the amateur system hurt others, too. "Under these absurd and antiquated amateur rulings, only a wealthy person can compete, and the fact of the matter is that only wealthy people *do* compete," she complained. "Is that fair? Does it advance the sport? Does it make tennis more popular—or does it tend to suppress and hinder an enormous amount of tennis talent lying dormant in the bodies of young men and women whose names are not in the social register?" Thus Suzanne Lenglen was an early leader in the fight against the establishment's stranglehold on tennis—a battle that took players forty years to win.

Perhaps inevitably, Suzanne's professional tour was short-lived. It was profitable—Suzanne reportedly received $25,000 in addition to her guarantee—and it had some exciting moments, including its opening before a crowd of 13,000 at Madison Square Garden in New York City. But most stops were far less successful. Like the other pioneer tours that sprang up over the years, Suzanne's lacked the drama of a real tournament. Suzanne also lacked competition. In nearly forty matches with Mary, she lost only two sets. Ultimately, Suzanne found the traveling tedious. A short tour of Great Britain followed her North American tour, and then Suzanne returned to Paris, where she became head of a government-sponsored tennis school for girls.

Suzanne's departure did not put an end to the dilemma facing amateur players. "Amateurs," both male and female, continued to take what they could. Helen Wills wrote extensively for periodicals and newspapers, sold sketches of tennis players, and, like Suzanne, wore fabulously expensive designer clothes. In 1931 Helen wrote, with more than a trace of sarcasm, "The only way now open for an amateur to avoid professionalism is for him to be rolled in cotton wool and moth balls between tennis seasons."

Anita Lizana of Chile won the 1937 United States title.

In 1930 the USLTA made a bid to open some tournaments to professionals, but the move was quashed by the International Lawn Tennis Federation (ILTF), the international governing body of the sport. Confronted with the ILTF roadblock, the USLTA in 1935 took a step backward and tried to enforce true amateurism. The USLTA adopted the "eight weeks rule," which stated that amateurs could accept expense money for only eight weeks during the year; during the other weeks they had to pay their own expenses. Helen Jacobs, in her memoir called the rule, which favored wealthy amateurs over the less well-to-do, "intrinsically unfair."

Despite the undercurrent of tension between players and the establishment in the late 1920s, amateur tennis flourished. It survived the great stock market crash of 1929 and the depression years that followed, and it endured despite increasing political unrest among European nations during the mid-1930s.

Even without Suzanne, women's tennis was glamorous and exciting. The women's game had a new, undisputed champion in Helen Wills and an international gallery of contenders, including Lili de Alvarez of Spain, Cecile "Cilly" Aussem and Hilde Krahwinkel of Germany, Simone Mathieu of France, Jadwiga Jedrzejowska of Poland, Anita Lizana of Chile, and Dorothy Round and Betty Nuthall of England. The Australian women, too, were beginning to enter the international scene. The Australians held their first national championships for women in 1922, seventeen years after their inaugural championships for men.

Cilly Aussem, only five feet tall, was the most successful woman player from Germany until Steffi Graf. Cilly won the French and Wimbledon singles championships in 1931.

Lili de Alvarez, a Spaniard born in Rome, was among the most popular Europeans. She was a beautiful, cosmopolitan woman, fluent in five languages. She wore the Lenglen bandeau with a twist, slanted to one side, and brought trousers—voluminous, calf-length slacks—to the game. She was a bold, exciting player who hit the ball on the rise and aimed for winners. She reached the Wimbledon final three successive times between 1926 and 1928 but never won the championship.

The pride of Germany was Cilly Aussem. Cilly hit the ball with little backswing, which gave her excellent disguise, and she hit her backhand with so much spin that the ball barely bounced. When Helen Wills first en-

Great Britain's Betty Nuthall, left, was the first player from overseas to win the United States women's title. Simone Mathieu of France won two French championships and later served with the French Resistance.

countered this bizarre shot, she incorrectly assumed the ball had hit a soft spot on the grass. Cilly defeated her compatriot, Hilde Krahwinkel, in the 1931 Wimbledon final to become the first German champion ever crowned at the All England Club. Hilde, a tall, slender woman, was three times the champion of France.

Another historically important player was Betty Nuthall. "Bounding Betty," who always smiled on the court, was said to be the most photographed woman in England. She showed much promise but lost interest in the game after her father's tragic death in 1925. Stuart Nuthall, who was also Betty's coach, had undergone a routine operation for tennis elbow and died from a complication of anesthesia. Encouraged by her mother, Betty eventually made a comeback, and in 1930 she became the first overseas player to win the United States women's singles championship.

England's best player of the 1930s was Dorothy Round, the last Englishwoman to win Wimbledon twice. She won in 1934 and 1937, years in which Helen Wills was absent. Dorothy, a Sunday School teacher who declined to play on Sundays, was a tenacious player who excelled from the backcourt. In the 1933 Wimbledon final she became the first player in six years to win a set from Helen Wills. Two years later she became the first foreign player to win the Australian women's championship.

Billie Tapscott and Joan Lycett, two women who have been largely forgotten, made contributions to women's tennis that cannot be underestimated. In 1929 Billie, a South African, became the first woman to play without stockings on a back court at Wimbledon. Two years later Joan, of England, became the first woman to walk barelegged onto the Centre Court.

France's new female star was Simone Mathieu, who was the French singles champion twice and runner-up five times. Simone, an exciting, temperamental woman, was known for upsetting top players in early rounds and for slamming balls around the court when angry. On one occasion Simone nearly hit Queen Mary in the Royal Box. On another, she had a linesman removed because he could not explain to her in French why he was calling her for foot faults. Simone did not tell the linesman she was fluent in English.

Despite her charisma, Simone could never match the popularity of her four countrymen, the "Four Musketeers," as they were called: Jean Borotra, René Lacoste, Henri Cochet, and Jacques Brugnon. The Musketeers, who won the Davis Cup six successive times between 1927 and 1932, inspired the French Tennis Federation to build a new complex of red clay courts in Paris. Roland Garros Stadium, named for a prominent French rugby player and daring aviator who was killed in action five weeks before the end of World War I, became one of the most famous arenas in tennis. It opened in 1928 with a women's

Dorothy Round was the last Englishwoman to win Wimbledon twice. She won her titles in 1934 and 1937.

team match between France and Britain.

Of all the notable women who competed in the 1920s and 1930s the strongest challenger to Helen Wills was her very own neighbor from Berkeley, Helen Jacobs. ''Little Helen,'' as she was called, had the misfortune to spend the peak of her career in the shadow of ''Queen Helen.'' For ten years Jacobs ranked second in the United States. She played Helen Wills in seven major championship finals and won only once.

Although Jacobs did not have the talent that Wills had, she is a special and memorable champion because she never gave up. She never saw ''Queen Helen'' as invincible. George Lott, a top American doubles player in the 1930s, said Helen Jacobs was one of his favorites. ''I always thought she got the furthest with the leastest,'' he wrote. ''She had a forehand chop, a sound backhand, and lots and lots of stomach muscles. She was buffeted from pillar to post by Helen Wills and still came back for more.''

Little Helen's perseverance led to four successive United States championships between 1932 and 1935, a record equaled only by Molla Mallory and Chris Evert. In 1936, in Wills's absence, Jacobs won her only Wimbledon singles title.

Helen Jacobs was famous for her historic duels with her nemesis Helen Wills, but she was a champion in her own right, winning four successive national singles titles.

Helen Hull Jacobs, the daughter of a mining engineer, was born in Globe, Arizona, in 1908. The family moved to San Francisco shortly before World War I and later moved into the very home in Berkeley where Helen Wills had lived. Like Wills, Jacobs learned the game at the Berkeley Tennis Club, took lessons from Pop Fuller, attended the University of California, and started a fashion trend of her own in 1933 when she became the first woman to wear shorts at Wimbledon. In personality, however, Jacobs was far different from Wills. She was outgoing, friendly, and popular among players and fans. Whenever she played Wills, she was the crowd's favorite.

Jacobs was fourteen years old when she began her long and bitter rivalry with Helen Wills in a practice set arranged by Pop Fuller. The seventeen-year-old Wills won the set, 6–0, in seven minutes. Jacobs was eager to play a second set, but Wills declined and walked away.

The rivalry between Wills and Jacobs became legend, in part because of their feelings toward each other. Both have repeatedly denied that they ever feuded. Jacobs wrote that ''during all the years in which we both were playing, we never once exchanged an unpleasant word!'' Wills wrote that Jacobs ''was hardly an enemy.'' Perhaps they were not enemies, but surely they were not friends. In truth, I think Helen Jacobs would have enjoyed being Helen Wills's friend; Jacobs liked everyone. But Wills, for whatever reason, could not tolerate a rival so close to home.

Bob Kelleher saw the two Helens together on and off the court numerous times and believed a ''frostiness'' always existed between them. ''Helen Wills was the daughter of a prominent physician; her mother was a lovely lady, and Helen regarded her family as being very much in the elite,'' Bob said. ''Helen Jacobs was not [of the elite]. It was obvious that she was tough and was going to be a threat to Wills. Wills just resented her. There was no cordiality between them at all.''

Kay Stammers, a leading British player in

Helen Wills, left, and Helen Jacobs vie during one of their many encounters at Forest Hills.

the late 1930s, said, "There was *definite* friction between them—particularly, I think, on Helen Wills's side. They met when they played tennis; but apart from that, I don't think they had a great deal to do with one another."

When the USLTA allowed Wills to choose the player who would accompany her to Europe in the spring of 1929, Wills declined to select Jacobs, who was ranked second, and instead chose Edith Cross, who was ranked third. Some saw the incident as a demonstration of Wills's dislike for Jacobs. Members of the San Francisco business community were so upset that they raised the money themselves to pay for Little Helen's trip. On the other hand, because Edith was an outstanding prospect and one of Wills's regular doubles partners, Wills's decision to select her over Jacobs may not have been as unseemly as it appeared.

Helen Wills dominated Helen Jacobs in their early championship matches. Wills won the 1928 final at Forest Hills, 6–2, 6–1, the 1929 Wimbledon final, 6–1, 6–2, the 1930 French final, 6–2, 6–1, and the 1932 Wimbledon final, 6–3, 6–1. Their next important meeting, in 1933, was not so one-sided.

By 1933 Helen Wills was ever so slightly past her prime. At Wimbledon she had won the championship but had lost her first set in six years. Suffering from a bad back, she then entered the United States championships against her doctor's advice, yet managed to reach the final. There she met Helen Jacobs, improved, eager, and armed with a new piece of strategy, courtesy of the master tactician herself, Suzanne Lenglen. Wills, Suzanne had advised, could be beaten with short, acutely angled crosscourts. Jacobs won the first set, 8–6; Wills won the second, 6–3. The women then took the customary ten-minute break. By the time Wills resumed play, the muscles in her back and legs had stiffened and she could hardly run.

In the eyes of the public, her medical problems failed to excuse her for what happened next. After falling behind, 3–0, Wills walked slowly to the umpire's stand, where, evoking memories of Suzanne Lenglen's infamous default against Molla Mallory in 1921, she told the umpire she was unable to continue. Helen Jacobs, in a gesture of sympathy, put her hand on Wills's shoulder, and the two women exchanged words. They parted without shaking hands. Wills then left the court and walked to the Forest Hills Inn, a distance of about two city blocks.

Jacobs has written that her exchange with Wills was cordial, but word leaked to the press that Wills, instead of accepting Jacobs's sympathy, had said, "Take your hand off

These are scenes from three celebrated matches between the two Helens. In the top photo, Wills, having been down match point, cannot hide her joy after winning the 1935 Wimbledon final. Bottom left, Wills defaults during the 1933 national final. At right, Wills accepts congratulations after the 1938 Wimbledon final but offers no sign of sympathy to the injured Jacobs.

me.'' That account, if true, could explain why the two women failed to shake hands.

Helen Wills did not return to the stadium for the awards ceremony. Instead, an official read a statement Wills had written on a piece of stationery at the Forest Hills Inn. ''In the third set of my singles match I felt as if I were going to faint, because of pain in my back and hip and a complete numbness of my right leg. The match was long, and by defaulting I do not wish to detract from the excellence of Miss Jacobs's play. I feel that I have spoiled the finish of the National Championships and wish that I had followed the advice of my doctor and returned to California. I still feel that I did right in withdrawing because I felt that I was on the verge of a collapse on the court.''

Later, the public learned that Helen, despite her injury, had wanted to play in the doubles final with Elizabeth Ryan that very day. Elizabeth, fearing the ramifications of such an appearance, persuaded Helen not to play.

SARAH PALFREY

"The Jacobs-Wills feud, as they called it, I never took that seriously. It was blown up more than it should have been. I guess because it was gossip. It wasn't dislike, but I think Helen Wills sort of considered herself better, and Helen Jacobs, being very competitive, thought she always had a chance and always wanted to try to beat her and felt a little ignored, let's put it that way. But I don't think there was the feud and dislike that the papers suggested.

"They were both on the Wightman Cup teams when Hazel Wightman was captain. What's that silly song, 'Nobody doesn't like Sara Lee?' Well, nobody didn't like Hazel Wightman. Both Helens liked her. There was no outward sign of conflict that those of us on the team noticed, the way we read in the papers. I never heard any bad, or even sarcastic, remarks. They were outwardly polite toward each other. Now some of the newspaper people may have heard something directly and, to be perfectly honest, I have no right to say they never did. There may have been a little envy on Jacobs's side. She wished she could beat Helen Wills. Who wouldn't?

"They were very different women. Helen Wills was accused of being a little icy and aloof. I never found her that way. I found her very friendly. Some people thought she was aloof. She just didn't talk very much. She concentrated hard on the court, but off the court, maybe she was a little more shy than people thought.

"She was always nice to me, and when I went to California for the first time she met me at the hotel in her car and took me on a sight-seeing tour all around San Francisco. I think that's because she knew I was a good friend of Mrs. Wightman. But she must have liked me, or she wouldn't have done it. She was very interested in what she was showing me: the museums, the Presidio. And she knew the history and told it to me, almost like a teacher. She took the trouble to do that, and there was no reason she had to. I was also a very good friend of Helen Jacobs. We won the national doubles three times, and Helen Wills knew that.

"I think Helen Wills liked being a celebrity. I think most champions enjoy being champions, but I do think she liked her privacy. I don't think she liked being stopped on the street, the way movie stars do.

"She was always the one who was Number 1 in my mind. I still think she could hold her own with some of the girls today. She never missed. Helen had a whale of a forehand. But her backhand was never quite that good. She had a very good first serve, which people forget. But she was a little bit slower than the girls today, and whether she could have covered the court and gotten to the drop shots and volleys, I don't know."

In the debate that followed the celebrated default, critics asked the obvious questions. Did Helen retire so that she could say she technically had not been beaten? Could she simply not stand the thought of losing to Little Helen? Or was she really on the verge of collapse? If so, how was she able to walk back to the inn?

Among those who believed Wills's story was former USLTA president Louis J. Carruthers, a longtime friend who had helped look after Wills when she came east as a young girl. In a 1956 letter, Carruthers wrote that Helen "told me personally that she was about to faint on the court. She was such a reserved and reticent person that any such outcome would have been almost unbearable."

Many years after the incident, Hazel Wightman recalled, "I listened to the broadcast of that match at home, and from the very beginning I had the weirdest sensation: I knew positively that something was wrong with Helen, that she was worried about her back injury and was afraid, deathly afraid, of falling and injuring herself permanently. I don't think that girl really knew what she was doing when she walked off that court or, for that matter, at any time during the match."

Wills, who indeed had a serious back injury, did not compete again for eighteen months. Nor did she ever return to Forest Hills. She played at Wimbledon, however, in 1935 and 1938, and both years met Helen Jacobs in the final.

In a tournament preceding the 1935 Wimbledon, Wills lost a match to England's Kay Stammers, 6–4, 6–0, and appeared vulnerable. Jacobs found her to be exactly that and for the first time in her life reached match point against her at 5–3, 40–30, in the third set. After an exchange, Wills hit a weak lob into the air. Jacobs, perhaps misjudging the ball in the wind, made a fatal error and allowed it to bounce. The ball failed to come up high enough for her to hit a clean overhead, and by that time, she wrote in her autobiography, "I was practically on my knees." Little Helen hit the ball into the net.

Helen Jacobs was still two games ahead, but the missed opportunity left her shaken. She lost her momentum completely, and Wills, rejuvenated, won four straight games and the match.

Helen Wills did not enter Wimbledon in 1936 or 1937, and Little Helen finally won her precious title there in 1936. To the surprise of many, Wills returned in 1938, presumably in an effort to break the record of seven singles titles, which she shared with Dorothea Lambert Chambers. Wills was thirty-two and had slowed down considerably. She was seeded first, but the favorite was a newer star from California, Alice Marble.

Helen Jacobs, who was not seeded, upset Alice in the semifinals, 6–4, 6–4, despite being injured. Helen had torn the sheath of her Achilles' tendon during her quarterfinal match against Poland's Jadwiga Jedrzejowska. With Alice Marble gone, the two Helens were in the final once again.

Jacobs, her ankle tightly wrapped, held even with Wills until 4–all. Then, at 40–30 on her serve, Jacobs lunged for a volley and landed heavily on her injured foot. Pain shot through her leg. She could walk with great pain, but she could no longer run.

An athlete today would not have taken another step for fear of risking a complete tear of the tendon, but Helen refused to leave the court until the match was finished. The memory of Wills's default at Forest Hills must have burned within her still. For slightly more than a set, Jacobs went through the motions as Wills blasted the ball for point after point. Hazel Wightman, who was then captain of the Wightman Cup team, walked onto the court and pleaded with Jacobs to stop, but Little Helen continued. She was proving something to herself and to those who looked on in silence. She was not quite as good as Helen Wills perhaps, but *she* at least would not quit.

Whether Helen Jacobs knew it or not at the time, she also exposed the private and mysterious Helen Wills by forcing her into a situation that demanded compassion when Wills had none to give. Wills, in typical form, never spoke to Jacobs and gave no sign of sympathy either during or after the match, which she won, 6–4, 6–0.

The spectators were appalled at Wills's coldness. Sarah Palfrey, a young member of America's Wightman Cup team and a friend of both Helens, recalled watching the match with her teammates. "We were embarrassed by Helen Wills Moody's lack of concern over

Alice Marble played tennis as no woman had before her. She could hit every shot in the game—with power.

Helen Jacobs's injury and inability to perform,'' she said.

Wills, after changing into her street clothes, told reporters, ''I'm so sorry about Miss Jacobs. It's too bad, but it couldn't be helped, could it?''

Hazel Wightman, who liked both women, said, ''It's a shame, but everybody seems to be blaming Mrs. Moody for finishing Miss Jacobs off so quickly. I think this is unfair. It was the only thing to do under the circumstances.''

If only Helen Wills had made one gesture of sympathy, she might have blunted the stories of a feud she claimed did not exist. Instead, she added a final page to the unhappy story of the two Helens. Helen Jacobs has said many times that after their last Wimbledon final together, she and Wills never saw each other again.

The 1938 Wimbledon was memorable for another sad event. On July 4, a few days after the tournament ended, Suzanne Lenglen died of leukemia at age thirty-nine. The courageous Suzanne, who had fallen seriously ill only a few months earlier, was near death throughout the final days of Wimbledon but lived long enough to know that Helen Wills won the title for a record eight times. At Wimbledon, Helen Wills paid tribute to Suzanne as ''the greatest woman player who ever lived.''

Alice Marble was the last in the series of colorful champions who flourished between the wars, and she was the start of something new. She was the first member of a generation of women who played power tennis.

Other women had played competently at the net before Alice, but none had put together a complete attacking game along the lines of the best men players. Alice, a streamlined athlete at five feet seven and 140 pounds, had all of the necessary attributes: quickness, consistency, height, strength, and the courage to play a high-risk game.

On the court, she was fluid and powerful, a picture of unrestrained athleticism. Her game was a poetic mixture of drives hit on the run, leaping volleys, and smashes struck with both feet in the air. Her serve was the first in women's tennis to be called great. She hit it with abandon, stretching, uncoiling, bending, and unleashing herself into the ball. No woman had done that before. Her first serve, which was fairly flat, streaked over the net on a line. Her second serve, hit with heavy spin, kicked high off the ground and to the left.

Alice hit her drives hard and deep and frequently caught the back lines of the court. Critics said she did not hit the ball as hard as Helen Wills, but, unlike Helen, Alice could rip her backhand drives both crosscourt and down the line. In versatility, she was another Suzanne Lenglen—but with power.

Like the serve-and-volley players who followed her, Alice was subject to lapses. She played a complex game, and until she reached her prime, she lacked the unwavering consistency of Helen Wills, who hit the same basic ground strokes time after time. Nevertheless, Alice had exactly the kind of game that would have troubled Helen. Had Helen and Alice met when each was at her peak, I think Helen probably would have been forced to add variety to her game. She could not have hit every passing shot crosscourt, or Alice would have gobbled up the predictable returns and volleyed them away for winners.

Alice's powerful serve and volley made her the best women's doubles player in tennis. She and Sarah Palfrey, undefeated during their four-year partnership, won two titles at Wimbledon and four at Forest Hills. In mixed doubles, which she played with Don Budge, Bobby Riggs, Gene Mako, and Harry Hopman, Alice won three championships at Wimbledon and four at Forest Hills.

Aside from Helen Wills and Suzanne Lenglen, Alice was the biggest drawing card women's tennis had seen. She captivated audiences not only with her strength and versatility but also with her appearance and personal style. She was statuesque in short-sleeved shirts and the shortest shorts yet seen in women's tennis—several inches above the knee. She wore a white jockey cap upon her golden hair. She was businesslike on the court yet often smiled or waved her racket when an opponent came up with a beautiful play.

Alice never achieved the records of players

like Helen Wills and Suzanne Lenglen, in part because her career was cut short at both ends. A siege of illness robbed her of valuable time early in her career, and World War II put an end to the great European tournaments right after she had reached her incredible peak at age twenty-five. She won the United States singles title four times between 1936 and 1940 but won only one Wimbledon singles title, in 1939. She turned professional in 1940, when she was twenty-six. Nonetheless, Alice is remembered as one of the greatest women to play the game because of her pioneering style and her sheer dominance while at the height of her career.

Kay Stammers, after losing to Alice, 6–2, 6–0, in a thirty-minute Wimbledon final in 1939, said, "Twice I have played against Mrs. Moody, but compared with the Alice of 1939, she was easy. Alice's game is so much more varied. She has every shot and makes them so easily, yet with such power." Charlotte Dod, the former Wimbledon champion, said Alice was the best of all the women players she had ever seen.

Alice was born in Plumas County, California, where her father worked as a logger and then as a cattle rancher. Alice wrote in her autobiography, *The Road to Wimbledon,* that her first memory was of milking a cow at age four. When Alice was six, she and her family moved to San Francisco. Alice's father died shortly thereafter, and her older brother, Dan, ruled the household.

Alice was an athletic child who loved playing baseball with her three brothers and their friends. She and the boys enjoyed going to the baseball park, where they watched the San Francisco Seals, a minor-league team. One day in 1927, one of the Seals, mistaking thirteen-year-old Alice for a boy, invited her to come down onto the field and play catch with him. Alice performed so admirably that she became the Seals' official mascot and bat girl. They dubbed her the "Little Queen of Swat."

By the time Alice was fifteen, her brother Dan decided it was time for her to give up baseball. "Allie, you've got to stop being a tomboy," he told her. "Here's a [tennis] racket I bought you. . . . I want you always to play and enjoy sports, but you must play a ladylike game."

Alice Marble receives assistance after collapsing during a team match between the United States and France at Roland Garros. She did not compete again for two years.

Alice was furious. She considered tennis a "sissy sport." Nevertheless, she began playing on the public courts at Golden Gate Park and was soon reveling in the physical demands of her new pastime.

Alice improved so rapidly that in 1931, at seventeen, she played in the national championships at Forest Hills. After losing in the first round, she received some important words of advice from a former champion, Mary K. Browne. Mary urged her to try fewer spins and trick shots and to perfect the basic forehand and backhand drives. Mary also urged Alice to find a good teacher.

Alice did. She worked with Howard Kinsey, the top San Francisco professional at that time, and the very next year, in 1932, she was ranked seventh in the United States. She then came under the guidance of a teacher who would change her life: Eleanor "Teach" Tennant. Eleanor, who had ranked third among American women in 1920, was a highly regarded professional in Los Angeles who was often called "Hollywood's best-known coach." Over the years her pupils ranged from actors and actresses like Clark Gable and Carole Lombard to champions like Bobby Riggs and Maureen Connolly.

Teach and another coach, Harwood White, worked endlessly to help Alice develop her twisting serve and powerful drives. Teach also made Alice train, believing that "five sets of singles in practice are equal to three in a match," a far more ambitious philosophy than the two-sets-a-day limit espoused by Helen Wills.

In 1933 Alice made the world take notice of a new kind of women's tennis. At the Essex County Club Invitation, a prestigious tournament in Manchester, Massachusetts, she won her quarterfinal match in sixteen minutes, in one stretch ripping off twenty-eight points in succession. It was, the Associated Press said, "the fastest tennis ever played" in the tournament's nine-year history.

Alice ranked third in the United States in 1933 behind Helen Wills and Helen Jacobs, but it was to become a year of crisis for her. Alice wanted to make her first appearance on the Wightman Cup team, and, as part of the unwritten political requirements, she had to play in a tournament run by the chairman of the Wightman Cup Committee, Julian S. Myrick. Myrick was a former USLTA president and still a power within the organization. His tournament, held at the Maidstone Club in Easthampton, New York, was a three-day event. Playing singles alone would not have been a problem for Alice, but Myrick, hoping to boost gate receipts, wanted her to play in both the singles and doubles. If she reached the finals in both events, she would have to play nine matches in three days.

Alice, who was resolute, tried to do the impossible. On the final day of the tournament, with the temperature over 100 degrees, she played four matches and 108 games. That evening, she collapsed. Doctors diagnosed her illness as mild sunstroke and anemia.

Alice played the remainder of 1933 at half speed, and the next spring a two-year nightmare began. She traveled to Paris with the Wightman Cup team for a specially arranged team match between the United States and France. Alice was not feeling well at the time, and the matches at Roland Garros, like those at the Maidstone Club, were played in extreme heat. Early in her first match, Alice tossed the ball up to serve and collapsed on the court. She was taken to the American Hospital.

Alice Marble and Britain's Kay Stammers take the court for their 1939 Wimbledon final. After losing, 6–2, 6–0, Kay said she would rather have played Helen Wills.

Six weeks later Alice sailed back to New York. After disembarking in a wheelchair, she was greeted by Teach, who had driven all the way from California, and by the USLTA secretary, who requested her expense account. Alice was examined by a doctor, who told her she had tuberculosis and would never play tennis again.

Teach took Alice home to California, but not before lambasting Julian Myrick. Teach blamed him for Alice's illness and said the USLTA should pay her medical expenses. According to Alice, Myrick said that was out of the question, as "I had cost them a great deal of money, the paying of my passage, the hospital and doctors' bills, and had not played in any of the matches."

Teach, undaunted, paid for Alice's medical care herself. She had Alice admitted to a sanatorium and worked overtime teaching tennis in order to pay the bills. Alice lived at the sanatorium for five months. During her stay she received constant encouragement from Teach. She also received an inspiring letter from one of Teach's pupils, Carole Lombard, who had overcome serious injuries suffered in an automobile accident.

When Alice left the sanatorium, she weighed 175 pounds. She went to live with Teach, and gradually her health improved. She began her rehabilitation by taking walks, progressed to skipping rope, and eventually had the strength to pick up tennis balls. Then, after a thorough medical examination, a doctor told her he did not think she had ever had tuberculosis but had suffered from pleurisy and anemia. The prognosis now was excellent, he said, adding, "Alice, you can play tennis again."

In 1936, two years after her collapse at Roland Garros, Alice returned to tennis. She began winning almost immediately, but a political obstacle remained. The USLTA, fearing reprisals if she fell ill again, at first refused her entry into the 1936 national championships. Finally, at the urging of Mary K. Browne, the USLTA officials gave Alice a chance to prove herself. They ordered her to play three male players on a single day. Alice did more than survive the endurance test: she beat the three men. She went on to win her first United States championship, defeating Helen Jacobs in a three-set final.

Despite her remarkable comeback, Alice was still far from her peak. She could play like a champion, but she did not always think like one. She went into a slump in 1937 and lost in the semifinals at Wimbledon and in the quarterfinals at Forest Hills.

Alice reached a turning point shortly afterward, while competing in the Pacific Southwest championships in Los Angeles. She has recalled many times that while walking past a private courtside box where Carole Lombard and Clark Gable sat, she heard Gable say, "Look honey, we all like Alice. She's a real nice person, but she doesn't have it."

Alice was stunned, then angry. "I went out on the court and won in twenty minutes," she said later. "I got fired up from that. He hurt my pride. It taught me to go out and win. I told Gable that night at dinner that he made me a champion."

Alice lost only one important match thereafter, a semifinal to Helen Jacobs at Wimbledon in 1938. At Wimbledon in 1939, critics agreed that Alice had set a new standard for the women's game. In the semifinals she defeated Hilde Krahwinkel Sperling, the 1931 Wimbledon runner-up, 6–0, 6–0, in twenty minutes. Her 6–2, 6–0 victory over Kay Stammers in the final was nearly as devastating. No woman since Suzanne Lenglen had so thoroughly dominated the Wimbledon field. Alice also won the women's and mixed doubles titles, and in so doing became the first woman to hold all three titles at Wimbledon and Forest Hills at the same time.

Following her 1939 Wimbledon victories, Alice enchanted all present at the Wimbledon Ball with her lovely contralto voice. But the outside world did not sing with her. While Alice and her peers were celebrating tennis, London and the rest of Europe were bracing for war—preparing air raid shelters, organizing hospitals, and recruiting volunteers to give blood. Two months later, England and France declared war on Nazi Germany.

Alice Marble never returned to Wimbledon. She won her second straight American triple crown in 1940 and then turned professional. Promoters guaranteed her $25,000 for a tour of fifty American cities with Mary Hardwick, Bill Tilden, and Don Budge. Regrettably, the tour failed to thrive. Alice was too good for Mary, Budge too good for Tilden. Thus the spectacular prewar era in women's tennis faded quietly away. But the explosive style of Alice Marble would not die. Women's power tennis had only begun.

Chapter 3

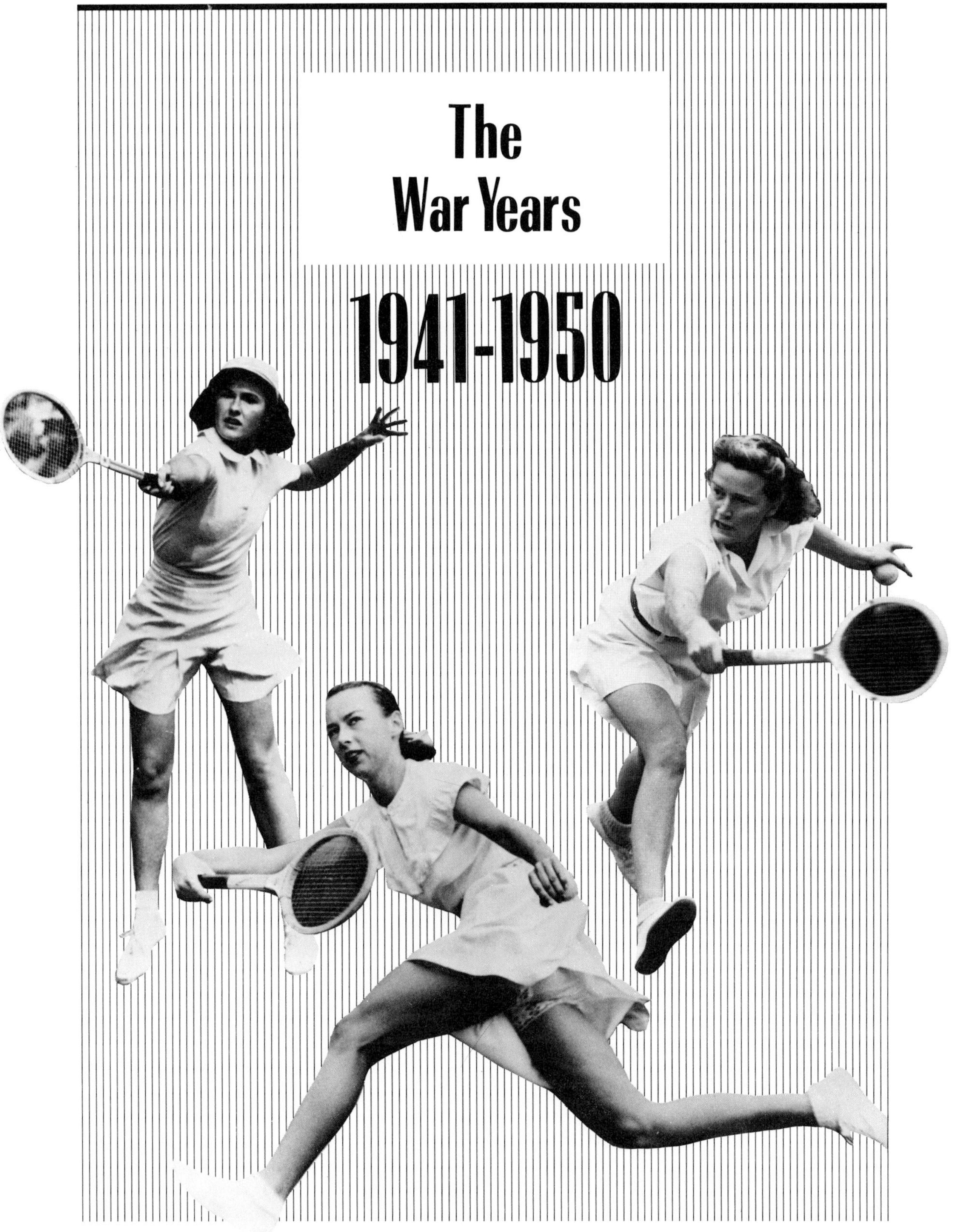

The War Years

1941-1950

Like men and women everywhere, tennis players were deeply affected by World War II. Many women tennis stars joined the thousands of other women who contributed during the war as factory workers, office workers, social volunteers, servicewomen, and entertainers. Simone Mathieu served in the French Resistance, creating a women's auxiliary group, and was honored for her achievements. Helen Jacobs joined the WAVES, the women's reserve of the United States Navy. Alice Marble sang for servicemen at hospitals and military camps. Mary K. Browne served with the Red Cross in Australia, where luxuries like tennis balls all but vanished. Brownie hungered for the sight of a tennis ball and was jubilant when she received three dozen from a friend in California.

Margaret Osborne, who would win three United States singles titles, worked as a clerk eight hours a day, six days a week, at a shipbuilding factory in Sausalito, California, carrying her brown-bag lunch, and then riding a bus to the California Tennis Club for practice afterward. Margaret and her doubles partner, Louise Brough (pronounced Bruff), entertained American soldiers by playing singles matches at more than fifty military bases. Margaret, who was then secretary-treasurer of the Northern California Tennis Association, compiled rankings with the association's president behind blackout curtains, which were used in all American coastal cities.

From 1940 through 1945, important competitions came to a halt throughout the world. The Wimbledon and French championships were disbanded in 1940 and the Australian championships a year later. Only in the United States did tennis continue at the highest level.

"Sports followers of recent eras cannot possibly appreciate what a slice World War II took out of people's lives," said Australia's Thelma Coyne Long, runner-up in Australia's last national championship before the war. "In 1938 I was the youngest member of an Australian women's team that went to Europe and America. Then came World War II, and the next time I had the opportunity to travel overseas was in 1949, eleven years later."

At Wimbledon and Roland Garros, the war came all too close. The All England Club was bombed sixteen times, the most serious damage inflicted by a 500-pound bomb that crashed through the Centre Court roof on October 11, 1940. The club grounds were pressed into service for use by the Red Cross and the National Fire Service, and soldiers drilled on the walkway outside the clubhouse. Norah Gordon Cleather, the club's acting secretary, kept farm animals in one of the car parks. "We are very proud of our little farm of pigs, poultry, and rabbits," she reported in 1943. Grazing on the courts, however, was not permitted.

The famed Centre Court, used only for tournament competition until World War II, was opened for special guests, including members of the Australian, British, and United States armed forces.

At Roland Garros in Paris, the scene was harrowing. German soldiers, who took over the grounds in 1943, used Roland Garros as a holding area for deportees waiting to be transferred to death camps. Only after the liberation of Paris in 1944 did tennis return to Roland Garros with an exhibition match between Frenchmen Henri Cochet and Yvon Petra. Simone Mathieu, dressed in her captain's uniform, umpired the match.

In America, most tournaments came to a halt during the war, but with the blessing of President Franklin D. Roosevelt, the national championships proceeded without interruption. Although the number of overseas entries dropped sharply and much of the glamour was lost, the event still drew crowds.

The United States nationals were more than just a form of entertainment during those years; they became a vehicle for raising money for the war effort. Portions of the gate receipts, however small, were donated to various war causes. Mary Hardwick, a former British Wightman Cup player who had moved to the United States, set aside her racket in 1941 and collected "Bundles for Britain" at a stand underneath the stadium at Forest Hills. During the national women's doubles championships that year at the Longwood Cricket Club, a table-tennis tournament benefiting the United States Service Organization

Overleaf, Sarah Palfrey, of Boston, top left, was the best woman volleyer of her day. Californian Gussy Moran, center, delighted Wimbledon spectators in 1949 with her lace panties. Pauline Betz, another Californian, overcame her rivals with stamina, determination, and an exquisite backhand.

Fund was held. Pauline Betz defeated Margaret Osborne in the final.

The American women tennis players who starred during and after the war were symbolic of the times. They were strong-willed and independent; many of them held jobs at some point in their lives, and most of them married relatively late. They wore basic, functional clothing and tennis shoes that were resoled over and over again because of the scarcity of rubber. They played aggressively and purposefully, and most of them liked to attack the net.

In one respect, they drew more attention than their counterparts of previous years. Because many of America's young male players had enlisted and were no longer competing, tournament directors frequently had no choice but to put women's matches on the spectator courts. "The women did not mind too much," Doris Hart wrote. "For once, *we* were the feature attractions and played on the front courts instead of being relegated to the 'pasture'!"

Still, the women stars during the war were hardly the celebrities they would be today. With the exception of the nationals, they were still appearing mostly in private clubs and before small crowds. They received less publicity than women in other years, because they had fewer tournaments in which to compete and because Wimbledon, the biggest tournament of all, was not being played. Furthermore, news of the war took precedence over everything else in the print media. I am not surprised that the most successful women players during the war years, Sarah Palfrey and Pauline Betz, are today among the least remembered of the American women title holders after World War I.

Sarah Palfrey won thirty-nine junior and adult titles, including a record three successive girls' eighteen-and-under championships, in a twenty-year period. She reached the final of the United States national singles four times, winning twice, in 1941 and 1945, as Sarah Palfrey Cooke. She never won a Wimbledon singles title, but as Sarah Palfrey Fabyan she won the women's doubles title twice with Alice Marble before the war. For ten years, beginning at age seventeen, she was a member of the Wightman Cup team.

Beautiful Sarah Palfrey was called "Little Miss Almost" until 1941, when, as a twenty-eight-year-old mother, she won her first of two United States singles titles.

Sarah Palfrey of Boston, only five feet three, enchanted crowds with her natural grace, her flair at the net, and her diminutive figure. Sportswriters marveled at her "exquisite daintiness" and her "eternal femininity." Some said she looked like a dancer.

Sarah's grace was completely natural. She never thought about her appearance when she ran for a ball. She just ran as fast as she could and looked like a sylph doing it. And if Sarah was considered feminine, she never thought of herself as dainty. "I felt like a tiger out there," she said.

Indeed, it was Sarah Palfrey the tigress who upstaged the great Ellsworth Vines, the reigning male Wimbledon champion, in the final of the 1932 mixed doubles championships at the Longwood Cricket Club. Vines, showing no mercy toward the petite Sarah, smashed an overhead right at her as her partner, Fred Perry, stood by helplessly. Sarah, having backed away from the net a pace or two, caught the screaming overhead squarely on her racket and knocked it off the forehand side for a clean winner. "It was one of the best shots I ever made," Sarah recalled. "Fred loved it. Vines never said a thing."

From the backcourt Sarah was consistent but not strong early in her career, but she was perhaps the best woman volleyer of her day. She was sought as a doubles partner by the game's finest, and she won thirteen national women's and mixed doubles titles between 1930 and 1941. For a span of four years, she and Alice Marble were unbeaten.

Sarah was greatly admired for her graciousness in victory and defeat. Allison Danzig, who covered tennis for *The New York Times* from the mid-1920s through the late 1960s, declared, "Sportsmanship has had no truer exemplar than the slip of a Boston blueblood who fought unrelentingly to win, but never at all costs, and ever mindful that it was a game."

Sarah was the fourth of six children born to the socially prominent Mr. and Mrs. John G. Palfrey of Boston, and later Brookline, a Boston suburb. Her father, a Harvard graduate, was an eminent lawyer. Sarah's mother, Methyl Gertrude Oakes, graduated from prestigious Smith College, where she was a member of the fledgling golf and tennis teams.

Sarah and her four sisters, Polly, Lee, Mianne, and Joanna, played during the summer on their private clay court on the family farm in Sharon, Massachusetts. After the family moved to Brookline, the Palfrey sisters polished their tennis games at the Longwood Cricket Club under the watchful eye of Mrs. Wightman, who once arranged for twelve-year-old Sarah to play in a doubles tournament with Bill Tilden. (Palfrey and Tilden lost in the semifinals, but an enduring friendship was begun.) All five Palfrey sisters went on to win at least one national junior title.

While attending the Winsor School in Brookline, Sarah was captain of the field hockey team, but tennis was always first in her heart. "No one ever tried to discourage me from participating in sports," Sarah recalled. "I was encouraged. And Mrs. Wightman, of course—without her, there wouldn't have been all those wonderful tournaments. Mrs. Wightman did a lot more than coach. She chauffeured the players to the club and back. She used to pick me up in her big, dark-red Cadillac. My mother did that, too. I don't know how they chauffeured so many people. But Mrs. Wightman and my mother were extraordinary."

Sarah honed her volleying skills and developed a sense of where to place the ball just by being on the same court with Mrs. Wightman. "Her tennis knowledge was instinctive," Sarah said. "It came to me, from her mind to my mind."

In 1940 Sarah married Elwood Cooke, who had reached the 1939 Wimbledon singles final against Bobby Riggs. The marriage did not endure, but it certainly helped Sarah's tennis. Elwood thought Sarah could strengthen her ground strokes, especially her backhand, and he recommended that she work with Tom Stow, a gifted teacher whose pupils included Don Budge and Margaret Osborne. Sarah agreed and traveled to California, where she worked with Stow almost every day for two months. Stow flattened out her sliced backhand in order to increase her power. As Sarah struggled with the new stroke throughout 1940, her losses mounted. She stayed with it, however, and in 1941, at age twenty-eight, she won the triple crown at Forest Hills. She beat the fading Helen Jacobs in the semifinals, and then beat the rising, twenty-two-year-old Pauline Betz in the final to become the first native Easterner to win the United States singles title since Maud Barger-Wallach in 1908. Sarah won the women's doubles title with Margaret Osborne and the mixed doubles with Jack Kramer.

At this high point in her career, Sarah chose to leave the competitive tennis world to be with her husband, who had enlisted as a naval officer at the outbreak of World War II. She gave birth to a daughter and later worked as a hostess at the La Jolla (California) Beach and Tennis Club. "Part of my job was to arrange bridge games, fix the flowers, and play tennis with the customers," Sarah recalled. "I got in lots of tennis." Indeed, Sarah practiced enough that she had no trouble making a comeback a couple of years later.

Succeeding Sarah Palfrey as national champion from 1942 through 1944 was Pauline Betz. She was a trim five feet five and had wavy, strawberry-blonde hair and greenish eyes. Unlike Sarah, she played from the baseline with remarkable consistency, with a backhand surpassed by none. Critics said that in the categories of serve, forehand, overhead, and volley, Margaret Osborne was superior to Pauline. Yet it was Pauline who was queen. If she could not beat you with power and style, she beat you with stamina and grit. The ultimate retriever, she flew around the court, diving for the most impossible shots. Eleanor "Teach" Tennant, who had coached Alice Marble, said Pauline had the strength and endurance of a stevedore. "If I were a second-rater," Pauline once said, "I'd quit."

In the years following her retirement some tennis experts called Pauline Betz one of the best women tennis players of all time. But she did not earn that accolade during her career—probably because her lone Wimbledon singles title in 1946 looked so insignificant compared with the eight won by Helen Wills and the six by Suzanne Lenglen. Wimbledon has always been the yardstick by which champions are measured.

In her own eyes, however, Pauline felt she received "plenty of recognition." Her status was high among those who knew tennis, and her active social life made her the talk of the circuit. Her long list of beaux included Jack Dempsey and Spencer Tracy.

The acrobatic Pauline Betz often leaped the net after a major success.

Pauline Betz was born in Dayton, Ohio. When she was eight years old, her father lost his job at Dayton Power & Light, and, as Pauline recalled, he took the family west "to look for something." Fortunately for Pauline's future, they settled in Los Angeles, the training ground of many champions, where a child could play tennis year-round for little expense.

Like Sarah Palfrey, Pauline was introduced to tennis by her mother, a high school physical-education teacher who apparently was alarmed by the tomboyish tendencies of her acrobatic little girl. One of Pauline's favorite tricks was to walk down the street on her hands to greet her father when he came home from work. Directed toward the more ladylike pastime of tennis, Pauline was soon hooked. She slugged balls against the garage door, pretending she was either Helen Wills or Helen Jacobs, her idols. As a wide-eyed girl of fourteen, she attended the famous Pacific Southwest tournament at the Los Angeles Tennis Club and watched the stars. Positioning herself behind the court, Pauline peered through the fence below the wind screen and became thoroughly enchanted with Don Budge's backhand, one of the great strokes in the history of the game. "I've always told Budge that story," Pauline recalled, smiling. "He likes that story."

Pauline began playing tournaments in her early teens but had no formal training until she was fifteen. She saved twenty-four dollars from her dollar-a-week allowance and bought twelve lessons with Dick Skeen, an excellent teacher.

The Betzes never had enough money for Pauline to travel east for the national junior tournaments, but in the long run, she said, it did not matter. "In California they had tournaments all the time, and you always had good competition."

In 1939 Pauline was awarded a tennis scholarship by Florida's Rollins College, where she studied economics and played Number 4 on a men's team that briefly featured Jack Kramer. Pauline graduated in 1943 and won a graduate scholarship to Columbia University.

In 1942, while a student at Rollins, twenty-three-year-old Pauline won her first United

PAULINE BETZ

"The first time I traveled outside California I was eighteen or nineteen years old. I went on the Florida circuit. I drove down with a couple of people, and we all split the expenses. It seems I always left home with a maximum of twenty-five dollars.

"The first time I went east to play, my mother drove me. It was during the summer, when she wasn't teaching school. A couple of people went with us, and we all shared the gas expense. Mother once told me she came across this little diary that she had kept of the expenses, and it would say something like, 'Breakfast, ten cents.'

"I'd say, 'How did we eat breakfast for ten cents?'

"She said—this was about 1939—'You could get three bananas for ten cents.' She said we each had a banana and a half in the car driving to the next tournament.

"There's such a difference the way it's done now and the way it was. It was pretty spartan then. Some of the people had plenty of money, but most of us didn't have much. But you could *do* it then. You could get by with it because some of the tournaments put you up.

"Once my mom and I slept on the beach in our sleeping bags. That was the first year I went to Forest Hills. If you got in at two or three o'clock in the morning, you didn't want to pay to stay somewhere all night. So you made it through the night in the car or somewhere, and then you could check in at the hotel in the morning.

"Later, the Wightman Cup picked up my expenses at Wimbledon. You also got expense money from tournaments—not very much, but you got some. I watched my pocketbook quite a bit. When I was the national champion, I was going to Rollins on a scholarship and was working part-time waiting tables. I could have gotten along without working, probably, but I loved making my own money.

"I remember being at the Westchester Country Club at an eastern grass-court tournament. Doris Hart and I were put up because we had high rankings. We each got a room, and nobody else did. We had four or five people sleeping in sleeping bags on the floors of our rooms. And we'd order breakfast up there, and everybody would eat breakfast. Somebody had a jar of peanut butter, the ever-present peanut butter. We had a great time.

"It was tough at the beginning, financially. It didn't seem that tough then, but in retrospect, it seems sort of incredible. But at the time you're striving toward a goal and you're having a wonderful time and you're young and life's great. The people who had money, whose parents could have afforded to give them anything, they weren't the ones who were winning.

"The only time I didn't like it was after I had won. I didn't really have the financial problem then, but I had the problem of trying to win, of trying to maintain it, where you got no credit if you won and lots of discredit if you lost. So I enjoyed the struggling years much more."

States singles title. In the final she met nineteen-year-old Louise Brough, a skillful all-round player from California. Louise, a heavy favorite, had gone unbeaten all year and had beaten Pauline twice previously that summer. When Louise played with confidence, she reminded critics of Alice Marble. With her high-kicking twist serve, she was untouchable. On this occasion, however, Pauline chipped away at Louise's attacking game with perfectly executed lobs and in so doing wore down Louise's confidence. "I lobbed into the sun," said Pauline. "Louise had a big overhead, but she was prone to being nervous. I think her nerves finally got to her." After the final point, Pauline gleefully leaped over the net.

Pauline successfully defended her national title in 1943, again beating Louise in the final, and in 1944, beating Margaret Osborne. Her bid for a fourth consecutive title was stopped in the 1945 final by the comeback of her old friend Sarah Palfrey Cooke. Sarah, then the mother of a two-year-old daughter, had been away from the competitive scene for most of the previous three years, but she had never strayed far from the tennis courts. While she and her husband were stationed in Pensacola, Florida, she had practiced with navy lieutenants until the eighth month of her pregnancy. Later in La Jolla, she practiced with Bill Tilden and gave exhibitions for the Red Cross. As a result, when she entered the 1945 national championships, her game was as sharp as it had ever been. She plowed through to the final without losing a set, beating the ever-difficult Louise Brough in the semifinals.

The final between Sarah Palfrey and Pauline Betz was played on V-J Day, September 2, 1945, several hours after the Japanese formally surrendered to the Allies on the battleship *Missouri.* The match, watched by a crowd of more than 10,000, was called one of the best ever played at Forest Hills. *The New York Times* described it as a beautifully fought match that had the spectators "in a state of almost breathless excitement" until the last point was played. Pauline broke Sarah's serve to take a 4–3 lead in the deciding set, but Sarah fought back with penetrating drives and put-away volleys. She triumphed, 3–6, 8–6, 6–4.

Sarah promptly retired from amateur competition, while Pauline Betz, stunned by her loss, returned to California and sought help from Teach Tennant. Pauline was too independent to allow Teach to control every aspect of her life and consequently was not as close to Teach as Alice Marble had been. Still, Pauline respected her as a teacher and a motivator. Teach worked on Pauline's serve and helped Pauline shorten the backswing on her forehand. Pauline would soon be ready for her finest year.

When the American women returned to Wimbledon for the Wightman Cup competition in 1946, they found an England scarred by war. At Wimbledon, the bomb that hit the Centre Court had reduced 1,200 seats to rubble. (Building restrictions prevented repairs from being completed until 1949.) Food was another problem. Meat, eggs, and sweets were impossible to find, and the word "chicken" on a restaurant menu usually meant pigeon. Fortunately for the Americans, a friendship with a naval officer's wife opened the door to the United States Embassy, where

Pauline Betz, left, has just defeated Margaret Osborne, 6–3, 8–6, in the final of the 1944 nationals. The title was Pauline's third straight at Forest Hills.

the players were able to eat balanced meals.

The inconveniences of postwar life in England, however, were of minor importance to a group of gifted athletes who had dreamed of Wimbledon for most of their lives. For them, the sight of the All England Club could not have been more moving. "I was awestruck," Margaret Osborne duPont recalled. "It was hard to believe you finally were there."

The American women were showered with attention by the British media and fans—"You were a celebrity over there," Pauline Betz said—and the Wightman Cup matches were played before capacity crowds.

The British Wightman Cup players, led by Kay Stammers and Jean Bostock—two great names in the 1930s—thought they had a chance to beat the Americans, but they were rusty from lack of tournament competition. Furthermore, they had no way of gauging the skill of the Americans—Betz, Brough, Osborne, Doris Hart, and Pat Todd—who would help extend America's dominance in women's tennis into the 1950s. Together these five women would win sixty-nine individual Wightman Cup matches against three losses between 1946 and 1962. They also would win twenty-eight singles titles in the four championships making up the Grand Slam (the Australian, French, Wimbledon, and American), a remarkable number in view of the lost opportunities during the war and the fact that not all of them had the opportunity to compete in Australia.

Doris Hart, a dynamic player despite a game leg, won Wimbledon in 1951 and the United States championships in 1954 and 1955. Patricia Canning Todd, the overlooked team member, won four of her five Wightman Cup matches, all in doubles, and was ranked among America's top ten women every year but one between 1942 and 1952.

The American Wightman Cup team of 1946 was once dubbed "the Betz Club" in honor of their leading lady. With their clubby nicknames—Bobbie Betz, Broughie, Ozzie, and Toddie—they might well have passed for a social clique, but the group was anything but clubby as a whole. Louise Brough said that, aside from Margaret Osborne duPont, her relationship with the other members of the team was "competitive and aloof." Margaret described Doris Hart and herself as "friendly enemies."

The coolness that existed then, however, can be likened neither to the gulf of silence that separated Helen Wills from Helen Jacobs nor to the unspoken rules of today's jungle that keep some doubles partners from so much as dining out together. One of Pauline Betz's most vivid memories of Wimbledon was of playing gin rummy with Doris Hart over breakfast at the Dorchester Hotel. Doris went to dinner and the movies with Pauline and later Shirley Fry. "All of us got along pretty well," Doris said. "We'd fight each other tooth and nail on the court, but it wasn't like we wouldn't talk to each other."

As Wightman Cup players in 1946, the Americans were positively united, and with their big serves and killer overheads they won all seven matches without the loss of a set. The victory was their most decisive against the British since 1923. "They were just too good for us," Kay Stammers recalled. "They were definitely the best group of players I had ever seen."

A correspondent for *The Times* of London marveled at Pauline Betz's backhand and Doris Hart's grace, and questioned whether any woman's service had traveled as fast as Margaret Osborne's. "There is not a great deal that can be said about the doubles," the writer said. "These Americans know this game and they play it like men. It may be that this team is as good as any ever sent over. . . . Our players know clearly now what standard has to be aimed at."

A week later, Pauline Betz extended her domination to the Wimbledon championships, where she lost only twenty games during the entire singles competition. She beat Louise Brough in the final, 6–2, 6–4. Only three other non-British women—May Sutton, Suzanne Lenglen, and Maureen Connolly—have won Wimbledon on their first try.

In the French championships, which followed Wimbledon in 1946, Pauline bowed in the final to Margaret Osborne, 1–6, 8–6, 7–5, after having a match point in the second set. ("I missed an overhead," was Pauline's laughing comment.) Pauline reasserted herself at Forest Hills, where she defeated Californian Pat Todd in the final, 11–9, 6–3, to become the seventh woman to win four United States singles titles.

On the eve of the national championships, tennis observers seemed uncertain of Pauline Betz's place in history. *Time* magazine said most experts dismissed her as "the best in a year with no greats." In *Time*'s editorial opinion she was "an obvious cut or two below the all-time greats, Suzanne Lenglen and Helen Wills Moody." Yet the editors must have sensed that Pauline was someone special: Her picture—a portrait that conveyed health, independence, and resolution—graced their cover. When Pauline had reached her sixth straight national final and captured her fourth title, *The New York Times* paid tribute to "as unconquerable a competitive spirit as the championship has known."

Pauline Betz was, in fact, the best of a very good bunch. One British tennis reporter, Peter Wilson of the London *Daily Mirror,* wrote in 1964 that Pauline's tenacious spirit and consistency at the baseline would have tested Maureen Connolly, "who never really cared for this sort of opponent." Pancho Gonzales, the former men's champion, also included Pauline in the same breath with Maureen Connolly. "Players like Maureen and Pauline seemed to be masters of the mind," Gonzales said. "They always seemed to know the right moves to make. They had a determination that was rare. They would never give up."

Pauline no doubt would have added to her accomplishments had she not turned professional, along with her good friend Sarah Palfrey Cooke, while still in her prime. Pauline had planned to make one more appearance at Wimbledon and Forest Hills in 1947, but when the USLTA discovered that Sarah's husband was making inquiries about a professional tour for the two women, it suspended Pauline from further amateur competition. The USLTA would not have granted a hearing on the matter until after the Wimbledon and United States championships had been completed.

Pauline was disappointed, but not devas-

The overpowering American Wightman Cup team of 1946 consisted of, from left: Patricia Canning Todd, Louise Brough, Pauline Betz, captain Hazel Wightman, Margaret Osborne, and Doris Hart.

tated, by the USLTA's action. "I'm sure I could have been reinstated if I had said, no, I wasn't going to turn pro," she explained later. "But by that time, I didn't want to play any more amateur tennis. I wasn't bitter, because I felt it was time to do something else." Then she added with a smile, "Now if there had been open tennis, *that* would have been marvelous. We all wanted it. But the USLTA had a stranglehold on tennis."

Sarah and Pauline preferred their well-paid nationwide tour in 1947 to making the circuit of amateur championships for twelve dollars a day in expenses, but it was backbreaking work. They played seven days a week and drove from city to city, traveling as much as 400 miles a night, frequently by themselves. The two often resorted to gimmickry to sell tennis at schools and colleges. "We wanted to give some instruction without putting the audiences to sleep," Pauline said. Pauline, alias "Susie Glutz," would appear on the court dressed in sloppy men's clothes (size forty shorts) and a rain hat, with a warped racket in her hand. Sarah, the straight woman, would iron out poor Susie Glutz's problems. Comedian Milton Berle once suggested that Pauline blacken her front teeth, but here Pauline drew the line.

Sarah and Pauline cannot remember exactly how much they made as professionals during their one-year tour; they put the figure in the neighborhood of $10,000 each. "I thought that was pretty good," Sarah said. Pauline was not complaining, either.

Sarah and Pauline also spent a month that year touring in Europe with Don Budge and Bobby Riggs. A few years later Riggs signed Pauline, who by then was Pauline Betz Addie, to tour with Jack Kramer, Pancho Segura, and Gertrude "Gussy" Moran. Pauline earned between $500 and $600 a week playing against Gussy, a high-ranking American who had paraded into the limelight in 1949 by wearing lace panties at Wimbledon. The side acts continued on this tour as well. Gussy wore several varieties of fake fur, including tiger and antelope, and on a few occasions Pauline tried to upstage her by wearing gold lamé shorts.

After their brief touring days were over, Pauline and Sarah got on with the business of raising children and nurturing the sport they loved so much. Sarah Palfrey and Elwood Cooke were divorced, and Sarah began a long, happy marriage to Jerome Danzig of New York, a television executive and onetime special assistant to New York Governor Nelson A. Rockefeller. (Jerome was not related to Allison Danzig of *The New York Times.*) Following Mrs. Wightman's example as a grand patron of the game, Sarah conducted clinics for underprivileged children, provided housing for international tennis stars competing at Forest Hills, wrote books and articles about tennis, served as a vice-president for *World Tennis* magazine, and became deeply involved in charity work.

Pauline, who married Bob Addie, a sportswriter for *The Washington Post,* taught tennis and lived a full life. When well into her sixties, she continued to teach tennis and keep the books at the Cabin John indoor tennis club in Bethesda, Maryland. Her backhand was still beautiful, too.

Pauline's five children inherited her love for tennis, and one of her sons, Gary, a teaching professional in Cincinnati, recalled being surprised by the discovery that men were better tennis players than women. "My dad never played tennis," Gary said. "I thought all the great players were women."

After Pauline's period of supremacy, the early postwar era was dominated by two friends and champions who are impossible to separate in history. Margaret Osborne duPont and Louise Brough were both powerhouses from California; they drove the ball hard from the baseline and attacked the net so frequently that critics said they played like men. Louise, of Beverly Hills, and Margaret, of San Francisco, carved out enduring records in singles—Louise at Wimbledon, Margaret in the United States—and together they set doubles records that endured for years.

As singles players, they both reached the finals so often that *The Times* of London referred to them as "the inevitable duPont and Brough." Between them they won every Wimbledon and United States singles title between 1947 and 1951.

The young Margaret Osborne, left, and Louise Brough were doubles partners, singles rivals, champions, and friends.

As a doubles team Ozzie and Broughie won twenty Grand Slam titles: twelve at Forest Hills, five at Wimbledon, and three in Paris. It is probably safe to say that they won no doubles titles in Australia only because they never competed there together. Louise made one trip to Australia and Margaret never went at all. Martina Navratilova and Pam Shriver were the only pair to approach the doubles record set by Margaret and Louise, and in 1988 they appeared destined to eclipse it.

Margaret Osborne duPont was at her best at Forest Hills, where she won three singles titles, thirteen women's doubles titles, and nine mixed doubles titles, for a total of twenty-five United States championships. That record is unsurpassed by any man or woman, and it remains unthreatened. Margaret Smith Court, who retired in 1976, is second with eighteen United States titles, and Louise Brough is third with seventeen. Margaret Osborne duPont also is unsurpassed in the number of years that span her first Grand Slam title, the United States women's doubles with Sarah Palfrey in 1941, and her last, the Wimbledon mixed doubles with Neale Fraser in 1962, when she was forty-four.

Louise Brough, in contrast, was in top form at Wimbledon, where she won four times between 1948 and 1955. She was one of nine women to win four Wimbledon singles championships; only she, Suzanne Lenglen, Helen Wills, Martina Navratilova, and I have won that many since World War I.

Margaret and Louise were virtually inseparable as young adults. Their old scrapbooks contain few pictures of one without the other. They roomed together on the road, and a typical finals day found them practicing together, having lunch together, and then competing together, in both singles and doubles. But the two women, one developed in northern California, the other in southern California, had vastly different beginnings, and in personality and court temperament, they were as different as topspin and slice.

Margaret Evelyn Osborne was born five years before Louise Brough and spent her earliest days on a farm in Joseph, Oregon. Her father's poor health forced the family to leave the farm when Margaret was ten. They moved first to Spokane and then to San Francisco, where Mr. Osborne managed a downtown garage. It was a humble beginning for a girl destined to marry a duPont from Wilmington, Delaware.

Margaret got her first glimpse of tennis soon after her family left the farm. While in Spokane, she passed some old dirt courts on her way to her piano lessons and stopped to pick up balls that sailed over the fence. When her mother gave her a racket, she was off and running. After the family moved to San Francisco, Margaret began playing seriously on the public courts at Golden Gate Park. Her mother encouraged her and drove her to tournaments. At seventeen, Margaret received her first formal lessons from Howard Kinsey, a former Davis Cup player who had become a well-known instructor. Kinsey helped her make ends meet by allowing her to write his articles for *American Lawn Tennis* magazine for a few pennies a word.

Another early influence on Margaret was the ubiquitous Hazel Wightman. Margaret was already established as a leading California junior when Mrs. Wightman stopped by the Berkeley Tennis Club to survey the local talent. Mrs. Wightman's presence always drew a crowd, and several newspaper reporters pressed her for her opinion of Margaret. As Margaret's mother listened, Mrs. Wightman replied that Margaret would never win a national championship. "She's too nice," Mrs. Wightman explained. "She doesn't have the killer instinct." Mrs. Osborne was irate, but Margaret vowed then and there that she would win a national championship.

She won her first, the national girls' eighteen-and-under title, in 1936 when she was eighteen years old. Mrs. Wightman had not counted on the ambition of the sweet-tempered young woman who wanted nothing less than to be a member of the Wightman Cup team, to win her national championship, and to finish first at Wimbledon, in that order. Years later, Margaret laughed about Mrs. Wightman's comment. "In a way it was a compliment," she said. "I considered her one of my very best friends in tennis."

Margaret's cheery and accommodating view of life must have helped her with her tennis. She slept long and well before her major matches, and she did not fret over her losses. She had the ability to remain calm, especially when confronted by adversity.

At Forest Hills, Margaret coped better than most with the irritants and distractions that were an accepted part of the nationals. She was able to ignore the sounds of commuter trains that sometimes screeched to a stop during an important point. She maintained her concentration and composure while making the long, quarter-mile walk from the clubhouse to the stadium court through the curious and pressing crowd. She dealt with the bedlam of the West Side Tennis Club's dressing room by avoiding it altogether; she changed her clothes in her room at the Forest Hills Inn instead.

Margaret had a reputation for playing her best in tight situations. Margaret Varner Bloss, her doubles partner in later years, said duPont never double faulted and never choked. No, Margaret duPont said, she could not remember ever choking, although Louise Brough gently disputed that statement in a rare disagreement. No one can dispute the fact, however, that Margaret was a far calmer player than her dear friend Louise.

Althea Louise Brough was born in Oklahoma City and moved to Beverly Hills with her mother when she was four. She was named for both her mother, Althea, who always pushed her to succeed, and for her mother's sister, Louise. Although Louise Brough's parents were separated, she had a comfortable childhood, devoid of financial worries. She developed an early interest in sports, and her competitive instincts were there from the start. "I always wanted to be the best—when I played baseball, when we had races in grammar school," Louise said. "I wanted to be the winner, and I usually was, because I was bigger and stronger than the other kids."

Louise and her brother, J.P., were introduced to tennis on the public courts six blocks from their home in Beverly Hills. Louise liked

Margaret Osborne duPont was one of tennis's greatest sportswomen. "There is no such thing as a bad sport," she once said, repeating a childhood lesson. "You're either a sport or you're not a sport."

the game well enough but lost interest the day her Aunt Louise made her wear a white school dress to the courts. "I was hating every minute of it because I was in that white dress. I didn't play for a long time," Louise recalled. Later, when her aunt gave her an old Bancroft racket, Louise's interest was rekindled. At thirteen, she received her first tennis lessons from Dick Skeen, who had taught Pauline Betz, and within a year was one of his most dedicated pupils.

Louise's mother, like Margaret Osborne's, was a driving force behind her career, but the similarities ended there. While Mrs. Osborne was a gentle observer who was not bothered by little Margaret's losses ("You'll get her next time," was her standard response), Mrs. Brough was an emotional participant who felt great pain when her daughter failed. "She was so supportive," Louise recalled. "But she didn't understand sports at all. She didn't understand that you could lose. She was very unhappy when I lost in junior tournaments. I think that drove me. I didn't want to go through that battle after I lost. It also made me mad, and a couple of times I threatened that I wouldn't play anymore. I don't remember what she said to me. I just remember it was anger. I'm not sure I didn't cry a little."

Louise drove herself, too. The result was an immaculate tennis game: a classic forehand and backhand and a paralyzing American twist serve.

As an up-and-coming teenager, Louise saw herself as a fierce and unflinching "fighter pilot," eager to gun down the stars. It was the fighter pilot in sixteen-year-old Louise that enabled her to attempt one of the more grueling feats in women's tennis in 1940: she competed simultaneously in two major tournaments in two different cities, ninety miles apart. The national junior championships at the Philadelphia Cricket Club, which had been delayed a week by rain, coincided with the women's nationals at Forest Hills. Louise, scheduled to play in both, commuted back and forth for her matches.

On one especially hectic afternoon, Louise and her Aunt Louise were rushing back for a match in Philadelphia after a match at Forest Hills when a tire on their car blew out. Determined to get to her match, Louise jumped out of the car, stuck out her thumb, and rode the rest of the way with a truck driver. Within an hour Louise was at the cricket club. "I think I got there half an hour or fifteen minutes before I had to play my match," Louise recalled. "But when you're young, things like that just don't bother you."

Louise Brough captured two rare triple crowns at Wimbledon, in 1948 and 1950. She nearly won a third in 1949 but fell short in the mixed doubles.

As time went on, however, many things did bother her. "After years of playing the same old people, you get tense," she said. "You just don't want to lose to them."

Louise invariably struggled at Forest Hills, with all of its unsettling distractions. Although she reached the finals of the nationals five times, she managed to win only one, losing each of the other four in three hard-fought sets. She lost the 1948 final to Margaret after having one match point; she lost the 1954 final to Doris Hart after having three.

Midway through her career Louise began having difficulty tossing the ball up straight

The ambidextrous Beverly Baker Fleitz, a frequent contender for major titles, hit the ball with both hands. In photo at left, she hits an overhead with her right hand; at right, she prepares for a left-handed forehand.

on her serve. In 1950, possibly as a result, she developed a severe case of tennis elbow in her right arm during her only trip to Australia. "It was windy over there and I was having trouble with my toss," Louise recalled. "I'd throw the ball different places, and they'd call a foot fault on me, and I got tenser and tenser. I'd reach back instead of having to throw it up again, but I did catch it a lot of times. And then I had a great big suitcase that I carried on and off planes with my right arm. I really think the suitcase had more to do with it than anything."

Louise Brough continued to compete long after her physical and emotional prime. Shirley Fry, who was four years younger than Louise, was saddened by the sight of Broughie tossing the ball up on her serve with a quivering hand and catching it, again and again. "She loved the game so much," Shirley recalled. "It's hard to break away from something when you've been so involved in it all those years. But it's hard to see a champion go down."

"I just played too long," Louise later said, with a wry smile that suggested she would play too long all over again if she had the chance. "You win Wimbledon and you don't want to quit. You keep waiting until somebody beats you and then you can quit. It's hard to give up a trip to Wimbledon."

Certainly, tennis's greatest stage could not have asked more of the four-time singles champion. Enclosed by the dark green walls of Wimbledon's Centre Court, despite the thousands looking down on her, Louise Brough was comforted by feelings of solitude and individuality that she found nowhere else on earth. She could not wait to go onto the Centre Court, she once said, so that she could be alone.

Louise's greatest victory at Wimbledon came in 1955 when, at thirty-two and struggling with her serve, she won her fourth singles title. Her victory, critics said at the time, put her on a pedestal near Suzanne Lenglen and Helen Wills.

Louise's opponent in the final, Californian Beverly Baker Fleitz, was powerful, ambidextrous, and seven years her junior. Beverly stayed at the baseline and hit nothing but forehands, switching her racket from one hand to the other. She had demolished Doris Hart in the semifinals, 6–2, 6–0, and was highly favored to beat Louise, whom she had beaten in their last four matches. Undaunted, Louise mapped out a game plan the night before the final: she would return every ball and

In a moment preserved from their wonderful rivalry, Louise Brough (near court) and Margaret Osborne duPont vie during their marathon 1948 United States final. Margaret won, 4–6, 6–4, 15–13.

disrupt Beverly's marvelous rhythm with a mixture of drives, slices, lobs, and drop shots. Louise trailed, 5–4, in both sets, had problems with her toss, grew tired near the end of the second set, and double-faulted on her first match point, yet won the match, miraculously, 7–5, 8–6. When Beverly hit a weak shot into the net on the second match point, Louise leaped into the air with joy.

Louise, who played some of her best matches at Wimbledon, was also at her best against Margaret Osborne duPont, no matter where they played. Against Margaret, her friend, she always felt relaxed. The feeling was mutual, and the two friends produced two of the longest women's finals ever in big-four tournaments. The first was the national singles final of 1948, which Margaret won, 4–6, 6–4, 15–13, after staving off a match point in the twelfth game of the final set—the longest set ever in women's singles at the nationals. (The match itself was the longest United States women's final since 1898, when women were still playing best-of-five-set matches.)

The two-hour duel, twice delayed by rain and played over a period of three hours, was dramatic and emotional for both women. The tension was heightened by some insensitive officials, who feared that darkness might prevent them from completing the match most spectators had come to see, the men's final between Eric Sturgess and superstar Pancho Gonzales.

"One time when it started to rain we didn't get off soon enough and my dress was pretty wet," Louise recalled. "We went in under the grandstand and one of the ladies took my dress to iron it dry. Then the rain stopped and we couldn't go on because I didn't have my dress. They blamed Margaret and me, and it wasn't Margaret's fault at all. It was a tense situation because I was waiting there for my dress and worrying that they were going to default me. They were so angry."

Even the spectators seemed hostile as they awaited the next match. Although the women compensated for their frequent errors on return of serve with dazzling net play, members of the gallery grew impatient during the

15–13 set and cried out, "Bring on the men! Bring on the men!"

Ozzie's and Broughie's second marathon was the 1949 Wimbledon final, a thriller that Louise won, 10–8, 1–6, 10–8. Margaret had four set points in the opening set, which she lost, and served for the match at 6–5, 30–love, in the final set. *The New York Times* called it a "long, tense match of almost faultless tennis." But *The Times* of London offered few superlatives, reporting that "The match was bound to suffer a bit from the fact that these two have met so often before . . . and from the similarity of their play, which is like men." Such comments show how unappreciated these great women were.

Margaret duPont, shown poaching in the foreground, and partner Louise Brough won twenty of twenty-four finals in Grand Slam tournaments. Margaret estimated that during their sixteen-year partnership, they lost no more than eight matches.

Surely the match dramatized their determination and fitness. The old rules of continuous play were still in effect at Wimbledon in 1949, and Margaret and Louise enjoyed no ninety-second rest period every two games as players do today. At Forest Hills women received a ten-minute break between the second and third sets, but not at Wimbledon. Once the match began, they never had an opportunity to sit down.

Margaret's and Louise's historic doubles partnership began in 1942 at the suggestion of Margaret's future husband, William duPont Jr. Will, a small, frail-looking man who presided over the Delaware Trust Company and had an affinity for horses and tennis players, was a longtime patron of the game. A mediocre player himself, he had befriended many tennis stars and knew almost everyone who played the circuit. One of his favorites was Alice Marble, who had arranged tennis matches for him and had played hundreds of sets with him.

Will spent most of the year at Bellevue Hall, a 400-acre estate with barns, a mile-long racetrack for his horses, three grass tennis courts, a cement court, two outdoor clay courts, and two indoor clay courts. Because he suffered from respiratory problems, he traveled west every winter to breathe the dry, warm California air. It was there, in 1941, that Will broke the news to Margaret that her doubles partner, Sarah Palfrey Cooke, was expecting a baby. "Why don't you consider Louise Brough?" he suggested. Margaret was twenty-four at the time, Louise nineteen.

Doris Hart described Margaret and Louise as "two bombs." Both had good serves, which were difficult to break. Both had good volleys and overheads. Louise's backhand return of serve from the ad court was superb, while Margaret had a wickedly disguised lob from the deuce court into the backhand alley.

In the eyes of Shirley Fry, the team also worked because it had a "captain" in Margaret and a "crew" in Louise. Shirley based her analysis on experience; she had played doubles with Louise in the 1956 Wimbledon championships, when Margaret was in temporary retirement, and they had lost in the semifinal round. "I won the singles and the mixed and might have won the triple crown," Shirley said. "But Louise and I were two crews. I was a forehand-court player and Louise was a backhand player, but that wasn't enough to pull us through."

Ozzie and Broughie never split up during their prime, the period from 1942 through

LOUISE BROUGH

"When I was working up to the top, those were happy days. As you stay on the top longer, there is more pressure building up. You get to the point where you're just playing not to lose, whereas earlier on in your career you're still trying to prove something. In the last few years, I felt I had to make every point, and the pressure was on me to win the points. Eventually it gets to you.

"When I won my first Wimbledon it was kind of unbelievable. After all the hard work, you're not sure it's real. You finally begin to realize it, and then you have to get out and play another tournament and prove it again.

"But you just love that Centre Court. It's like your own. Once you've been out there often enough, you feel very much at home, and that's where you want to play all your matches. It didn't bother me to play in a big arena. And I loved the grass at Wimbledon.

"When I went back for the Centenary in 1977, Wimbledon hadn't changed much. There were more people and they had made improvements, but actually it all feels the same with the grass, the Centre Court, the routine. I try to remember what it was like playing, and all I can think of is *how does anyone go through this?* The waiting and the weather and the noise and the crowds—I can remember how awful it was. We'd have to wait almost all day for the rain to clear up, and we'd be on pins and needles waiting for that match to happen. It just seems like it would be too much, just not worth it. Looking at the Centre Court now, from my standpoint, I wonder if I wouldn't just faint if I had to walk out there. And yet in the days when I was playing, it didn't even faze me.

"My only regrets are that I didn't try harder. I think I goofed off a few times and didn't realize it at the time, but I look back now and I feel I could have done a lot better. The opportunities were there to win things that I just missed out on. In my younger days I think I could have won a couple of more championships if I'd had the right mental attitude.

"The first time I got to the finals of the nationals when I was nineteen, I really didn't appreciate the importance of it and lost. I can remember feeling that I had won all the tournaments up to the national final and I thought, well gee, I really haven't done enough to deserve this. I feel that if I had had a coach around, the way the players do today, I might have gotten myself up a little more. I didn't realize what it meant until I realized how hard it was to win.

"I didn't see my career in a historical perspective, either. That was probably why I didn't do better. Now it has become such a big game. They're always remarking that it's a record here and a record there. It's much more obvious that it's going to be in the books, and I didn't think about that at all.

"I wish the young players on the tour could take more time to improve their games. They can't afford it, I guess. They're all such sluggers that they don't seem to have the variety.

"The young players don't care about the history of the game, at least in my opinion. But I felt the same way. When I played I couldn't care less who played before I played."

1950, when they won nine straight United States titles. They disbanded in 1951 when Margaret retired to have a baby and Louise temporarily left the circuit to rest her tennis elbow, but they competed together at selected events in the middle 1950s, winning three successive United States titles in 1955, 1956, and 1957.

If the achievements of Louise and Margaret were extraordinary, so was their friendship, which was—and is—unique in the annals of the women's game and which neither interfered with nor suffered from their competitiveness on the court. Although they were "friendly enemies" with their other peers, as Margaret has said, they were always friendly toward each other. "We have different personalities," Margaret said, "but we never clash.'' Most players vying for the top spot in tennis are unable to maintain close ties. Doris Hart and Shirley Fry were doubles partners, friends, and rivals in the late 1940s and early 1950s, but they were not as equally matched as Margaret and Louise. Doris usually had the upper hand. Margaret Court and I were distant toward each other as we battled for the Number 1 position, and while Martina Navratilova and Chris Evert became close with the end of their careers in sight, Chris had kept her distance from Martina for many years.

Margaret, who married Will duPont in 1947, was more than just a friend to Louise. Bellevue Hall, the duPont residence, became a home base for Louise, a stopping-off point between eastern tournaments where she was able to find good food, a warm bed, and a place to practice, rain or shine. ''Margaret always took care of me,'' Louise recalled. ''When we were at the duPonts', there were no expenses.''

One summer during the war, a summer without Wimbledon, Will duPont asked Margaret and Louise—each separately—what their favorite color was. Coincidentally, both replied red.

''He said he was going to give us both 'something' if we won the national doubles and that it would be red,'' said Margaret.

''He never did tell us what it was,'' said Louise.

Weeks later, during the national doubles final against Doris Hart and Pauline Betz, Margaret and Louise lost the first set and were losing the second when Louise began thinking to herself, ''Now we're going to lose that surprise.'' But with a few breaks they squared the set and powered ahead to victory. Louise was back in California when she received her red surprise: a ruby and diamond pin in the shape of a tennis racket, with her initials in the center and perfect little platinum strings.

''So we really won something,'' Louise said. ''At that time, there were no prizes. We got little silver platters. We were lucky, I guess, if they engraved our names on them. In 1942 all they gave were certificates.''

Indeed, for Ozzie and Broughie the 1940s and early 1950s were halcyon days of tennis, travel, and Bellevue Hall. Tennis players from the Philadelphia area descended on the estate every Sunday for a day of competition and an elaborate lunch. The lucky ones were invited to dinner as well. The tariff occasionally exacted by Will duPont was small: if the turf on his mile-long racetrack was unusually bumpy, he asked the players to walk around the track and pick up rocks and stones that might injure the feet of his thoroughbreds.

For Margaret, however, there was another, more subtle price to pay. When she married Will she was twenty-seven years old, successful, and independent. He was forty-seven years old, successful, and independent. He was also the boss. He allowed his wife a long rein, to be sure, but there was a rein. ''I knew what I was getting into,'' Margaret said. ''I never regretted it.''

Her only regret was that Will would not let her travel to the Australian championships. ''They didn't start to invite people down there and pay their expenses until I got married, and that was wintertime and Will's vacation time, and I just never got to go. He threatened to divorce me if I went to Australia, so I never went. He had that respiratory trouble, and he wanted me to come to California with him. He thought I should be with him. That was that.''

Will also did not like to stay at tournament sites once a championship was over, even if his wife had something to celebrate. ''We never had any tennis parties after the matches, because we always had to take the 8:30 train back to Wilmington that night. This was so Will could be up and going the next morning. I can remember having a bottle of champagne in the Pennsylvania Railroad Station one year, sitting at the counter. That was probably the biggest celebration I ever had. But it didn't matter. It was such a nice, satisfying feeling, to have won.''

More than four decades after their last doubles match together, Margaret and Louise still corresponded on birthdays and at Christmas, but both were leading very different lives. Louise, married in 1958 to Alan Clapp, a dentist, finally retired after more than twenty years of teaching tennis. She was still active in her middle sixties, keeping her game at a high level, helping to manage the family finances, and tending to the gardens at her home in Vista, California. "I'm much happier in my later years," she said. "I wasn't really as happy playing tennis."

Margaret and Will were divorced in 1964, two years before he died. After her divorce she shared a home and a successful thoroughbred breeding and racing business in El Paso, Texas, with her other doubles partner, Margaret Varner Bloss, who was widowed. The two women named their horses with tennis in mind—Six Love Six Love, Two Imposters, Fast Smash, and Be a Smash. One filly was named Mrs. Wightie in honor of the aging Hazel Wightman, in hopes that it would "help keep her alive."

Margaret Osborne duPont, who served the Southwestern Tennis Association as the El Paso-area vice-president from 1971 through 1985, continued to compile the SWTA's women's rankings in her sixty-ninth year, but she no longer played tennis. In San Francisco, the city named a block of six tennis courts the Margaret Osborne duPont Playground in her honor. Sadly, the sweetest tribute to Margaret, her namesake Mary Margaret Bloss, daughter of Margaret Varner Bloss, was killed in a riding accident at age ten.

In 1949, a year dominated by Louise Brough and Margaret Osborne duPont, the most publicized woman tennis player was one who never won a championship at Wimbledon or Forest Hills. Gertrude "Gorgeous Gussy" Moran is better known today than many of the women whose achievements far outdistanced hers. A man of Gussy's modest stature would never have survived in the annals of tennis lore. But a woman's fame was based on different standards—especially after World War II, when men wanted their wives to leave their jobs in factories and return to their traditional feminine roles. The same male sportswriters who grew tired of watching "the inevitable" Louise Brough and Margaret Osborne duPont fell over their typewriters when they got a look at pretty Gussy Moran. When Gussy wore panties trimmed with lace at the 1949 Wimbledon—an act that was tantamount to going out on the court in lingerie—many members of the press corps turned her into a superstar.

"It used to bother me a bit that they didn't write up the tennis," Louise said many years later. "All they wrote about was Gussy's panties."

Gussy was, in fact, a good tennis player. She reached the semifinals of the United States nationals in 1948, beating third-seeded Doris Hart in the quarterfinals before losing to Margaret Osborne duPont, 10–8, 6–4. Gussy also triumphed in her one and only Wightman Cup appearance, a doubles match, in 1949.

Nevertheless, Gussy never gave herself totally to the game. She was an entertainer first, a tennis player second. She was a Rita Hayworth in tennis whites, a pinup girl with shiny chestnut hair pulled tightly back, a brilliant smile, and long, suntanned legs. "She had a beautifully modulated, laughing voice, and her skin had a lustrous California gleam," Ted Tinling wrote in his memoir, *Sixty Years in Tennis*. "I thought of her as a person who actually shimmered."

Gussy delighted in the role of glamour girl and was a master at wooing the male tennis writers. During one press conference at which she was measured for a new outfit, her vital statistics were announced as 37–25–37½. At another she performed an unexpected striptease behind a semitransparent screen.

Gussy reached her peak in 1948 and in the spring of 1949 swept the singles, doubles, and mixed doubles titles at the National Indoor Championships. She did not maintain that level of play for long, however. Distractions began cropping up—movie stars, for example. Then, on her first trip to Wimbledon, she hired Ted Tinling.

Tinling, a six-foot-five-inch couturier, had been active in tennis for more than three decades, first as an umpire and player on the Riviera in the days of Suzanne Lenglen. In 1927 he became an official liaison between Wimbledon's tournament committee and the players. Four years later he launched his career as a designer of women's fashions.

In 1947 Joy Gannon, an English player, was the first to wear Tinling's dresses at Wimbledon. She was also the first to wear color; her dresses were white with pink or blue hems. The following year Ted designed a color-trimmed dress for another British player, Betty Hilton, and immediately ran into controversy. Betty wore her dress during the Wightman Cup competition, which preceded Wimbledon, and Mrs. Wightman, captain of the American Wightman Cup team, protested. Wimbledon officials subsequently told players that white clothes alone were acceptable.

Gussy, who had heard of Tinling's revolutionary dresses, wrote to him and asked him to make her "something feminine" for her Wimbledon debut in 1949. Tinling, for his part, was eager to clothe the striking Californian. His creation was a pretty white dress of rayon trimmed in satin. In keeping with the times, the dress hung just a few inches above Gussy's knees. When Gussy insisted that Tinling make panties to go under the dress, he complied, but because he thought them dull looking, he added a ribbon of lace around the edges. "And why shouldn't they be pretty?" he asked. "I never could understand tennis players who wore nice dresses but showed dreary garments underneath."

Surely Tinling was not so naive as to think the panties would go unnoticed. But it is doubtful that he designed them intending to create an international spectacle. Then again, maybe he did.

Although the Wimbledon establishment—the same establishment that once had required women to wear stockings and ankle-length dresses—was shocked by the panties, the rest of the British Commonwealth went wild. No doubt people had grown tired of the plain styles worn by the other women during and after the war, when silk and lace were in short supply. Gussy was inundated with requests. The Marx Brothers called. The London *Daily Express* plastered her on its front page five times in one week. Wimbledon enjoyed its biggest crowds since the war. "Maybe an extra thousand a day," Tinling said, "and all to see Gussy's panties."

Through it all, the ever-dignified *Times* of London never raised so much as an editorial eyebrow. When Gussy Moran lost in the third round to a relatively unknown player, *The Times*, never mentioning the panties, reported that the overanxious Gussy was victimized by "the octopus of publicity."

Indeed, the octopus helped strangle Gussy's promising amateur tennis career. "I was always self-conscious," she said several years later. "After the lace panties, everyone always was staring to see what I was wearing, and I couldn't concentrate on tennis."

As for Tinling, a public tongue-lashing by Wimbledon chairman Sir Louis Gregg prompted his resignation as official liaison. He had become internationally famous as a dress designer, however, and Wimbledon officials had not heard the last from him. In years to come he frequently would test their limits with dresses banned as too colorful or too risqué.

In the summer of 1950, Gussy retired from amateur tennis and signed a professional contract with promoter Bobby Riggs. Gussy earned about $25,000, a lot of money in those days, but she endured one shellacking after another in her matches with Pauline Betz.

Gussy remained an avid follower of tennis and its fashion trends, long after her playing days were over. She expressed mock outrage in 1958 when Wimbledon banned Karol Fageros's gold lamé panties, a Tinling creation, and added, "The next thing they will be doing is taking away women's suffrage."

The memory of Gussy Moran lasted long after she vanished from the tennis scene. People who cannot identify Pauline Betz or Louise Brough know that Gussy Moran was the one who wore lace panties. Although I think it unfair that players like Pauline, Louise, and Margaret duPont were not as famous as Gussy was, Gussy's notoriety did help women's tennis. She made people take notice of the women's game. That was good, because we had some real champions in the making in 1949, and they would deserve as much of the spotlight as they could get in the decade ahead.

Chapter 4

The Achievers

1951-1958

While crowds were still swooning over Gorgeous Gussy Moran, the look of women's tennis was changing. The 1950s were not so different from the 1940s, but they had their own distinct character and champions. As the decade began, Floridian Doris Hart and her doubles partner, Ohioan Shirley Fry, were steadily progressing toward the major titles they would ultimately win. In California, a stocky little sixteen-year-old named Maureen Connolly, winner of more than fifty junior titles, was challenging her elders. And within the American Tennis Association (ATA), the black counterpart to the all-white United States Lawn Tennis Association, a tall woman from Harlem, Althea Gibson, was rapidly becoming too good to hold back.

Althea Gibson was a lean and muscular athlete, who in her prime stood five feet ten and weighed 140 pounds. Her long arms and legs gave her incredible reach and mobility on the tennis court and earned her the nickname "Spider" among her friends. Her strongest shot was her serve and, after that, her overhead. "I'll take the overheads," she told her doubles partners, both the men and the women. Although she lacked consistency until late in her career, she had potential from the beginning, and lots of it.

Althea was a shy trailblazer, some said a lonely one, who was never entirely comfortable in her role as tennis's Jackie Robinson. She kept her frustrations to herself and did nothing that could be considered militant. Her racket spoke loudly for her, perhaps erratically at first, but more and more eloquently as the years went by. The hard road she traveled and her brief but commanding stay at the top make her one of the most memorable champions of all time.

Althea Gibson grew up on West 143d Street in the slums of Harlem. The walkup apartment she shared with her parents, three sisters, and a brother was a thirty-minute subway ride from the West Side Tennis Club, an all-white enclave that could not have seemed more remote to Althea had it been located in Siberia. Althea's parents had moved to Harlem when Althea was three years old, abandoning their cotton farm in the small town of Silver, South Carolina, during the Depression in pursuit of a better life.

When she was old enough, Althea took to the streets. She played hooky from school, stole food from street vendors, played every variety of ball game, and was generally aimless and uncontrollable. "I was, you might say, mischievous," Althea said. "I roamed the streets of New York City as a vagabond, I don't know why. Maybe I was afraid of my daddy giving me good whippings." Althea's father, a garage mechanic, punished her when she skipped school or came home drunk after visiting her uncles.

Her father also taught her how to box, with the hope of turning her into a professional boxer, but Althea preferred hitting balls with sticks. The 143d Street block between Lenox and Seventh avenues was a Police Athletic League (PAL) play street, which was closed to cars during the day so that children could play there safely. Paddle tennis was a prime activity, and Althea had established herself as champion of the block when her PAL supervisor, Buddy Walker, decided she should try tennis. Buddy bought Althea her first racket, instructed her to practice against the wall of a handball court, took her to some public courts (where she drew a gallery the first time she ever played), and introduced her at the interracial Cosmopolitan Tennis Club in Harlem. Althea, in her fourteenth year, impressed many of the club members, who took up a collection to buy her a membership and pay for her lessons. Her teacher was Fred Johnson, the club's one-armed professional.

For Althea, it was a strange new world. "I really wasn't the tennis type," she wrote. "But the polite manners of the game, that seemed so silly to me at first, gradually began to appeal to me. So did the pretty white clothes. . . . After a while I began to understand that you could walk out on the court like a lady, all dressed up in immaculate white, be polite to everybody, and still play like a tiger and beat the liver and lights out of the ball."

Althea won the ATA's national girls' title in 1944 and 1945, but she was still far from single-minded about the game. She played the saxophone, bought for her by boxer Sugar Ray Robinson, bowled until the wee hours of

Overleaf, the 1950s featured a cast of unique champions. It included, from left, Maureen Connolly, who won the United States championship at sixteen; Althea Gibson, the first black player to win the French, Wimbledon, and United States titles; and Doris Hart, who won major titles despite a bad leg.

the morning, played in a women's basketball league several times a week, and worked at one job after another. She cleaned chickens, waited on customers at a Chock Full o' Nuts shop, operated an elevator, and worked as a mechanic in a machine shop.

The turning point of her life came in the summer of 1946, when she competed in the ATA's adult championships and caught the eye of two ATA officials, Dr. Robert Johnson of Lynchburg, Virginia, and Dr. Hubert Eaton of Wilmington, North Carolina. The two physicians thought Althea had a chance to reach the top in tennis, and they came to her aid.

A plan was made: During the school year Althea would stay in Wilmington with the Eatons, starting high school all over again at nineteen; during the summer, she would live with the Johnsons and travel the ATA circuit. (Dr. Johnson would later nurture the career of Arthur Ashe.)

Dr. Eaton recalled that when Althea arrived at the railroad station in Wilmington, she was carrying Sugar Ray's saxophone in one hand

Althea Gibson, an attacking player, was so confident at the net that she was not afraid to rush in when her opponent was already there.

Althea practices at the West Side Tennis Club at Forest Hills for the first time in her life in July 1950. A month later she became the first black to compete there.

and an old pasteboard suitcase held together with two belts in the other. "She was wearing an old skirt," Dr. Eaton said. "She'd never owned a dress."

Together the two doctors gave Althea the opportunity to change her life. They coached her, taught her tennis etiquette, and above all, treated her like a daughter. Althea, throughout her life, called both of them "Dad."

During the summers Althea also had her share of fun. "Dr. Johnson and I and a few other young players would travel all over the ATA circuit," Althea remembered. "We'd all get stacked in the car and go. Dr. Johnson and I were mixed doubles partners. We won countless ATA mixed doubles titles."

In 1947 Althea won the women's ATA national championship, her first of ten in a row. Winning that title was a terrific accomplishment, but something was missing; with rare exceptions, Althea was still competing only against blacks.

Even so, Althea gave no sign of restlessness or rage. She claimed that during the 1940s she did not even *dream* of playing at Wimbledon and Forest Hills, because she thought she would never have the opportunity. "I wasn't disappointed, because I was learning something every time I struck a ball," she said.

Those were the days when blacks in the South still sat in the backs of buses, watched movies from the balconies, and used segregated rest rooms. The landmark Supreme Court decision in *Brown* v. *Board of Education,* which prohibited segregation in the public schools, was still several years away.

In tennis, however, the color line was beginning to fade, and if Althea was not dreaming about the great all-white tournaments of the world, the all-black ATA *was*. The ATA, founded in 1916, had been holding national championships for both men and women since 1917 and had produced two notable women's champions, Isadore Channels in the 1920s and Ora Washington in the 1930s. These women, who won twelve ATA national singles titles between them, never had the opportunity to compete in tournaments sanctioned by the all-white USLTA. It was not until 1948 that Dr. Reginald Weir, a veteran player, became the first black to compete in a USLTA tournament, the National Indoor Championships. The ATA, encouraged by Weir's important breakthrough, wanted Althea to go one giant step further.

Althea's first break was her acceptance into the USLTA-sponsored Eastern Indoor Championships, which were played during the winter of 1949 near her childhood home, at the 143d Street Armory in New York. Althea reached the quarterfinals, an excellent showing. The next week, she competed in the National Indoor Championships and again reached the quarterfinals. Althea probably was ready to vault into the international tennis scene then, but ATA officials remained cautious. They wanted to be sure; they preferred to be a year too late with Althea rather than a year too soon.

In the winter of 1950, Althea entered both the Eastern Indoor and National Indoor championships for the second time and showed marked improvement, winning the former and finishing second in the latter. Her performances eminently qualified her for the United States championships at Forest Hills. She was on her way. Or was she?

Althea still had competed only in indoor USLTA tournaments on hard surfaces, and tennis insiders heard rumors that she would not gain entry into Forest Hills unless she proved herself on grass. If that were true, Althea faced a major obstacle. Most of the grass-court events preceding the nationals were invitationals played at country clubs—and Althea was not receiving any invitations.

On July 1, 1950, *American Lawn Tennis* magazine printed a guest editorial by former champion Alice Marble, lambasting the tennis community for failing to open its tournaments to the rising black star. "Miss Gibson is over a very cunningly wrought barrel, and I can only hope to loosen a few of its staves with one lone opinion," Alice wrote. "If tennis is a game for ladies and gentlemen, it's also time we acted a little more like gentlepeople and less like sanctimonious hypocrites. . . . If Althea Gibson represents a challenge to the present crop of women players, it's only fair that they should meet that challenge on the courts." Should Althea not be given the chance to succeed or fail, Alice added, "then there is an uneradicable mark against a game to which I have devoted most of my life, and I would be bitterly ashamed."

Shortly after Alice Marble's eloquent indictment appeared, Althea tried without success to enter the New Jersey State Championships at the Maplewood Country Club in Maplewood. Tournament officials rejected her, Althea said, because they had insufficient information about her qualifications. It was obviously a ludicrous cover for the club's racist attitudes. How could a runner-up at the National Indoor not be qualified?

Althea finally got a chance to compete on grass, when the Orange Lawn Tennis Club in South Orange, New Jersey, accepted her into the important 1950 Eastern Grass Court Championships. She won her first match, proving to everyone that she deserved to be there. Althea subsequently played in the National Clay Court Championships in Chicago, where she reached the quarterfinals before losing to Doris Hart. In mid-August, Lawrence A. Baker, president of the USLTA, announced that "based on her ability," Althea Gibson had been accepted into the national championships at the West Side Tennis Club at Forest Hills.

Although Althea was nervous before her first match, she was not overwhelmed by the historical importance of the occasion. "I just wanted to get onto the court and show my talent as a tennis player," she insisted. "I didn't think about the racial issue or anything. I didn't think, 'Here I am the first Negro.' I was accepted as a tennis player when I walked to the court. All I thought about was how am I going to play this game and win?"

Althea made her debut quietly on distant court Number 14, where she defeated Barbara Knapp of England, 6–2, 6–2, in the opening round. (The following summer, in stark contrast, Wimbledon officials honored their first black contestant by scheduling her opening match on Centre Court.) Althea played her second-round match at Forest Hills on the grandstand court, and the fans who jammed every available seat saw a thriller.

Alice Marble, who championed Althea's cause, escorts her friend back to the clubhouse. Althea has just won her historic first-round match in the 1950 national championships.

Althea's opponent was Louis Brough, the reigning Wimbledon champion, former United States champion, and Number 3 seed. Louise was not terribly worried about Althea when they took the court, but Althea, after playing nervously and losing the first set, 6–1, began to capitalize on her aggressive serve-and-volley game and won the second set, 6–3. Adding to the drama were the darkening skies and increasing winds of an impending storm.

The women fought through a tense third set, Louise surging ahead, 3–0, and Althea clawing back. Lightning began to flash. Althea finally went ahead for the first time in the match, 6–5. She led, 7–6, when the cloudburst hit, sending players, officials, and fans running for cover. A lightning bolt struck one of the stone eagles on the top of the horseshoe-shaped stadium, and the eagle hurtled to the ground.

"There is no doubt in my mind, or in anybody else's," Althea Gibson wrote, "that the delay was the worst thing that could have happened to me. It gave me a whole evening—and the next morning, too, for that matter—to think about the match. By the time I got through reading the morning newspapers I was a nervous wreck."

Of course, Louise Brough had to wait, too, and her battles with nerves were well known. She arrived the next day at the grandstand court at the appointed time, only to wait some more. "Because Althea was black, and because it was the first time she had played in the nationals, the press was all over her," Louise recalled. "I was out there waiting. You're not supposed to hit a ball before you start your match again; you just start where you left off, but I went out and hit a few serves. The umpire said it was not legal. Then the head referee came out and said go ahead and hit as many serves as you want. Finally, it was like the red carpet was rolled out. Althea arrived with the press following her."

Eleven minutes later, it was over. Louise held her serve to tie the score at 7–all. The next game was fiercely contested; Louise won it on the eighteenth point, when Althea double-faulted. Louise held serve again to take the set, 9–7, and the match.

Louise lost her next match to Nancy Chaffee, and Margaret Osborne duPont beat Doris Hart in the final, 6–4, 6–3, for her third and last United States singles title. Althea Gibson was just another second-round loser at Forest Hills in 1950, albeit a special one. Her day at Forest Hills would come, but not for seven long years.

Doris Hart, after years of contending for the great titles in tennis but never winning them, finally won her cherished Wimbledon singles title in 1951. Nothing had ever come easily for the slender player with the damaged knee. Ten years earlier, Doris had shown tremendous potential, beating Pauline Betz in the Southern Championships and nearly beating her again in the first round of the national championships at Forest Hills. The Forest Hills crowd had cheered wildly for the underdog Doris, but the tenacious Betz had prevailed, 5–7, 6–0, 11–9. It seemed that the gentle, churchgoing Doris was close to the top, but such was not the case. In the decade that followed her early show of promise, she often doubted that the greatest tennis titles would ever be hers.

Indeed, because of the serious health problems she suffered as a child, Doris had good reason to wonder. She was a toddler of fifteen months when her family noticed that she was walking with a slight limp, the result of an infection under the right kneecap. The family physician, Dr. David Todd, was away on a hunting trip, and a specialist mistakenly treated her for rheumatism. Inappropriately treated, the infection spread rapidly and Doris became seriously ill. A trio of specialists, fearing gangrene, recommended that the leg be amputated to save her life, but Doris's father, Robert Hart, would not consent until he got an opinion from Dr. Todd.

The doctor was summoned home and immediately vetoed the decision to amputate. He decided to operate and drain the poisonous fluid from the knee. Dr. Todd sent Doris's mother out of the house on a made-up errand and performed the operation without anesthesia right on the kitchen table. Robert Hart and a nurse held Doris's arms and legs. Years later, many people who watched Doris play tennis assumed incorrectly that she had suffered from poliomyelitis, but in fact she had had osteomyelitis, a bone infection.

Doris's health problems did not end with her leg infection. During her prolonged recovery from the operation, she contracted chicken pox *and* scarlet fever. She also underwent a mastoid operation. As a result Doris did not learn to walk until she was three years old.

The doctors believed that Doris would always walk with a limp, and they never imagined that she would be able to participate in sports. But the Hart family never gave up. They moved from St. Louis to Florida when Doris was four, and every day Doris's parents took her to the ocean to soak her leg in the salt water.

Doris took one more step backward at age ten, when she underwent surgery for a double hernia. "I was in the hospital so long, not like today," she recalled. "And the hospital was around the corner from where we lived, right next to Henderson Park. My room overlooked the park and the tennis courts. My older brother, Bud, had just started hacking around with tennis. Then, when I got better, the doctor said, 'Why not let Doris try it?' "

Doris received her first racket from Bud, who would become the most profound influence on her career. The two pals spent every moment possible on the courts together. When they were not playing, they were helping sweep and line the courts to earn money to pay for the twenty-cent hourly fees. "We'd hang around there all day," Doris said. "Bud played a lot with me. Other people did, too, but Bud was the one who did everything for me. He was ranked twentieth in the men's [in 1943]. He could just annihilate me. I remember coming home crying, 'He beat me, 6–0.' But it was good for me, because then I'd go out and play girls my own age and it would seem like nothing."

With Bud's help, Doris rose quickly through the ranks, winning the national junior title and achieving a top-ten national women's ranking at age sixteen. She would remain among

America's best for fifteen years. Although her right leg caused her to shuffle more than run on the court, she compensated by becoming a magician with her racket: she had a greater variety of shots than anyone in her day. Her drop shots were especially cunning. She reasoned that if she could not run as fast as her opponents, she would make *them* do most of the running by placing the ball in all areas of the court. She accomplished her task with a look of effortless grace. Had Doris been blessed with two normal legs, I think she would have been one of the greatest ever to play the game.

Doris, however, was destined for many years to be the tennis world's favorite runner-up, a classic underdog who nearly always won the favor of the crowd if not the championships. The great players of her time, Louise Brough, Margaret Osborne duPont, and later Maureen Connolly, were almost always a bit too good for her, and they were as unsympathetic toward her plight as any professional would be today. "So many people *were* sympathetic," Margaret duPont recalled. "But we players couldn't be, not when we were trying to beat her. The leg didn't impair her movement that much or she couldn't have won what she did."

Doris was runner-up at Wimbledon in 1947 and 1948 before finally winning in 1951, and she was runner-up at the United States championships in 1949, 1950, 1952, and 1953, before winning in 1954 on her thirteenth try.

Wimbledon was the tournament Doris loved the most; she always got goose bumps there. "It inspires you," she said. "Just going in the changing room and getting ready, I'd get hyper about it all. There is so much history. People who come there love tennis; they know the game and respect good play. I always said if you're going to play your best tennis, you'll do it at Wimbledon."

Many of Doris's favorite memories of Wimbledon were of times shared with Shirley Fry, with whom she won eleven big-four doubles titles. Doris remembered the time she and Shirley rented a flat in London and stood in a queue every morning to buy groceries. "This was maybe the fifth year after the war, and they were still tight on food. People would be standing there and all of a sudden they'd be turning around and looking at us. Finally they couldn't stand it and they'd say, 'Aren't you Miss Hart and Miss Fry?' We'd say yes and then they'd want us to get in their place in the queue. They couldn't believe we'd be doing what they were doing. But we enjoyed it all."

Another time, Doris and Shirley arrived at Wimbledon knowing they would be unable to use their tickets for the players' viewing section. Each had three matches to play that day. "It's a shame to let them go to waste," Doris said. She and Shirley walked over to the standing-room queue outside the All England Club, approached two kindly looking older women, and offered them seats to the Centre Court. The women, who had never had Centre Court seats, were elated. The next day, Doris and Shirley walked into the dressing room and were greeted by a bouquet of flowers and a thank-you letter from their two devoted new fans.

Incidents like these were typically British, and for the most part they were confined to Wimbledon. One might think that the French, who adored Suzanne Lenglen in the 1920s, would have continued to embrace women's tennis after Suzanne stopped playing. But France's love for the women's game died when Suzanne departed and was not revived until the 1980s. In the 1950s, when Doris and Shirley played at beautiful Roland Garros in Paris, the French regarded women's tennis as second-rate entertainment. The women often played their matches in the mornings or late afternoons before sparse crowds.

Doris and Shirley have never forgotten the nerve-racking and infuriating prelude to one of their two singles finals. A car provided by the tournament was supposed to take them to Roland Garros. Doris and Shirley had been pacing the hotel lobby for some time, looking nervously at their watches, when the reality of the situation hit them: the tournament officials had forgotten them. "We were frantic," Shirley recalled.

The officials finally remembered their women's finalists, but when the car arrived the traffic was bumper to bumper. When Doris and Shirley walked on the court, the specta-

DORIS HART

"I had the bad leg all my life, so my movement was not as great as that of some of the girls. I worked very hard on anticipation. I worked hard on the drop shot, which really helped me in my career, and I worked on half volleys, stepping in and taking the ball right after the bounce. I knew I couldn't stay out there and rally fifty times a point.

"A lot of those half volleys were at the baseline. I never retreated. When my brother, Bud, and I played sets, he'd mark the court maybe two feet behind the baseline, and if I moved back beyond that line, I'd lose the point. So it made me stay up there and take deep balls on the half volley. People used to say, 'That's such a chancy shot.' But for me, it wasn't. I felt just as confident doing that as someone else would have been, hitting a regular forehand.

"My serve also helped me a lot. If I was down, 15–40, I could still put in a few good ones and pull it out. I had a good forehand. I hit it flat and could slice it, too. I hit my backhand flat or with slice. The slice was very good on grass. Many of the tournaments were on grass then, not like today.

"The leg bothered me my whole life. It was painful, particularly in England, because it was so damp. I had surgery on it twelve years ago and it's much better now. But I still can't bend my right knee to any extent. I never could when I played. In England, I used to have the lady rub something on it and put the heat lamp on it before I played to loosen it up. But it always bothered me.

"I never went to see a doctor about it, all the years I was playing. I was afraid they'd say I had to have surgery. Then, I had been teaching all these years and it just got so painful, and my leg was bowing in more. So I went to an orthopedic doctor. When he saw me in the office, he said, 'I knew some day you'd be in to see me.' As it turned out, I had torn cartilages and bone chips and arthritis, so he broke my leg deliberately, realigned it, and cleaned out the knee. I was in a cast for four months. Now it's stronger than it has been in my life. If I had known I was going to be lucky, I might have done it years ago."

---

tors, who had been waiting for more than half an hour, whistled and booed. "I presumed the crowd didn't know what had happened," Shirley said.

It is difficult to imagine such a scene occurring at Wimbledon. Officials there would never forget to pick up their finalists, first of all, and if the finalists *were* late through no fault of their own, I think the ushers would have spread the word.

Although the Wimbledon establishment was behind the times on some issues (women's clothing, for instance), the officials *never* failed to treat women with respect. The All England Club provided them with many courtesies: chauffeuring, lunches, a masseuse, and a comfortable dressing room. Furthermore, Wimbledon honored the women with a fair number of appearances on the Centre and Number 1 courts. No other tournament in the world treated women so well.

For Doris, the 1951 Wimbledon was the best of all. After reaching the final, she played almost perfectly and crushed Shirley Fry, 6–1, 6–0, in thirty-four minutes. Doris later wrote that for the first time in her life, she had played her best tennis when it mattered most.

Shirley lost every game she served in the match, but she did not lose her sense of humor. When she hurried to the net to shake Doris's hand, she asked, "Do you want to play it over?"

Doris won more than the Wimbledon singles on that special day in 1951; she won the triple crown. She won the women's doubles, playing with Shirley, and after a change of clothes and a short rest, the mixed doubles with Frank Sedgman. Only three women, Suzanne Lenglen, Alice Marble, and Louise Brough, had previously won the Wimbledon triple crown.

After a long and exhausting afternoon, Doris was sitting with Shirley in the women's locker room when the phone rang. It was Colonel Duncan MacAuley, secretary of the All England Lawn Tennis Club.

"Doris, have you changed yet?" Colonel MacAuley asked.

"No, I'm on cloud nine," Doris replied.

"Then will you and Shirley please come to my office?"

There, awaiting Doris and Shirley, was the Duchess of Kent. Also champagne.

"Miss Hart, I've always rooted for you," the Duchess told her. "I want to toast you."

Doris Hart loved those memories. "When I went back for the 100th anniversary in 1984, the Duchess's son, the present Duke of Kent, told me, 'You were one of my mother's favorites.' Things like that never happened in the United States."

Unfortunately for Doris Hart, her stay at the top of women's tennis lasted only a few short weeks. In 1951, her year of triumph, she was not even ranked Number 1 in her own country. Although sixteen-year-old Maureen Connolly had not traveled to Wimbledon that summer, she was ready to be queen.

Doris Hart, a winner in 1951 after many tries, accepts the Wimbledon salver from one of her biggest fans, Princess Marina.

Maureen Catherine Connolly's nickname, Little Mo, was inspired by the World War II battleship *Missouri,* and to the women she beat she was as powerful and ruthless as "Big Mo's" sixteen-inch guns. History has never

Doris Hart compensated for her lack of mobility with superb racket control. She could place the ball wherever she chose.

produced a more precocious or dominating champion than this California teenager. Before a horseback-riding accident caused her to retire at age nineteen, she had won three Wimbledon championships, three United States championships, two French championships, one Australian championship, and the first Grand Slam—the four major championships in a calendar year—ever achieved by a woman. Driven by a desperate fear of losing and, as she later admitted, a hatred for her opponents, Maureen Connolly dominated women's tennis for three and a half years, winning each of the nine Grand Slam tournaments she played from the national championships of 1951 through Wimbledon of 1954. During her reign at the top, she lost only five matches: one to Louise Brough, two to Doris Hart, one to Shirley Fry, and one to Beverly Baker Fleitz.

Maureen was the first postwar champion whose career was not adversely affected by World War II. Part of the new generation of tennis stars, she was only a child when the war was robbing older players of opportunities to travel and compete.

Maureen was most comfortable playing from the baseline. As a child she had developed a fear of volleying after being struck by an overhead at the net. Like other baseline players throughout history, she developed into a champion more quickly than those who worked to perfect a more complicated, all-court game. In 1951, two weeks shy of her seventeenth birthday, she defeated Doris Hart and Shirley Fry to become the youngest United States champion since sixteen-year-old May Sutton triumphed in 1904. At seventeen, she became the youngest Wimbledon winner since Charlotte "Lottie" Dod won back-to-back titles at fifteen and sixteen in 1887 and 1888.

The young Maureen had a fun-loving side, a glimmer of happy teenage normalcy that prompted designer Ted Tinling to put smiling cats and furry poodles on her tennis dresses. She loved horses, she loved dancing, and she loved to go out on dates. In her publicity photos she appeared to be a cheerful young woman.

Nevertheless, the lighter side of Little Mo's personality was frequently overshadowed by the consuming passion with which she viewed and played out her life in tennis. Tennis was everything for Little Mo. She measured her self-worth by her victories on the tennis court, and she imagined that others judged her by that same narrow and uncompromising standard. The real Maureen Connolly, the public later discovered from her autobiography, *Forehand Drive*, was not as happy as she looked. "I have always believed greatness on a tennis court was my destiny, a dark destiny, at times, where the tennis court became my secret jungle and I, a lonely, fear-stricken hunter," she wrote. "I was a strange little girl armed with hate, fear, and a Golden Racket."

On the court Maureen's absorption in the game was total and unwavering, her anger fused into fierce concentration. Her face rarely changed expression, and she rarely smiled. "All I ever see is my opponent," she once

Despite her excellence, Maureen Connolly was extremely superstitious. On her left arm she wears her lucky bracelet, a gift from her mother many years earlier.

said. "You could set off dynamite in the next court and I wouldn't notice."

"Maureen did not go out to lose," said Shirley Fry, who was one of Little Mo's strongest rivals. "*Never* did she go out to lose. Her concentration was so tough. She could be down, 5-0, 40-love, in the final set and not be beaten."

Maureen punished the ball with her backhand and forehand drives, aimed for the lines, and hit them. The harder her opponent hit, the better she played. She turned her upper body as she prepared to strike the ball and then unleashed her weight into every shot.

"She hit the ball this close to the line," said Doris Hart, gesturing with her hand, her thumb and index finger an inch apart. "A lot of players today hit the ball a couple of feet inside the line, whereas Maureen hit it inches inside the line."

Little Mo fascinated the tennis public. She charmed many with her cuteness, yet alienated others with her cold demeanor and her relentless stream of victories. No woman player since the days of Suzanne Lenglen and Helen Wills had generated so much interest and debate. A London *Daily Express* correspondent called her "an efficient clockwork machine" and "a subdued tennis robot," while Lance Tingay of the London *Daily Telegraph* wrote, "It is, perhaps, one of the drawbacks of greatness that Miss Connolly's cold efficiency should be regarded as a personal characteristic. Off the court Miss Connolly is a charming youngster. She is remorseless only when she begins to play."

Had tournament tennis been open to professionals in the 1950s, Maureen would have become wealthy. Instead, as with so many other talented players before her, she could only protest the system that allowed tournament promoters to pay top amateurs a fraction of their value and always surreptitiously. Like Suzanne Lenglen, Maureen came to the defense of the "exploited" amateur athlete and urged tennis officials to "drop the mask of hypocrisy" and "pay the players a standard fee."

Although Maureen's rivals believed she was routinely paid, she admitted to having received a $400 appearance fee on only two occasions. Players also believed Althea Gibson was paid, but Althea said she was not. "If I was, it probably was peanuts, not thousands of dollars. Just enough to go in and buy a sandwich."

Bob Kelleher, chairman of the USLTA's Amateur Rules Committee in the 1950s, told me he did not know of a single dollar that was paid under the table to Maureen or Althea. "But they were part of an era when it was absolutely common knowledge" that players were being paid. "People would look the other way, but everybody knew."

The amateur system became so corrupt in the 1950s, he went on, that Jack Kramer, by then a promoter of professional events, complained that the men were making more money as amateurs than he could offer them as professionals. "Don Budge was a Grand Slam winner, and while he was still an amateur, everybody commented on the fact that he lived very well and drove an expensive car."

Certainly, men like Budge were making far more than women like Maureen Connolly and Althea Gibson. The majority of the women probably made nothing at all. For them, open tennis would come twenty years too late.

Maureen Connolly was born in San Diego on September 17, 1934. She was raised by her mother, who was divorced when Maureen was three years old, and by an aunt. Her mother, Jessamine Connolly, remarried but the marriage did not last. Mrs. Connolly tried to push her daughter toward a dancing career, arranging for tap-dancing lessons when Maureen was five. But even as a child, Maureen was not one to be forced into anything she herself did not choose to do. She was so disruptive during a dancing tryout that her mother had no choice but to abandon the idea.

Maureen's first love was horses, but because her mother did not have the money to buy a horse, Maureen pursued other endeavors. She became infatuated with tennis at age nine after watching two proficient men whizzing balls back and forth on the cracked cement courts at the University Heights playground two doors from her home. Mau-

Seventeen-year-old Little Mo faces an army of photographers during a practice session in Surrey, England, several weeks before she won her first Wimbledon singles title.

reen was soon picking up balls for the handicapped playground coach, Wilbur Folsom, who had a prosthetic leg. Folsom gave Maureen lessons in return. She vowed from the start that she would be the best in the world.

Although Maureen was a natural left-hander, a trait that would be regarded as an advantage today, Folsom persuaded her to change. In his experience, women who played left-handed did not become champions. (Indeed, a left-handed woman did not win at Wimbledon until Ann Jones triumphed in 1969.) Maureen developed rapidly as a right-hander while practicing three hours a day, five days a week. At age twelve she came under the guidance of Teach Tennant, Alice Marble's former mentor.

Teach improved Maureen's game technically and molded her into an unyielding competitor by sheltering her and refusing to let her socialize or even practice with the other women players. The tactics worked, but Maureen later blamed Teach for contributing to her unhappiness. Maureen also blamed Teach for intensifying the hatred that consumed and depressed her. In her autobiography, written in her early twenties, an older, more sensitive Little Mo gave a startling description of her fierceness. "This was no passing dislike, but a blazing, virulent, powerful, and consuming hate. I believed I could not win without hatred. And win I must, because I was afraid to lose. The fear I knew was the clutching kind you can almost taste and smell and the specter of defeat was my shadow. So, tragically, this hate, this fear became the fuel of my obsession to win."

In 1948, when Maureen Connolly was just fourteen and beating all but the very best women in the Los Angeles area, Teach predicted that Maureen would soon become "one of our great champions." Helen Wills said that she had "a greater tennis temperament at this stage than even Suzanne [Lenglen]."

During that year Maureen had the first of her many memorable confrontations with Shirley Fry. The two met in the Pacific Southwest championships, and Shirley needed three sets to win. "And here I was ranked in the top five," Shirley said. "Maureen was tough and getting tougher."

In 1949, still fourteen, Maureen became the youngest player ever to win the national girls' eighteen-and-under championship. She repeated as junior champion in 1950, but by 1951 she was ready to represent the United States on the Wightman Cup team. She was by then known as "Little Mo," the nickname given her by Nelson Fisher, a sportswriter for *The San Diego Union.* A few weeks later Little Mo became the women's national champion.

Maureen temporarily lost something in the process, however: her friendship with Doris Hart. As a child Maureen had idolized Doris, who was ten years older, and she was overcome with happiness when Doris later befriended her. Before playing each other in an early round of the 1950 United States championships, Doris had tried to calm Maureen, who was terrified about making her first appearance before thousands on the stadium court. Doris proceeded to beat her soundly.

In 1951, when Maureen and Doris met in the semifinals, the situation had changed. Maureen was a serious contender for the title, and Teach considered Maureen's friendship with Doris, the reigning Wimbledon champion, a serious liability. Teach reasoned that if Maureen played a woman she revered, she would lose.

Teach therefore invented a lie. She instructed Maureen's chaperone to tell Maureen that Doris Hart really considered her a spoiled brat. When Maureen asked Teach if it were true, Teach assured her it was. Maureen later said, "No idol fell faster or with a more shattering crash than Doris Hart. I was shocked, stunned, then I saw blinding red." She said that when she faced Doris Hart in the semifinals, "I never hated anyone more in my life!"

During the match, with Doris Hart leading, 4–0, a light rain began to fall. Doris wanted to stop, but the officials ordered the women to keep playing. Maureen, spurred on by the crowd's roars of approval, played with abandon and took the set, 6–4. Only then was play suspended. Maureen finished off Doris the next day, 6–4. Maureen walked off the court crying with happiness, while Doris walked off crying in sorrow. Doris, after all her years of trying, probably thought the national championship would never be hers.

In the final, before a crowd of only 2,500, Maureen met Doris's close friend Shirley Fry, whose hunger for victory was fueled by many sources. Shirley had been trying to capture her nation's title ever since 1941, and for the first time her parents had come to Forest Hills to watch her play. Shirley was also motivated by revenge. Maureen's victory over Doris rankled her, and Maureen knew it. Maureen probably did not know, however, that Shirley also wanted to prove a point to Teach. Said Shirley: "Many years before—although I didn't know this until later when my dad told me—Teach had come through Akron with Alice Marble for an exhibition. My dad asked her if she would look at my game, because he wanted to send me to California to be taught by her. She told him I didn't have natural strokes, that I was too mechanical, and she wasn't interested. That was another reason why I wanted to beat Maureen."

Shirley lost the first set, 6–3, but then raised her game. Yanking Maureen around the court with masterful placements, she raced through the second set, 6–1, leaving Maureen feeling exhausted and defeated. Unfortunately for Shirley, the ten-minute break before the third set saved Little Mo. After a leg massage and pep talk from Teach in the dressing room—"You *must* win!"—her spirit and strength were revived.

At the end of the close third set, Shirley twice coming within a point of tying the score at 5-all, it was Teach, not Maureen, who was near collapse. *The New York Times* reported

Maureen Connolly shares one of her last happy moments with her coach, Teach Tennant, the woman who molded her into a champion.

In an example of classic strategy, Shirley Fry hits an approach shot down the line to Maureen Connolly. Maureen beat Shirley in that match to win the 1951 nationals at age sixteen.

that after Mo won the set, 6–4, Teach "had to be administered to in a box in the marquee as her pretty little protégée let out a scream of joy and ran forward to greet her beaten opponent." After leaving the court, Maureen fell into Teach's arms. Crying with happiness and relief, she told her coach, "Now we can go home and work on the offensive game."

Sometime later, Maureen was appalled to discover that Teach had lied to her about Doris. She apologized to Doris, and their friendship was renewed.

During the 1952 Wimbledon the following summer, Maureen ended her relationship with Teach. The rift between the strong-willed coach and the strong-willed teenager yearning for independence began a few days before Wimbledon, when Maureen, practicing in cool weather without a sweater, strained a muscle in her shoulder. A trainer declared the injury minor, an inflamed muscle, but another medical source said Maureen had torn the muscle and risked permanent damage if she played at Wimbledon. Teach, distraught, wanted Maureen to default, but Maureen, who felt that the injury was not serious, wanted to play. Speculation abounded. Some players believed the story was a hoax, a ready-made excuse in case Maureen lost. Maureen's confusion turned to anger when she heard secondhand that Teach had said she was through with her.

Despite Teach's opposition, Maureen played at Wimbledon. She won her first match, 6–2, 6–0, in twenty-two minutes. Her easy victory was not as surprising, however, as what happened next. Maureen called her own press conference, something even veteran players did not do in those days, and "fired" Teach publicly, without having told her first. Teach no longer represented her views, Maureen told the dumbfounded members of the press. Ted Tinling later wrote that Teach "never really recovered from the shocks of those few days."

With Teach no longer at Maureen's side, concerned members of the USLTA persuaded Maureen and her mother to consult with a respected doctor. His verdict: Maureen did not have a torn ligament but only fibrositis, an inflamed muscle.

Little Mo's resolve was soon to be tested again in the fourth round against Susan Partridge. After Maureen won the first set, 6–3, Susan slowed the pace and hit lob after lob. Maureen's rhythm was disrupted, and while hitting overhead after overhead, her shoulder began to ache. Susan won the second set, 7–5. Maureen later said that in her moment of unforeseen desolation, she searched the stands fruitlessly for her Teach.

In the final set, Susan Partridge inched ahead, 5–4, 30–15, against Maureen's serve, two points from victory. When Maureen then served a fault, the thought crossed her mind that if she double-faulted, Susan would have match point. "For the first and only time in my career, I became almost ill with a nausea which threatened to choke me," she wrote. Maureen won the point for 30–30. The crowd, pulling for Susan, groaned.

In the few seconds of quiet between points, Maureen was jolted by the cry of an American serviceman that rang through the silence: "Give 'em hell, Mo!" The words gave her a surge of adrenaline, and she won that game and the next two for the victory.

After winning two more matches, Maureen faced Louise Brough in the final. Louise led, 5–4, in the first set, but she began to have serving difficulties. Maureen won, 7–5, 6–3.

Later in the summer of 1952, Maureen successfully defended her title in the nationals. In the semifinals, playing against Shirley Fry, good luck was with her. The match began on an outside court, but in the middle of the second set, with Maureen down one set and possibly headed for defeat, the officials decided to move the women into the stadium, where more people could watch. Shirley, who had led, 4–2, in the second set, lost her momentum, and Maureen came back to win.

Shirley Fry could laugh about that match more than thirty years later, but I can only shake my head. Shirley and Maureen should have been on the showcase court in the first place; it was the national semifinals, after all. Furthermore, moving them in the middle of their match was unforgivable. Unfortunately, women in the 1950s were treated like second-class citizens almost everywhere they played.

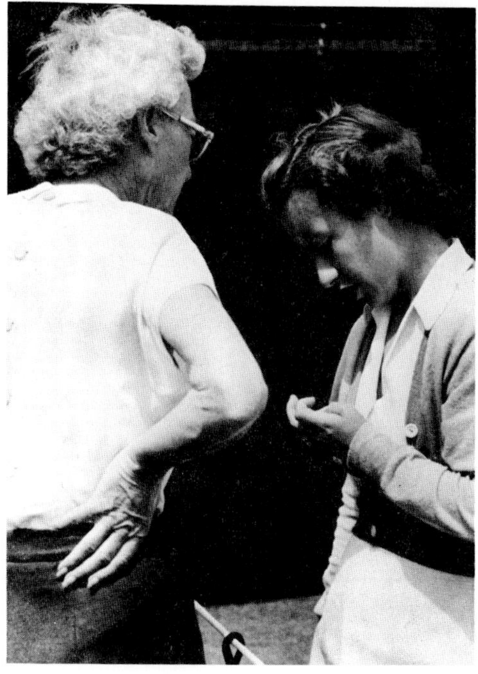

The pupil-coach relationship between Maureen Connolly and Teach Tennant was dissolving rapidly when this photograph was taken, shortly before the 1952 Wimbledon began.

By 1953 Maureen had found a new coach in Harry Hopman, then the Australian Davis Cup captain, and a new chaperone in his wife, Nell, a motherly woman and an Australian tennis official. Nell, Maureen would say later, helped her learn to play tennis without hating her opponents.

Encouraged by her new Australian connections, Maureen set her sights on the Grand Slam. She wanted to be the first woman, and the first player since Don Budge, to win it. (Budge won his slam in 1938, a year after he conceived of the idea.)

Maureen began her quest by winning the Australian title. She beat her doubles partner, Julie Sampson, in the final. In the quarterfinals of the French championships, Maureen lost her only set of her Grand Slam to a difficult opponent from the past, Susan Partridge, then Mrs. Philippe Chatrier. Maureen beat Doris Hart in the final, 6–2, 6–4, for her second big-four triumph.

Maureen proceeded to Wimbledon, and when she crushed Shirley Fry in the semifinals, 6–1, 6–1, Roy McKelvie of the London *Daily Mail* wrote that she had "reached the stage of being unbeatable.''

The tennis world regarded the 1953 Wimbledon final as one of the greatest women's finals ever played at the All England Club and probably the greatest match of both Doris Hart's and Maureen Connolly's careers. Maureen felt that in beating Doris, 8–6, 7–5, she had approached ''the mythical perfect game.'' Doris felt an equal rush of pride, even in defeat. ''When I walked off the court,'' she later said, ''I felt as if I had won.''

Maureen played Doris yet again in the 1953 final at Forest Hills and won, 6–2, 6–4, in forty-three minutes. The Grand Slam was hers. It was a stunning achievement, but the response of the press was remarkably restrained. In line with the prevailing attitude toward women's tennis, the front page of *The New York Times* bore a photograph of Tony Trabert, winner of the men's singles title, while Maureen Connolly's picture appeared on the sports page.

The 1954 French and Wimbledon championships were the last majors Little Mo won. She beat Ginette Bucaille of France in the final in Paris, and she defeated Louise Brough in the final at Wimbledon.

Maureen went home to San Diego to rest and engage in one of her favorite pastimes, horseback riding, a hobby always frowned upon by her former coach, Teach Tennant. Maureen by this time had her own horse, a Tennessee Walking Horse named Colonel Merryboy, a gift from some of her admirers in San Diego. Maureen and her friends were riding on a narrow side road when a noisy cement truck passed between them. Colonel Merryboy whirled. The truck's rear mudguard caught Maureen's right leg, throwing her to the ground. The impact tore the muscles below her knee and broke and exposed the bone. Maureen never played competitive tennis again.

Could she have come back? Some said yes; Maureen and her attorneys said no. Maureen sued the cement company, demanding $265,000 in damages. A jury voted, nine to three, to award her $95,000, the amount she could have expected to earn as a professional.

Maureen testified in court that several attempts at a comeback were thwarted by pains in her leg. She also testified that she had planned to turn professional in October 1954, shortly after the national championships. Two physicians, meanwhile, said that she had lost much circulation in her foot and that if circulatory problems worsened, amputation might become necessary.

Maureen's peers on the tour viewed the incredible turn of events with raised eyebrows and little sympathy. ''I think she could have played,'' Doris Hart said in retrospect. ''But she had a lawsuit going and they told her not to play. She didn't even go near a tennis court. It's awful to say, not that she wished for something like that to happen to her, but she really didn't care about playing anymore. She had won everything there was to win. It was not like today, where you keep going because of all the money. There was really not that much incentive for her.''

When Little Mo announced her retirement several months after the accident, she said, ''I just don't enjoy tennis anymore.'' It was a shocking statement that was never fully explained. Perhaps Little Mo had grown disillusioned because of her injury. Perhaps she realized she would never again be the player she once was. I met Little Mo when I was fifteen, and I shivered upon seeing the deep and terrible scar in the back of her leg, just below the calf muscle.

Away from the fierce arena of competition, Maureen Connolly found happiness as the wife of Norman Brinker, a member of the 1952 Olympic equestrian team, and as the mother of two daughters, Cindy and Brenda. The teenager who appeared so cold and remote grew into a woman who loved sharing her knowledge with young people. She coached the British Wightman Cup team on its trips to the United States during the 1960s, and she wrote articles about tennis for *The San Diego Union*, the London *Daily Mail*, and *World Tennis*.

She continued to play tennis despite her injury and the ominous forecast by her doctors in court. ''I still hit with Maureen after the accident,'' Pancho Gonzales, the men's champion, said. ''She didn't move as well, but she hit the ball really well.'' Maureen also played with a promising young ten-year-old named Chris Evert, who remembered that "her ground strokes were really hard and crisp and deep."

Gonzales liked to speculate on the outcome of a match between Maureen and Chris. "They would have had some great matches," he said. "I can imagine that if Maureen and Chris had played a match it would have lasted forever."

I agree that they would have had great matches, but only if Maureen had been born in Chris's day or Chris had been born in Maureen's day. Maureen was not as strong physically as Chris because Maureen, like all her contemporaries, did not train with weights. Furthermore, Maureen did not play long enough to reach her prime and never developed as complete a game as Chris's. Maureen's serve was always weak, the result, perhaps, of being forced to play right-handed when she was naturally left-handed.

In the mid-1960s Maureen Connolly Brinker became ill. Doris Hart was at Wimbledon, serving in the role of Wightman Cup captain, when she last saw Maureen. "She and Norman were on holiday with another couple in Europe," Doris said. "We were sitting there, talking. I can remember I said, 'You really look well.' And she said, 'Yeah, that's good, but Doris, I'm having the worst pains in the lower part of my back. And when I get home, I'm going to go in and check it out.' And then I heard she had cancer. She lived for only three more years."

Six months before her death, Maureen and her close friend, Nancy Jeffett, established the Maureen Connolly Brinker Tennis Foundation, dedicated to promoting junior tennis.

On June 21, 1969, two days before the start of Wimbledon, Maureen Connolly Brinker died. She was thirty-four years old. Her life, like her career, was fulfilling but too short.

Little Mo played in nine Grand Slam championships during her brief career and won every one of them. Her name was engraved on the Wimbledon salver three times.

Maureen Connolly, winner of the Pacific Southwest championship, poses with three former champions: from left, May Sutton Bundy, Helen Wills Roark, and Marion Jones Farquhar.

In 1954, with Maureen out of competition because of her leg injury, Doris Hart finally won her nation's championship at Forest Hills. Doris had lost four previous finals and came close to losing this time, too. She played her old nemesis, Louise Brough, who had one match point at 5–4 in the third set and two more at 6–5. On one of the match points, Doris recounted, "I missed the first serve and I just babied in the second one. It went right to her backhand, which she loved—she used to slice her backhand and rush the net—and I thought, 'Oh no, here it comes.' But she hit it in the bottom of the net. When I won that game for 6–all, I knew I had it."

After winning the match, 6–8, 6–1, 8–6, and her first national singles title, Doris experienced foot cramps. It was a long hike from the stadium back to the clubhouse, but Doris's brother, Bud, was there, just as he had been from the time she was a little girl, and he assisted her. When they arrived at the women's locker room Bud yelled, "I'm bringing Doris in!" and walked right in with her. "He still laughs about it," Doris said.

The next year, 1955, Louise Brough won her fourth and last Wimbledon with a heroic effort against Beverly Baker Fleitz, and Doris Hart repeated as national champion with a 6–4, 6–2 victory over Englishwoman Pat Ward. Doris then retired from amateur competition and became a teaching professional. She also wrote her autobiography, *Tennis with Hart,* and endorsed a Spalding racket, which carried her name and a little red heart on the throat. In 1988 she was in her twenty-ninth year of teaching at the Hillsboro Club in Pompano Beach, Florida.

Doris Hart's friend Shirley Fry also had her long-awaited moments at the top of women's tennis. Shirley considered herself past her prime by the time she was Number 1 in the world in 1956. Her best days, she believed, coincided with those of Maureen Connolly, against whom she played some of her most memorable matches. Nevertheless, Shirley was good enough in 1956 to win fourteen of seventeen tournaments, including the big ones, Wimbledon and Forest Hills.

Another feat secured her place in the record books: following in the paths of Maureen Connolly and Doris Hart, she became only the third woman to win all four of the national titles making up the Grand Slam at least once during the course of her career. (By the end of 1987 only four more women had done it: Margaret Smith Court, Martina Navratilova, Chris Evert, and I.) In addition to winning the United States and Wimbledon championships in 1956, Shirley beat Doris Hart to win the French title in 1951 and Althea Gibson to win

Shirley Fry of Akron, Ohio, broke the long string of American champions from warm-weather states when she won Wimbledon and the United States titles in 1956.

SHIRLEY FRY

"This is how tough it was. My parents couldn't travel with me when I was young. I had a dollar a day. Needless to say, I didn't eat breakfast. I would try to keep seventy cents for the evening meal. But you could get a hamburger for twenty cents and a drink for ten. I did that right on up through the juniors, when I was eighteen.

"Of course, we were supposed to be true amateurs. You weren't even allowed, supposedly, to accept rackets. My dad stuck strictly to the rules, even when Wilson and Spalding offered me rackets. Eventually, with my travels, I did accept rackets. And then it got to be that you were allowed expenses–if they were offered, of course! And really, only the top ones got them. The tournaments that wanted the top people would pay transportation. I'm sure Maureen Connolly got under-the-table money. Doris Hart and I never did.

"I remember going to Egypt to a tournament in 1951. Doris and I had written and made arrangements, and they had agreed to pay our fares. And at the last minute, Louise Brough decided to go, too. When I got to Cairo, they said they weren't paying my way because they were paying Louise's way. Doris said, 'Don't worry about it. I'll help you out if you need it.' But I was mad. That's all I needed–a little stronger incentive. I beat Doris and Louise to win that tournament in Cairo. Then we went on to Alexandria to play and I got to the doubles final, and Doris said, 'Now's your chance. Don't play the doubles final until they pay you.' They paid me.

"I didn't break even over a year. It cost money to play. It cost $350 to go over to Europe and back on the boat. I'd say it cost $1,000 for a summer in Europe. Trying to make ends meet was an endless job.

"People fly now, but we didn't have jets then. Whenever Doris and I could, we took the *Queen Elizabeth* and the *Queen Mary*. We were celebrities on the boat. It was five days from New York to England. We sat at the Captain's table or the head table, and we had fun.

"There were a lot of fun tournaments then for men and women, like the Pacific Southwest championships in L.A. We went to a lot of nice parties. Ali Khan was at a party when he was dating Rita Hayworth. There were escorts for Doris and me. Jimmy Stewart and his wife were at a party the tournament gave for Maureen Connolly. We met quite a few people because of Maureen. She loved to party. And she loved to sing.

"The best thing about tennis was seeing the world. I played on cow-dung courts in Durban, South Africa. I rode a camel in Egypt. I saw the Pyramids. What fun it was, traveling around the world."

---

the Australian championship in 1957.

Shirley June Fry was born in Akron, Ohio, in 1927, two years before the stock market crash triggered the Great Depression. Akron, the rubber capital of the world, was especially hard hit, and its people suffered keenly. "I remember the beggars who came to the door," Shirley recalled. "Mother handed out sandwiches. If they went to the front door where my dad's office was, they got money. No one *had* that much money, so I was lucky to be able to play tennis. It wasn't a cheap sport, either, at that time, but my dad believed in sports. We had all the equipment, always. When I started to play tennis, my dad started restringing tennis rackets. When we went and played ice hockey, he got the grindstone and sharpened skates for everyone."

Shirley was introduced to tennis at age eight on the white clay courts at the nearby University Club of Akron. Her father, Lester Fry, oversaw her development. He set up games for her with good male players, and he arranged for her to go by bus to tournaments–by herself. When Shirley was nine, Mr. Fry tested the ingenuity and independence of his pretty little daughter by sending her by bus to the Cleveland Exposition. Shirley looked over the exhibits and made it back home without a hitch. At age ten, she traveled alone to Philadelphia, where she competed in a tournament. The next year, she traveled alone to Forest Hills to watch the women stars compete for the Wightman Cup. Lester Fry also set goals for Shirley. In 1936, when Shirley was only nine, he started her scrapbook and wrote on the first page: "Wimbledon—1945."

Shirley faced several obstacles, however. Unlike Floridian Doris Hart and the Californians, who could play tennis year-round, Shirley played tennis for only six months of the year until she was eighteen. Nor did she have the advantages of expert training, as did Louise Brough, Margaret Osborne du-Pont, and Little Mo. As a result, she was not a classic player but a gritty one, who relied on quickness and resolve. Shirley said that as a child she won by lobbing and retrieving. "I never thought that someone wasn't beatable. I knew my talents weren't as good, but that didn't mean I couldn't luck through a match if I hung in there." As an adult, Shirley became known as the fastest player in her day, and she concentrated harder and better than everyone except Little Mo.

Shirley first appeared in the women's nationals at Forest Hills at fourteen, the youngest contestant until that time. The next year, at fifteen, she reached the quarterfinals before losing to Pauline Betz. Thirteen years later, however, Shirley still had not won the championship.

"After a while, even her staunchest supporters began to give up hope and say maybe she just didn't have it," Sarah Palfrey said. She speculated that Shirley's father might have pushed her too hard when she was a child, or "perhaps, it was just bad timing and bad luck, coming along as she had at the same time as Doris Hart and Maureen Connolly."

At the end of 1954, at age twenty-seven, Shirley retired from the game, moved into a small apartment in St. Petersburg, Florida, and worked as a copygirl for the *St. Petersburg Times.* "I had a sore elbow and felt I had had enough tennis," she explained. But Shirley missed her sport enough that two years later, when she was invited to replace Maureen Connolly on the 1956 Wightman Cup team, she plunged back in. "Heck," Shirley thought, "why not go to Europe one more time?"

Playing for the pure fun of it ("there was no pressure"), Shirley proceeded to win three successive big-four singles titles. At Wimbledon she beat Althea Gibson in the quarterfinals and in the semifinals beat defending champion and Number 1 seed Louise Brough, who she felt was "going downhill fast." The victories put her in the final against twenty-one-year-old Angela Buxton, the first British singles finalist since Kay Stammers in 1939.

Angela made her first and only Wimbledon singles final with a little help from second-seeded Beverly Baker Fleitz. Beverly, runner-up the previous year and favored to win in 1956, discovered in the middle of the tournament that she was pregnant. Beverly immediately defaulted to Angela in the quarterfinals. Shirley, who regarded Angela as a far easier opponent than Beverly, later wrote thank-you notes to Beverly and her husband.

The stakes in the Wimbledon final, already enormous, leaped skyward when Angela's proud father, a noted figure in the import-export business, promised to give Angela a *dock* if she won. To provide Shirley with equal incentive, the city of St. Petersburg promptly offered the million-dollar *St. Petersburg Pier* as a prize for Shirley if she won.

Shirley defeated Angela Buxton, 6–3, 6–1, and immediately cabled her father: "Worth all the trouble. Love, Shirley." On her return home St. Petersburg gave her a ticker-tape parade, a new car, and a plaque affixed to the million-dollar pier.

Shirley went on to win the 1956 United States title by beating Althea Gibson, 6–3, 6–4, and closed out her playing career with her one and only tour of the Australian circuit. She had always wanted to go to Australia but had never before received an expenses-paid invitation. In 1956, however, Australians were clamoring to see Althea, the first black star in tennis, and Shirley, the world's best woman player, was a natural choice to go with her.

Shirley, then twenty-nine, went to Austra-

BUD COLLINS
NBC Television, *The Boston Globe*

"I covered tennis on a limited basis beginning in 1955 for the *Boston Herald.* I moved to the *Globe* in 1963, and after that I appeared much more frequently on the world scene, you might say. I started doing television in 1963 for WGBH-TV in Boston, the public station. We did the national doubles in 1963, but those were just local telecasts until 1968, when PBS for the first time had the capability to go nationwide. Then I started doing the U.S. Open in 1968 for CBS.

"I always enjoyed women's tennis. The first assignment I ever had was to cover a women's tennis tournament, the Massachusetts Women's Championships, in 1955. We had very limited coverage of tennis, but the tournament was run by Hazel Wightman, who was the donor of the Wightman Cup, and they were always careful to treat her well. The sports editor was rather apologetic about sending me there. I was new on the staff and he treated it as though it was something the new person had to do. But I enjoyed it very much. When the sports editor saw that I liked it, he was a little disturbed. He said, 'You may like this game, but it's not of any great interest. So don't get too excited about it, because you're not going to cover much,' which was absolutely true.

"We used to have another tournament, to the north of Boston, called the Essex County Club Women's Invitational. It was part of the Eastern grass-court circuit, which was all the tennis that mattered in those days. About 200 or 300 people would attend. They might get 500 for the finals.

"The Essex County Club was a very exclusive, Brahmin club—a very F. Scott Fitzgerald sort of place, right on the sea. The people were wealthy, but it was New England wealth. Everybody was casual, very khaki and denim. The players would all stay in very elaborate, private homes. I think they enjoyed it. There was a nice party every night, a clam bake; they could go swimming and horseback riding. They didn't get paid. There was no money under the table, although I think the year Althea Gibson got there they might have paid her a little something. They had their biggest crowds that year. Althea drew the only black spectators ever seen there.

"The tournament was very nice, but it was one of those things that really epitomized tennis and that Billie Jean knew they had to get away from. It was just for the members and their friends. Tennis wasn't going to go anywhere in situations like that. And as soon as open tennis came in, the club dropped their tournament. They didn't want to pay anyone.

"Years later I drove by there. I wanted to show my wife the place and we happened to be in the neighborhood. And I said, 'This is where I spent some of my most pleasant weeks.' The courts are still there. They still play on grass. They originally had an old wooden grandstand that held maybe 300 people, but they tore that down.

"The only people who wrote about tennis regularly [in the 1950s] were Allison Danzig of *The New York Times* and Al Laney of the *New York Herald Tribune.* They covered all the tournaments during the summer. I first went to Forest Hills in 1956, and only because Althea was a story then. The press box was merely three or four short rows, and, except for a few reporters from the foreign wire services, nobody from outside New York was there.

"It was a much more pleasant game to cover then. When the players came off the court you sidled up to them and walked to the clubhouse with them. With the men, there were no locker room restrictions. If you cared to go up there, the player was glad to see you. With the women, you'd tell the attendant at the door, 'I'd like to see so-and-so when she's through showering,' and she would say, 'Of course, I'll tell her.' "

lia and did not return for two years. She had decided she would marry the next eligible man she met. The man happened to be Karl Irvin, an advertising executive for J. Walter Thompson and a USLTA umpire. Karl was on assignment in Australia, calling lines in his spare time. Shirley beat Althea in the final of the Australian championships and was soon celebrating at the altar. She did not come home to America until her first son was nine months old.

In the mid-1980s I found Shirley Fry Irvin—still pretty and bubbly at age sixty—living alone in Farmington, Connecticut. Her four children had grown up and moved away, and her beloved Karl had died of a heart attack on the tennis court in 1976.

Shirley, who taught tennis for many years, could no longer play much; aching knees had forced her to turn to golf. She also walked regularly in a nearby park, accompanied by her golden retriever, Wimbledon's Royal Duchess.

In September 1987, she received the USTA's Service Award for her contributions to tennis. "I might have expected it thirty years ago," Shirley said of the occasion. "But it means much more to be remembered at this late date. I hope I have contributed to tennis over the years. It has given so much to me."

Althea Gibson and Darlene Hard take the court for their 1957 Wimbledon final. They are carrying the bouquets traditionally brought to women finalists in the dressing room before the match.

The Althea Gibson who won back-to-back Wimbledon and United States titles in 1957 and 1958 was a much improved version of the player who failed to win a single big-four title from 1950 through 1955. Althea was destined to be a late bloomer from the moment she came into the world on a cotton farm in South Carolina. When the white tennis world opened its doors to her, she was nearly twenty-three years old. When she finally hit her stride in 1957, at age twenty-nine, there was no one better. "Behind Althea Gibson," *Time* magazine reported that year, "women's tennis curves off into mediocrity."

Although Althea's game lacked consistency at times, she overpowered opponents with her serve, her volleys, and her overhead. "I tried to play ruthlessly," she said later. "I had the biggest serve in women's tennis. As a matter of fact, somebody wrote, 'Her serve was remarkably like a man's.' Well, it probably felt like that to my opponents. It was hard, and it was well placed."

Althea was one of the first players to take advantage of the new foot-fault rule of 1955. Unlike the old rule, which required players to keep both feet behind the line until the ball was struck, the new rule allowed a player to swing the back foot over the line *before* hitting the ball. As Althea served, she leaped into the ball and pounced toward the net.

Despite Althea's many accomplishments and the uniquely difficult challenges she faced, she remains one of our most underrated champions. I agree with Angela Mortimer, the 1961 Wimbledon champion, who said that Althea "never received the recognition her powerful tennis and her great athleticism deserved." The era in which she played was partly to blame, but there were other reasons, too.

Those close to Althea thought her warm, but few people in the white tennis world had the chance to know and understand her. Althea did not merely set herself apart from the rest of the field, as did many champions before her and after; she intimidated her opponents. I sensed that while in the dressing room with her at the Pacific Southwest championships in the late 1950s. She was taller than everyone else, which made her imposing to begin with, and she had a swagger and an arrogant demeanor that added to that aura. I thought she was trying to exert her superiority over the other women before going onto the court. Being supremely confident in competition is one thing, but as Gardnar Mulloy, one of her mixed doubles partners, said in 1957: "The trouble is she doesn't come down to life size off [the] court."

Althea also created some hostility, perhaps inadvertently, during her matches. "Playing against Althea was not terribly pleasant," said Louise Brough. "She had a way of stalling and doing things that she perhaps was not aware of, but we all thought she was doing it on purpose." Althea later denied that she ever purposely stalled. "That's their version," she said. "I don't believe I ever stalled in a match."

Althea undoubtedly was under enormous pressure, not only from herself but from the black community. "Althea really had a cross to bear," said Darlene Hard, Althea's roommate for two and a half years on the tour. "She was trying to be the first black to succeed in tennis; she was pushing. I think sometimes she caused the trouble. Sometimes she didn't. How do you know? It's hard to step back and objectively say this happened or that happened, because I think we all have problems in communicating. Althea worked through it."

Occasionally, Althea's frustrations surfaced. *World Tennis* reported that after repeated foot faults during the 1957 Victorian Championships in Melbourne, Althea became so upset that she "hit a ball straight into the gallery," missing the Australian prime minister "by a bare two feet." Having slammed a few tennis balls around myself in the 1960s and 1970s, I can identify with the frustration Althea must have felt.

The five years that followed Althea's initial splash at Forest Hills in 1950 were a mixture of achievement and disappointment. She graduated from Florida A&M University in 1953 and accepted a position teaching physical education at Lincoln University, then an all-black school, in Jefferson City, Missouri. In tennis, however, she continued to struggle. She broke into America's top ten in 1952, rose to seventh in 1953, and slid to thirteenth in 1954.

After Althea Gibson became the first black tennis player to win Wimbledon, New York City honored the champion from Harlem with a ticker-tape parade.

Althea, her confidence flagging, decided to retire from amateur competition in 1955 and join the Women's Army Corps. She explained her decision in her autobiography, *I Always Wanted to Be Somebody*: "I'm just not good enough. I'm probably never going to be. And I'm sick of having people support me, taking up collections for me, buying me clothes and airplane tickets and every damn thing I eat or wear. I want to take care of myself for a change."

Then, in the autumn of 1955, her career took an unexpected turn, and she decided not to join the Army after all. The State Department invited her to be part of a goodwill tour of Southeast Asia. Althea went and won virtually every event she entered. In 1956 she bolted toward the top of the women's game, winning twenty-one tournaments in all, including her first big-four title, the French, with a 6–0, 12–10 victory over Angela Mortimer.

Suddenly she was ranked second in the world behind Shirley Fry.

As Wimbledon got under way in 1957, with her chief rival, Shirley, in retirement, Althea knew the Number 1 ranking was within her grasp. After winning her semifinal match against Christine Truman, a sixteen-year-old English newcomer, Althea told reporters, "Praise be, this could be my year."

Her instincts were right on target. Playing in unseasonable, 100-degree heat, Althea defeated Darlene Hard in the final, 6–3, 6–2, to become the first black player, male or female, to win Wimbledon. "At last!" Althea cried, after the final point was played. "At last!"

Moments later, Queen Elizabeth II presented the woman from Harlem with the gilded salver. "It must have been terribly hot out there," the Queen said to Althea, smiling and shaking her hand.

"Sure was, Madam," Althea replied. "I hope it wasn't as hot up there for you."

Sports Illustrated reported that the Wimbledon crowds treated Althea with "silent respect" during the early rounds and raised "only an apathetic cheer" when she received the golden salver. The more appreciative city of New York would give Althea a ticker-tape parade, and the mayor would hold a luncheon in her honor at the Waldorf-Astoria Hotel.

Two months later at Forest Hills, Althea defeated thirty-three-year-old Louise Brough, 6–3, 6–2, to win the 1957 United States championship. Althea received her trophy, filled with white gladioli and red roses, from Vice-President Richard M. Nixon. Addressing the crowd, Althea thanked God for her ability and said she hoped she would wear her crown with dignity and humility. "Her remarks," said *The New York Times,* "were followed by the longest demonstration of hand-clapping heard in the stadium in years."

Althea retained her Wimbledon title in 1958 with an 8–6, 6–2 victory over Angela Mortimer. Althea was so confident at this stage of her career that she could pull off even the riskiest and most difficult shots when she felt she had to make them. When Angela held a set point at 5–3 in the first set, Althea responded by hitting a searing forehand drive to Angela's backhand corner. The shot nicked the line.

Althea also held on to her United States crown in 1958. She defeated nineteen-year-old Ann Jones of Britain in the semifinals and Darlene Hard in the final.

Having won everything she had ever wanted to win, Althea retired from amateur tennis in 1959, bringing a decisive end to a decade of unique events in the women's game. Althea probably would have added to her collection of titles had she remained an amateur, but she had no incentive to do so. "I couldn't eat trophies," she said wistfully.

Althea then signed a $100,000 contract with the Harlem Globetrotters to play exhibitions during their halftime intermissions. Her opponent was Floridian Karol Fageros, an attractive player who was not nearly as good as Althea. Although the money Althea received for the six-month tour was unprecedented at the time for a woman tennis player, much of it was used for expenses. "That $100,000 had to take care of everybody on our part of the tour," she explained. "We had to pay salaries out of that to people we traveled with, people who laid out the court, our driver. After it was over I believe I had a little bit left over for myself, enough to get an apartment in New York in those years." The Globetrotters did not renew the contract.

In the years that followed, Althea turned her attention to golf and became good enough to join the Ladies Professional Golf Association tour. She taught tennis in New Jersey for several years but experienced bad luck when the clubs at which she worked closed. Althea served as New Jersey State Athletic Commissioner in the mid-1970s. In 1977 she ran unsuccessfully in the Democratic primary election for the New Jersey state senate.

Althea Gibson always expressed satisfaction that the next generations of young women were able to become wealthy playing tennis. "That's beautiful; I'm happy for them," she said. "I just sometimes feel I should have had some of it. But that's the way it goes. I was, would you say, too soon? I'm not mad about it or anything, but I think about it now and then, maybe saying to myself, 'My goodness. Look what I missed!' "

Chapter 5

Open Tennis Arrives

1959-1969

Open Tennis Arrives

Overleaf, Brazil's Maria Bueno, left, was a champion despite her fragile health. Her career was interrupted by illness and injuries. Angela Mortimer of Great Britain, center, used her excellent ground strokes and unwavering determination to win a Wimbledon singles title in 1961. Margaret Smith Court, right, Australia's first woman superstar in tennis, won twenty-four singles titles in Grand Slam events, a record that probably will stand forever.

The 1960s were a mixture of old and new, an era of diverse and colorful champions and a decade of growth and change. No longer did Americans rule the major tournaments. The players who learned the game in the years that followed World War II entered their prime in the 1960s and gave tennis a global flavor. Six women from four continents won Wimbledon in this decade: Maria Bueno of Brazil, Margaret Smith Court of Australia, Angela Mortimer and Ann Haydon Jones of England, and Karen Hantze Susman and I of the United States.

A new international team championship for women, the Federation Cup, dramatized the growth of women's tennis. Unlike the Wightman Cup, which involved only Great Britain and the United States, the Federation Cup competition, born in 1963, featured a field of sixteen nations.

Five years later, in 1968, tennis came of age, as the major championships were opened up to professionals as well as amateurs. With the dawn of "open tennis," players began competing for legitimate prize money, an incentive that lured a tidal wave of athletes into the game. In spite of these important developments, the early and middle 1960s were in many ways like the 1940s and the 1950s. We played a few great championship matches in front of crowds numbering in the thousands, at Wimbledon, Forest Hills, and Roland Garros, and the rest of our matches took place before small crowds—in the hundreds if we were lucky—at private country clubs. Tournament promoters went on paying the best players under-the-table appearance fees, while lower-ranked players got barely enough to live on. Most of the sport's kingpins were against "open tennis" with honest prize money for all players, thinking it would spoil the game, which they saw as essentially a country-club sport for society's elite.

Nevertheless, we had an inkling as early as 1960 that at least some influential tennis officials were starting to see things differently. Those with vision and foresight in the international tennis community, including some members of Britain's Lawn Tennis Association (LTA) and the United States Lawn Tennis Association (USLTA), said they wanted to change the game because they were disgusted with the hypocrisy of illicit payments in an amateur sport.

Bob Kelleher, president of the USLTA from 1967 to 1969, said he had been "rather violently" in favor of open tennis because he felt sham amateurism was corrupting youth. "We purported to be an amateur game and we had rules that you could not get paid in any way, and actually all the good young kids, especially the Californians, were paid under the table to use a particular tennis racket. They also were paid to come play in tournaments, in violation of the rules. I felt that it was as crooked as anything could be. The only solution was to have open tennis and let them be pros if they wanted to be and amateurs if not."

Those in favor of open tennis were further alarmed by the drain of talent out of the great amateur tournaments and into the struggling professional sideshows. The top men were leaving the amateur game one by one in an effort to earn a decent living for themselves and their families. Jack Kramer, Pancho Gonzales, Frank Sedgman, Vic Seixas, Tony Trabert, Rod Laver, Lew Hoad, and Ken Rosewall were among the defectors.

Although only a few women stars had turned professional—Pauline Betz and Althea Gibson among them—more women probably would have left the amateur ranks if the male promoters had offered them the opportunity. Some of these women might also have banded together, as Pauline Betz and Sarah Palfrey had, to create their own opportunities. But as Shirley Fry recalled, "We were programmed: get married and have kids." Thus, playing on and on as a tennis star with little pay was an attractive option for a woman who was not ready to start a family. For the men who were supposed to be breadwinners, however, the amateur life was degrading and often unviable.

Those who wanted to abolish the distinction between professional and amateur brought the issue to a vote at a meeting of the International Lawn Tennis Federation (ILTF), a body composed of the various national federations, in Paris in July 1960. Led by Britain, the United States, France, and

Australia, the national federations voted, 134–75, to open up eight major championships to professionals in 1961. Unfortunately, the measure failed to win the necessary two-thirds majority by five votes. The USLTA tried to revive the issue a year later, but the ILTF let the matter slide. For seven more years hypocrisy continued, and amateur tennis went on as before.

Maria Esther Bueno was among the biggest stars of the new era. She came from São Paulo, Brazil, and she brought something new and glistening to the game. Her volleying was fluid and instinctive, and although she was only five feet six and 118 pounds, the ball shot off her racket like an arrow when she served. Her natural grace, combined with her ballerina's figure, made her wildly popular; her victories, added to these attributes, made her a superstar. "La Bueno," as she was affectionately called, heightened global awareness of women's tennis from Rome to Melbourne.

After Althea Gibson retired in 1959, Maria came to the forefront of women's tennis by winning both the Wimbledon and United States singles titles at nineteen. Critics called her the most exciting player since Alice Marble and compared her with the incomparable Suzanne Lenglen. Although an attack of hepatitis threatened Maria's career when she was twenty-one and already twice a Wimbledon champion, she battled back to the top and did not leave the game until she had won a total of three Wimbledon titles, four United States titles, and three Italian titles.

Maria was a genius on the court. To her the joy of tennis was not merely winning a point, but winning it beautifully; she was satisfied only with a victory that was artistically achieved. Maria's zeal for perfection did not come without a price, however. She became frustrated and impatient when her physical performance could not keep pace with her imagination, and this led to her downfall on more than one occasion.

It was said that her genius was like an electric current that could be turned on or off, and during those spells when she grew tired or bored, a healthy lead could vanish instantly. But just as suddenly the electricity would return to swing the momentum in her favor once again.

Maria Bueno of São Paulo, Brazil, was a ballerina on the court who reminded tennis aficionados of Suzanne Lenglen.

Maria was the first woman tennis player since Suzanne Lenglen to captivate Continental Europe. The Europeans had always enjoyed women, but they had not necessarily enjoyed watching women play tennis. The Italians were notorious for scheduling women's matches on back courts and at unpopular hours. Rino Tommasi, an Italian radio sportscaster, remembered watching the final

MARIA BUENO

"Every time I go back to Centre Court to watch, it's a feeling that I don't have anywhere else. There is only one feeling. It doesn't matter whether you get paid a million dollars or if you don't get paid anything at all. You're always out there to do your best. If you're playing, you're playing to be Number 1. I'm sure the feelings they have today are exactly the ones we had.

"I always felt appreciated as a woman athlete, especially in England. The crowds were always with me, even when I played in Rome. The Italians somehow always thought women's tennis was very boring. But when I first played there at Foro Italico, they had most of my matches on center court, which was never done for the women. Even when I played the Italian players in Italy, one of the things everybody dislikes doing the most, I never had any trouble. I was very lucky and was able to communicate well with the crowds. So I had them on my side most of the time.

"When I played at Wimbledon and played Christine Truman, who was a very great favorite of the crowds, and when I played Ann Jones, the crowds were so fair to me. I must say I've enjoyed very much playing at Wimbledon. Playing on Centre, to me, was like creating something. I was happy that I could let the audience know what I was doing, how I was feeling and how important it was to me.

"To me tennis was more of an art than a sport. I was a very natural player. Everything was done by impulse or intuition. I could never be programmed like most of the players are today. Maybe it would have helped me if I had had some special advice. But I think I would never change. I'm a natural player who goes along creating at the moment.

"I was never satisfied if I did not play beautifully. I was always going for perfection and the impossible shots. If you look back, the clippings always said I was going for the impossible shots, going for the difficult ones, going for the lines, always making it difficult for myself.

"If I hadn't had so many injuries, I would have done much, much better, because I never had two seasons running when I was totally fit. I think it was very short, the period that I played. It was ten years, but I don't think I played full-time for more than six or seven. I felt it was very short for me, doing something I wanted to do so much. The difference now is that I don't see too many people enjoying what they are doing. It was hard to have to retire, but there was no way I could keep going."

---

of the women's Italian championships in the mid-1960s. At that time, the women's and men's tournaments were held simultaneously at the beautiful Foro Italico in Rome. "Margaret Smith was playing Lesley Turner on court 6 and there were six spectators," Tommasi said. "The center court was packed to watch a doubles match with an Italian player. I felt sorry for the girls. I felt sorry also for Italy, because it was terrible."

The Italians, like the rest of the Europeans, embraced La Bueno, placing her on a pedestal and on center court. "Bueno! Bueno!" the crowds chanted when she played.

Maria helped excite the tennis public in Australia, too. She made her debut in the Australian championships in 1960, and although she lost in the quarterfinals to that nation's first great female champion, seventeen-year-old Margaret Smith, she won the hearts of the crowd.

"Maria Bueno did a lot for women's tennis," Margaret recalled. "It was at that time, just when I was coming in, that people started to take a lot more notice of women's tennis. People were drawn to her because she was very graceful. Whenever we played there was a tremendous crowd."

Maria enhanced her star quality by dressing to the hilt in beautiful swirling dresses designed by Ted Tinling. "I think it helps your attitude and game if you look well and feel good," Maria said. "Ted and I would discuss the dresses before he made anything. First it had to be very comfortable and practical. We made history with his dresses.''

Ted, who was a celebrity himself by this time, thanks in part to Gussy Moran's lace panties, did not hesitate to go out on the fashion limb for Maria, who was one of his most glamorous models since Gussy. The dress that created the greatest stir was unveiled during the 1962 Wimbledon championships. It was white except for the lining below the waist, which was shocking pink. ''Every time I served, it would show,'' Maria said, laughing. ''This caused a great deal of commotion.''

Commotion? As I recall, the whole Centre Court crowd was shocked. The British gasped (or perhaps sighed) every time Maria's dress flew up, but I remember thinking the dress was wonderful. After that, color started catching on everywhere, though not at Wimbledon. The next year the all-white rule was again firmly in place.

Maria Bueno was introduced to tennis at age five by her father, Pedro Bueno, a veterinarian who enjoyed playing the game. Mr. Bueno bought Maria a membership at the Clube de Regatas Tietê in São Paulo, a rowing club with swimming pools and tennis courts located across the street from their home.

Maria had no formal lessons, adopting instead her own eclectic methods of self-improvement. ''I would copy anybody I liked to watch, any of the club players,'' she said. Maria yearned to have a serve like Bill Tilden's. She studied a book that featured several photographs of Tilden's serve and spent hours trying to imitate his majestic motion.

She practiced mainly with the best male players at the club, including her brother Pedrinho, and by age fourteen she was touted as a prodigy. She won the Brazilian women's championship that year and took a set from Shirley Fry, one of the best women players in the world. At seventeen Maria began to tour internationally. In 1958, at eighteen, she won the Italian women's singles title and the Wimbledon doubles title with Althea Gibson.

Maria was seeded only sixth at Wimbledon in 1959. Britain's Christine Truman, winner of the French championships, was seeded first. Playing with uncharacteristic emotional consistency, Maria fought her way into the final against Californian Darlene Hard. Darlene had beaten Maria in their six previous encounters, but this time Maria played almost flawlessly. She won, 6–4, 6–3, with the help of seventeen aces, ending a run of American triumphs that extended back to 1938. In South America, Maria—the first Brazilian to win Wimbledon—became an instant celebrity.

''Tennis wasn't big at all for men *or* women in Brazil,'' Maria said, remembering the attention showered upon her when she returned home, including a twenty-one-gun salute and a parade. ''Being a girl and by myself, I had gone out to conquer the world. Statues and airmail stamps were made.''

For a while Maria Bueno continued to do what her country had come to expect of her. She won the 1959 United States championship at Forest Hills, beating Christine Truman in the final, and successfully defended her

Maria Bueno enhanced her star status by wearing beautiful, feminine tennis dresses designed by Ted Tinling.

Wimbledon title in 1960 with an 8–6, 6–0 victory over Sandra Reynolds of South Africa.

Then, in the spring of 1961, after capturing her second Italian title, Maria traveled to Paris for the French championships and was stricken with hepatitis. She and Darlene Hard defaulted their doubles final to Sandra Reynolds and Renée Schuurman of South Africa, and Maria spent the next month confined to bed in her Paris hotel room. Darlene also contracted the disease.

"When I was able to get up and travel, that's when I went home," Maria recounted. "I was really in very bad shape, and I stayed in bed for eight months after that. It was just one of those unfortunate situations that I never had too much assistance from people who were supposed to have helped. Coming from Brazil, I was so far away from everything and everybody."

Maria returned to competition nearly a year later, but her illness had weakened her. She was suffering from elbow problems, and her confidence had been eroded by her long absence. When she lost to me, nineteen-year-old Billie Jean Moffitt, in the Wimbledon quarterfinals in 1963, David Gray wrote in the British newspaper *The Guardian* that Maria "played as though she was her own ghost." To the sportswriter, who was not alone in this opinion, "it seemed beyond belief that she could ever win a great singles title again."

But Maria Bueno was stronger than she looked. She simply needed more time to recover and pull herself together. La Bueno would be back, and sooner than anyone imagined.

The best player in the United States from 1960 through 1963 was Darlene Hard. She retired in 1964, four years before open tennis, with a total of twenty-one Grand Slam singles and doubles titles to her credit and only $400 in her bank account.

"But I didn't do it for money," Darlene said. "We toured for country and flag and to play better and to be Number 1 or whatever we were working for. I was the last of the amateurs. In our day I won Forest Hills and I got my airfare from New York to Los Angeles. Whoopee. I won Wimbledon [doubles championships] seven times and I got ten pounds each time, which was like eighteen dollars. But we still went for the titles. We went for the glory. It kept us out there year after year. I was happy. I loved it. I loved tennis."

Darlene won the United States singles championship twice and the French once; in doubles she won eighteen big-four titles—thirteen in women's doubles and five in mixed. She might have won more singles titles but for two weaknesses in her game. She had an erratic forehand, and she did not believe in herself. Her two Wimbledon finals, against Althea Gibson in 1957 and Maria Bueno in 1959, were anticlimactic for her, she said, "because I didn't seem to produce the same tennis I had while getting there. I seemed to be happy being there and not eager to take Number 1, I don't know why. I was always Number 2 in the world, and I always knew that. I wasn't trying to set any records. All I knew was I didn't want to lose."

In doubles, however, where her forehand could take a back seat to an aggressive serve-and-volley game, Darlene was almost unbeatable. She could team up with any partner and win. Darlene won her thirteen major women's doubles titles with seven different partners: Beverly Baker Fleitz, Althea Gibson, Shirley Bloomer, Maria Bueno, Jeanne Arth, Lesley Turner, and Françoise Durr.

Darlene's most incredible doubles victory came at the 1969 United States championships, renamed the U.S. Open, five years after she had retired from regular competition. She and Françoise Durr of France, playing together for the first time, defeated Margaret Smith Court and Virginia Wade in the final, 0–6, 6–4, 6–4.

"We were down, 6–0, 2–0," Darlene recalled. "I looked up at the scoreboard and said, 'Frankie, we've got to do something. Those zeros are so huge. They're as tall as we are.' Frankie said, 'Darlene, how can you joke at a time like this?' I said, 'We're playing so badly, if we don't start joking and getting loose we're going to lose, love and love.' Frankie said, 'Stop clowning and go back and serve.' So I said OK and we won the match."

Years later Darlene still laughed about that

Darlene Hard, one of the most successful doubles players in history, was among the last of the great amateurs.

victory. "I loved it," she said. "That was a big moment. And let me tell you, we went home with $500 each. For me, that was the biggest amount of money I'd ever seen. Five hundred smacks!"

Darlene was a ponytailed blonde and a crowd pleaser, a good-natured player who always had a smile on her face. She made friends everywhere she went. Although she had no children of her own—one of her great regrets—she did have godchildren all over the world. "I waited until forty to get married, and then that ended in three and a half years," she said. "So I don't have any kids. What a waste."

While still a tennis star, Darlene hoped to be a pediatrician. She took her college entrance exams before playing in the semifinals of a tournament and scored high enough to earn an academic scholarship to Pomona College in Claremont, California. At Pomona Darlene completed her premedical requirements, but she grew bored when she had to face liberal arts courses like history and music appreciation and left school to rejoin the tour.

At five feet six and 140 pounds, Darlene was always battling her weight, a state of affairs she had no trouble joking about. "I just can't pass up anything on the menu," she once said. Players in those days did not measure their percentage of body fat with computers, nor, with the notable exception of Margaret Smith Court, did they train with weights. "We didn't know what strengthening a muscle was," Darlene said.

Darlene, who grew up in Los Angeles, was influenced by several champions from the past. As a child she delighted in watching Louise Brough at the Los Angeles Tennis Club. Years later she received personal instruction from Alice Marble. Alice had watched Darlene play a match at the Los Angeles Tennis Club one day, and as Darlene approached the clubhouse, thinking she had played rather well, Alice said, "Would you like to play better?"

"She worked with me hours and hours," Darlene recalled. "My ranking went from seventh to ninth and back to seventh over a two-year period, and then I went straight to the top."

Darlene's other mentors were Hazel Wightman and Sarah Palfrey Danzig. When Darlene went east she always spent several days with Mrs. Wightman in Longwood. They became so close that even while Darlene was playing elsewhere on the East Coast, she would drive to Mrs. Wightman's home once a week to mow her lawn. Darlene also benefited from a three-month stay with Sarah. They practiced together daily, with Sarah hitting Darlene nothing but forehands. Afterward, Darlene went off to win the French championship.

In the late 1980s, nearly twenty-five years after her retirement, the once carefree Darlene was putting in eleven-hour days as a computer-systems operator for the University of Southern California. She was still playing tennis, but not seriously. She had to give up her job as a teaching professional because of skin cancer.

Darlene had not kept in touch with anyone from the tennis tour, not even Maria Bueno or Sarah Palfrey Danzig. How would she like to be remembered? "I think just forgotten,"

Christine Truman, left, and Angela Mortimer treated Wimbledon fans to an all-British final in 1961. Angela triumphed in three sets.

she said. "Yes, I think just swept into the cracks. I didn't play tennis to do anything."

But of course Darlene Hard accomplished a great deal while playing tennis. No one can sweep twenty-one major singles and doubles titles into the cracks.

The 1961 women's singles championship at Wimbledon took on an air of uncertainty: Maria Bueno was ill in a hotel room in Paris and Darlene Hard, also ill, was at her side. It was far from clear who the possible champion might be. In the end, Wimbledon had its first all-British final since 1914: Angela Mortimer versus Christine Truman.

Angela was a very good player, though not a great one. She was neither quick nor powerful, and she never learned how to get full extension on her serve. Nevertheless, she was one of the most tenacious people I ever met. "Every match I ever won had been the result of practice and determination and hard work," she wrote in her memoir. "Perhaps I had worked harder than most champions. I knew that I was not truly one of the greats."

Angela won the French and Australian championships once during the 1950s and played in her first Wimbledon final against Althea Gibson in 1958. By 1961, however, she was suffering from a sore arm and at twenty-nine was thought to be past her prime.

Christine Truman, only twenty, was favored to beat Angela. Although six feet tall and not particularly agile, Christine had a wonderful forehand and the capacity to play brilliantly. She reached the Wimbledon semifinals on her first try, at age sixteen in 1958, and she won the French and Italian championships in 1959. In one of her most notable victories, she upset Althea Gibson in the 1958 Wightman Cup competition and led the British team to its first postwar triumph.

Christine's sportsmanship and gentle demeanor made her one of the most popular British players ever. Despite her imposing height, she conveyed the image of a nice British schoolgirl. She was exactly the kind of sweet-tempered and wholesome woman the English adore.

Christine led Angela in the Wimbledon final, 6–4, 4–3, when she tried to retrieve a shot off the net cord and slipped on the grass, which had been dampened by rain. When Christine stood up she grabbed the back of her right thigh in pain. She continued to play but never regained her form. Angela emerged the victor, 4–6, 6–4, 7–5.

The 1961 Wimbledon was my first and a special one indeed. Karen Hantze of San Diego and I were the first unseeded team, and the youngest, to win the women's doubles. Karen was eighteen, and I was seventeen. My coach, Clyde Walker, was dying of cancer, and I wanted to win for him because he had always believed in me. Before I left for England, I saw him for what I knew would be the last time. Clyde, who had always wanted to coach a champion, followed Karen's and my progress in the newspapers and talked to the nurses about us. His wife, Louise, later told me that every match Karen and I won at Wimbledon kept him alive another day. The day after Karen and I won the championship, he died.

Karen and I wanted to go to the Wimbledon Ball to celebrate, but because neither of us had a dress, we spent the evening in our hotel room, packing. I can still see Karen folding every piece of clothing, just so. She was methodical on the tennis courts, too; she drove Wimbledon officials to distraction by taking so much time between points.

Karen always did things at her own pace and with a certain stubbornness that I liked. When she fell in love with a high-ranking doubles player named Rod Susman, some USLTA officials tried to break off the romance, fearing that Karen would lose interest in her tennis. They told Karen to stop seeing Rod, but Karen did not comply. As she later said, romance "is a natural thing; you don't spend *all day* looking at a tennis ball."

In 1962 Karen and I won the doubles again, and Karen—then Mrs. Rod Susman—captured the singles crown in one of the most surprising women's championships of all time. *The Times* of London noted before the start of the tournament that "there are several dangerous loose cards in the pack," including Britain's Christine Truman, Australia's Judy Tegart and Jan Lehane, and America's Nancy Richey. The reporter was right about the dangerous cards, but he might have added two others, Karen and me. While Karen was breezing through the draw (she won the tournament without dropping a set), I caused a stir of my own by upsetting top-seeded Margaret Smith.

Margaret, who would win three Wimbledon singles titles as Margaret Smith Court, had a long and trying relationship with Wimbledon's Centre Court. It began in 1961, when she nearly lost in the first round to Nancy Richey and then fizzled in the fourth round against Christine Truman after leading, 4–1, in the third set. Both matches took place on Centre Court and earned Margaret the reputation for having "Centre Court jitters."

When Margaret returned to Wimbledon in 1962, she was being touted as the world's best player and the greatest athlete women's tennis had ever seen. She had won three successive Australian championships, and she had just won the Italian and French and every other big tournament leading up to Wimbledon that year. Nevertheless, Margaret was only nineteen and still very much the shy, small-town girl from Albury in New South Wales. It was not easy for her to carry the hopes of her country, which had never produced a female Wimbledon champion. I can

The winning Wightman Cup team of 1962 poses with the trophy. From left are Karen Hantze Susman, Margaret Varner, captain Margaret duPont, Darlene Hard, myself, and Nancy Richey.

Karen Hantze Susman, right, appears with Vera Sukova of Czechoslovakia before beating her in the 1962 Wimbledon final.

remember thinking that had she not been under so much pressure she would have done better.

About six months before Wimbledon, I had a premonition: I was going to play Margaret in the first round, and I was going to win. Incredible as it sounds, Margaret and I *did* play each other in our first match.

When we met on Centre Court, I was still an unknown—"Little Miss Moffitt," a bubbly, nearsighted eighteen-year-old with 20-400 vision and "pert, pointed glasses." But I surprised a few people. Margaret was serving for the match at 5–3, 30–15, in the third set, when I hit a beautiful winning backhand down the line to win the next point. Margaret suddenly caved in and went down to defeat in a bundle of nerves. Never before had a first seed lost her first match at Wimbledon.

That strangest of Wimbledons ended with eighth-seeded Karen Hantze Susman facing Vera Sukova of Czechoslovakia. Vera lost the first set to Karen, 6–4, but was leading, 3–2, in the second set when she turned her ankle and lost her momentum, just as Christine Truman had the year before. Karen then glided to victory.

Two years later, at the age of twenty-one, Karen left the international circuit for the traditional role of wife and mother. (Rod became a successful life-insurance broker.) Karen has had a few nostalgic moments looking back on what she missed, but she knows she made the choice that was right for her. I knew she and Rod would be happy in the marriage the USLTA did not want to happen. And they have been.

The summer of 1963 was a memorable one for women's tennis. It marked both the beginning of the Federation Cup team championships and the arrival of Margaret Smith as the new queen.

In the 1950s Mrs. Wightman's dream of seeing a women's international team championship involving many nations was revived, when several women began lobbying vigorously to open up the Wightman Cup competition to countries other than Britain and the United States. The staunchest backers of an expanded Wightman Cup were Margaret duPont, a longtime cup captain, and three Australian women: Thelma Coyne Long, the Australian champion in 1952 and 1954; Nell Hopman, a former touring player who was then a Victorian Tennis Association official; and Floris Conway, an administrator within the New South Wales Tennis Association. The Australians were especially eager to have an international team competition. At that time, they boasted five top women—Lesley Turner, Jan Lehane, Robin Ebbern, Mary Carter, and Margaret Smith.

After England steadfastly refused to open up the Wightman Cup competition, Thelma Long had a brainstorm. In 1960 she began urging Margaret duPont and two key USLTA officials, president Ed Turville and committee member Mary Hardwick Hare, to establish a championship entirely separate from the Wightman Cup. Once the USLTA had embraced this concept, progress came quickly. The structure was appealing and the timing was right; women's tennis in 1960 was clearly on the rise internationally.

As enthusiasm for a women's team championship mounted, Margaret duPont offered to donate a cup. She and Thelma Long were actually in the process of drawing up rules for the team championship when Mary Hardwick Hare preempted them, proposing the championship at an ILTF meeting in Paris in 1962. The ILTF passed the proposal without argument and announced that the first Federation Cup matches, featuring sixteen teams, would be held in June 1963 in London, in conjunction with the ILTF's fiftieth anniversary.

Unlike the Wightman Cup, which had turned into a show of American dominance, the Federation Cup produced lively rivalries. Because a Federation Cup team match consisted of two singles and one doubles, compared with five singles and two doubles in the Wightman Cup, a nation needed only two top players to field a team. During the first nine years, Australia won the Federation Cup five times, the United States four. Czechoslovakia later emerged as a tennis power and won the trophy four times between 1975 and 1985.

In the inaugural Federation Cup championship at the Queen's Club in London, the United States beat Australia in the thrilling final, two matches to one. Darlene Hard and I won the decisive doubles, overcoming Margaret Smith and Lesley Turner after being down double match point, 3–6, 13–11, 6–3.

Margaret, who beat me in the 1963 Wimbledon final, went on to establish herself as one of the enduring giants of the game. Many of her records probably never will be touched. Between 1960 and 1975, despite two separate year-long absences from the tour, she won sixty-two Grand Slam titles in singles, doubles, and mixed doubles, including twenty-four Grand Slam singles titles. In singles she won the Australian championships eleven times, the French five times, Wimbledon three times, and the United States five times. Margaret had the advantage of playing her nation's championship year in and year out at a time when many top players could not afford to travel to Australia, but even without all those Australian victories, her record would be remarkable.

In 1970 Margaret achieved one of her greatest ambitions. She became the second woman (Maureen Connolly was the first) to win *the* Grand Slam—all four major championships in a calendar year.

Despite her historic feats, Margaret never completely conquered her nerves. "She would not serve double-faults at 5–0, 40–0, but it was quite possible that she would at 5–all, deuce," said Ann Haydon Jones. Louise Brough, who had won four Wimbledon titles between 1948 and 1955 in spite of her own debilitating jitters, said she used to get nervous just watching Margaret play.

"People used to say she was nervous on the big occasion," said Rex Bellamy, veteran tennis correspondent for *The Times* of London. "My answer to that was fine, she was nervous, but how many players would like to be as nervous as Margaret was when she could still win all those championships? We have to remember that she dominated tennis—or was at least the best of a very good crop—at the time when Maria Bueno was playing, and Billie Jean King."

Said Margaret: "When I felt tremendous and knew that I was playing well, I didn't feel anybody could touch me. But then I had my times when I struggled within myself and I had to build myself up, which I often did on the practice court. I could seem to bring myself up during a lot of the major tournaments, and I could play through it. If I was in a bad patch, I could pull myself out."

Margaret hated losing under any circumstances, and she never gave up. She set high goals for herself, making the Grand Slam a top priority before she was twenty. "I loved to win, and I liked being at the top," Margaret said. "When I lost, it normally made me much more determined to get up and show them that I could do it. Often after I lost a tournament I'd be out practicing harder than ever to make up my mind I wasn't going to lose the next one."

The Times's Bellamy told a revealing story: "I saw her win when I knew she was so ill that a lot of players would not have gone on the court. It was a relatively minor tournament sometime in the late 1960s at Torquay, but it had a good entry. In this particular year, the tournament was in progress and Margaret was ill. My wife and I went up to visit Margaret in her room and she could hardly talk. She had a desperately bad cold. We talked about what happens in a situation like this. Do you withdraw? Do you lose gracefully? Tank, as they say in the trade?

"And Margaret said—I forget her words exactly—'I never learned how to do that. I can't do that.' So the next day she was on the court with Joyce Barclay, a British Wightman Cup player who was then very competent, very ambitious. Joyce led by something

Margaret Smith Court, the first woman tennis player to use weights, worked out with trainer Stan Nicholes five mornings a week when she was in Australia. "I was skinny and raw, and he built me up into a real athlete," Margaret recalled. Margaret could win matches on strength and endurance alone. The bottom photo at right dramatizes why we called her "The Arm."

MARGARET SMITH COURT

"I don't think back on my playing days very often. My life has changed so much and has become so full in other areas that unless somebody finds me or speaks to me about my tennis, I never really think about it.

"I always loved tennis. I can't say I always enjoyed all the traveling and the hotels, but I always knew it was a talent that I had, and I always knew, even when I was a little girl, that it was a gift from God that I had. I just loved it. I loved all sports. I always felt very free when I was playing.

"But no, I never have missed it. The last time I ever went back and played I knew my heart wasn't there anymore. I just knew having been at the top that I couldn't stay out there and just go down and down. I knew it was time to stop, and from the time I stopped I never ever wished I was back there. I was done and I had fulfilled all the goals that I had aimed for.

"Right through, the press was pretty good to me. But I think in my early years that the British press did put a lot of pressure on me, and I think that's probably why I never did as well at Wimbledon as I should have. I got a thing within myself, and I never really enjoyed playing at Wimbledon, or played my best tennis there. I felt more comfortable playing in the U.S. Open or the French, because I won a lot more of those tournaments.

"I think probably if I had known what I know now from the word of God I would have won six Wimbledons and not three, but I don't think of it as a regret. Where I once had insecurities in my life, I know how much the Lord has changed me in those areas. They're not there anymore. Perhaps where there were nerves, they aren't there anymore. Or perhaps in an area of fear, that's not there anymore.

"I think insecurities come from your background and whether you were born a positive person. I think a lot of it has to do with your surroundings, how you're brought up in those areas to have confidence in yourself.

"Being tall and athletic, that was a security to me. That was one of my greatest weapons and abilities. I think believing in yourself has a lot to do with words. You are what you say you are, and I think if you come from a very positive family you believe in yourself from the time you're a little one. Your children will be what you say they are. Words are important and powerful. And having come to know God's word and how positive Jesus was, he always spoke the answer and never spoke the problem. In America a lot of your athletes were always tremendously confident, whereas we as Australians hadn't had that built within us. I think that has changed tremendously."

---

like a set and 4–1, and I remember thinking if ever there was a time for Margaret to lose a match gracefully and get back to bed and get healthy again, this was it. But she came back and won, because she could never tolerate the idea of defeat."

Margaret held herself apart from her rivals, who saw her as aloof and unwilling to give an inch. "I knew that I couldn't let myself get close to too many people, particularly when I was playing at the top," she said.

She described her relationship with Maria Bueno as a "long, bitter rivalry," and certainly Margaret and Darlene Hard were not friends. "I don't think Darlene enjoyed playing me, and I sensed that," Margaret recalled. "There was something there. I think I was the young one coming in—the threat."

Margaret and I, during our competitive days, were never the best of friends. In the 1960s we were competing too hard for the same prizes to feel warmly toward each other. In the 1970s the tension became greater when Margaret declined to join my fight to establish a women's tour. Today, however, Margaret and I enjoy standing next to each other in parades of champions. Players learn to relax and appreciate each other after they have retired.

Margaret was only a year older than I, but

she had a big head start on me. She began playing full-time when she was fifteen, but because I was going to Los Angeles State College I did not make that commitment until I was twenty-one. Margaret had won the Australian championship five years in a row before I even saw Australia. After losing to me in the first round of Wimbledon in 1962, she beat me fourteen straight times during the next four years. But once I got my game together in 1966, when I was twenty-two, I had the edge. Of our last twenty matches, I won twelve.

Margaret said that playing me was a mental and physical challenge for her, because I was rarely quiet on the court. When I made a great shot, I pumped my fists and shouted "*Yes!*"; when I erred, I screamed at myself to do better and slapped my thigh.

In 1987 Rex Bellamy, veteran tennis writer for The Times *of London, said Margaret Court was the greatest player he had ever seen. She won a record sixty-two Grand Slam titles in singles, doubles, and mixed doubles.*

Margaret put it this way: "I knew I was playing Billie Jean's temperament as well as her shots, and I had to have self-control. It was a battle in every way when I was playing her. But I knew that I could match her in other ways and ignore her antics, and I didn't let them get to me as some players did."

I think Margaret was being kind in her assessment of me. Some players thought I had ulterior motives when I exulted or berated myself; they thought I was trying to intimidate them. But unless I reached a feverish emotional pitch, I could not play my best.

Margaret Smith, born on July 16, 1942, grew up in a small house on the outskirts of Albury, New South Wales, where her father worked as a foreman in a cheese- and butter-processing plant. Her family was not wealthy.

Margaret's first "racket" was not a racket at all but a piece of wood she had found. Her family could not afford to buy her a real one. A sympathetic neighbor saw Margaret playing in the streets with her piece of wood and gave her an old racket. Judging from Margaret's description, the racket must have predated the days of Helen Wills. The head was squared off at the bottom, and the thick wooden handle had no leather grip.

Margaret soon began playing tennis, on the sly, at the Albury Tennis Club, a private club with twenty-five courts not far from her home. The eight-year-old Margaret, who was not a member, would creep under the fence with her neighborhood friends (all boys) and play until she and her friends were spotted and told to leave. Finally, the club professional, Wal Rutter, softened his stance and began holding clinics for the children on weekends. Margaret won her first tournament before she was ten, still using her ancient racket.

Like Maureen Connolly, Margaret was a natural left-hander who learned to play tennis with her right hand. "I think probably I would have had a better serve if I had played as a lefty," Margaret told me. "It probably would have been more natural to me. But I don't regret it because at that time I didn't know any different. There were no women players in the world who were known as left-handed.''

Margaret quit school and left home when she was fifteen to work with Keith Rogers and Frank Sedgman, the former Australian champion, in Melbourne. Margaret lived with the Sedgmans and earned money working at Frank's office. Robert Mitchell, a wealthy Melbourne businessman, paid for her lessons and even sent her to charm school in an effort to make her feel more at ease with herself.

To add strength to her tall, scrawny figure, Margaret began working with Olympic trainer Stan Nicholes. This was a first in women's tennis; no woman had ever participated in a rigorous fitness regimen. ''I loved it,'' Margaret said. ''I really enjoyed that side of it more than the tennis. I always found it very easy, where for some people it was such hard work.''

Margaret won her first Australian championship in 1960 at the age of seventeen. She upset Maria Bueno in the quarterfinals and beat Australian Jan Lehane, one of the first women to use a two-handed backhand, in the final. ''I was a nobody in Australia,'' Margaret said. ''I became a hero overnight.''

Nevertheless, officials within the Lawn Tennis Association of Australia (LTAA) regarded Margaret as emotionally and physically immature, and they did not allow her to travel to Paris and Wimbledon with the Australian team that year. When Margaret traveled abroad the next year, in 1961, friction arose between her and team manager Nell Hopman. Nell's ambition as team manager was to return from the eleven-month tour with a profit for the LTAA, even if it meant staying in inexpensive hotels and ordering Continental breakfasts for her charges instead of the preferred steak and eggs. Margaret was so upset that she withdrew from the team in 1962 and traveled independently, her expenses being underwritten by Robert Mitchell. Despite her loss to me in the first round of Wimbledon, Margaret was fabulous in 1962, winning three of the four Grand Slam singles titles.

In the 1964 Wimbledon final, Margaret lost to the woman who was not supposed to win another major title, Maria Bueno. Maria, who had astounded the tennis world the previous September when she beat Margaret in the final at Forest Hills, won her third and last Wimbledon by beating Margaret, 6–4, 7–9, 6–3. Margaret had won fifteen successive tournaments coming into Wimbledon, including the first two legs of the Grand Slam, but her ''Wimbledon jinx,'' as she called it, reappeared. She overslept the morning of the final and awoke at 11:30, only ninety minutes before her match. She then went out and double-faulted three times in the first game. Margaret came back, however, and the match was described as the best women's final at Wimbledon since Maureen Connolly beat Doris Hart in 1953. Frank Butler, writing for the British newspaper *News of the World*, stated that ''for drama, tenseness, and entertaining play, it made the men's final a complete bore.''

If the occasion was a bitter one for Margaret, it was a joyful one for Maria and her

I am pictured in the backcourt here, but I was at my best at the net. Only five feet four and a half inches tall, I was one of the smallest net-rushing champions in history.

world of admirers. In Brazil Maria had suffered all the bruises of a fallen star. Not only had her country failed to help her when she was ill and stranded in Paris in 1961, but the government had also withdrawn her diplomatic passport, which meant she was forced to pay duty on her trophies.

"I had a bad elbow, I was sick. I had everything against me, and then I came back," Maria said. "It was a great personal victory for me. Every victory is big, but winning Wimbledon after all this meant a lot. I remember the newspapers here—they had headlines I never forgot. They said, 'The Girl the Whole World Wanted to Win.' "

I grew up in Long Beach, California, not far from the ocean. My father, Bill, worked for the Long Beach fire department, and my mother, Betty, was a homemaker. My younger brother, Randy Moffitt, was a natural athlete like me and became a major-league baseball pitcher. Randy and I both loved performing under pressure.

As a child I never dreamed that I would one day win a record twenty Wimbledon singles and doubles titles or that I would help change the game of tennis, but I always knew I was going to do something special with my life. I loved going to the library, signing out books and poring over maps. Even as a young girl I knew I wanted to travel.

When I was about eleven, a friend of mine, Susan Williams, invited me to play tennis at the Virginia Country Club. I had never played before. "You'll have to wear white," Susan told me, and of course I had nothing to wear. My mother, who had sewn all of my clothes from the time I was a baby, made me some white shorts, and Susan, who was the best player in Long Beach, lent me a racket. I had a great time.

I also played softball that summer, and a few days after my tennis debut the softball coach at Houghton Park told me about the free group tennis lessons held at the park every Tuesday. I immediately started saving up for a racket, plunking nickels and dimes into a mason jar. When I had accumulated eight dollars, I took the jar and went over to Brown's Sporting Goods on Atlantic Avenue, where I was shown a racket with a violet throat and violet-colored strings. "This is probably what you're looking for," the man said. It was fine with me.

Here I am as a plump and bubbly teenager, wearing one of the many dresses my mother made for me.

I was entranced from the moment I began hitting the ball with my new racket. I knew that day what I was going to do with my life. When my mother picked me up at Houghton Park, I told her I was going to be Number 1 in the world. She tried to bring me down to earth by reminding me about my homework and piano lessons, but I know she was secretly delighted. At least tennis was *ladylike*. Mother had already told me I could no longer play touch football in the front yard, and that had crushed me. I loved to run and cut corners fast, feeling the wind in my hair, changing direction, thinking, deciding.

"Always be a lady, Billie," my mother would say.

And I would ask, "Mother, what does that *mean*?"

The Los Angeles Tennis Club was a hub for tennis in Southern California at that time; you could see Pancho Gonzales, Jack Kramer, Louise Brough, and Althea Gibson play there. I used to watch Louise Brough whenever I could. She always smiled and said hello. I also watched Tony Trabert, Ken Rosewall, Lew Hoad, and Darlene Hard. I studied them to see what made them good. If Gonzales was giving Dennis Ralston a serving lesson, I watched and tried to learn as much as I could. It was a tremendous opportunity because Gonzales, in my opinion, still has the best service motion of all time—it is sheer poetry.

Money was always a problem for me as a child. The Long Beach Tennis Patrons paid most of my entry fees, which were two dollars or three dollars, but they were not able to give me everything I needed. I remember the time Perry Jones, who ran the Southern California Tennis Association, insisted that I travel with a chaperone to Middletown, Ohio, for a girls' national championship. Because I did not have enough money to fly with a chaperone, my mother and I rode the train and slept—sitting up—for three nights. After the tournament, the other girls boarded flights to Philadelphia for the next event, while my mother and I took the train back to California.

The people who really helped me when I was young were my coach, Clyde Walker, and Alice Marble. I used to get rackets from Joe Bixler, an equipment representative for Wilson Sporting Goods, and because I reminded him of the way Alice used to play, he came up to me one day—I was fifteen—and said, "Would you like to meet Alice Marble?" I was ecstatic. My parents called Alice, and she said she would be happy to teach me. For three months my parents drove me to Encino every weekend so that I could work with her.

Alice understood tennis. She helped me understand the relationship between the face of the racket and the ball, and she also taught me not to get too close to the ball. A woman with enormous strengths, she was also a master at understanding her weaknesses. She knew how to think and to find solutions on the tennis court. Just listening to a champion like Alice helped me think like a champion. Although I had only three months of weekends with her, my national ranking rose from nineteenth in 1959 to fourth in 1960.

The turning point in my career came in late 1964. I was in my third year as a history major at Los Angeles State College, and I was engaged to Larry King, a prelaw student there. I still had my dream of being Number 1 in tennis, but I had yet to win a major singles title. I finally realized that I would never know whether I could make it unless I made a commitment to play full-time.

I was able to make that commitment when Robert Mitchell, the same businessman who had helped Margaret Smith, offered to pay my way to Australia so that I could train under the great Australian coach Mervyn Rose.

This is one way to express the thrill one feels after winning a Wimbledon title. Altogether, I won twenty of them in singles, doubles, and mixed doubles, a record that still stands.

I told my friends I was going to Australia to become the best player in the world. It was a frightening admission, but it helped to drive me. Merv Rose was exactly what I needed. He made radical alterations in my game, changing my swooping, wristy forehand and backhand into the crisp, efficient strokes of a champion.

My breakthrough came during a match I lost to Margaret Smith in 1965. It was my first final at Forest Hills, and I led Margaret, 5-3, in both sets before losing, 8-6, 7-5. To come so close and lose was devastating, but I was exhilarated by the knowledge that I finally had the skill to beat her. After the match, I walked along Continental Avenue in Forest Hills with my good friends Frank Brennan Sr. and his wife, Lillian. I told Frank, who helped coach me, "I'm so upset I can't breathe. But I know now that I'm good enough to be the best in the world. I'm going to win Wimbledon next year."

I did win Wimbledon in 1966. I beat Margaret in the semifinals with the help of a new shot, a forehand down the line. Then in the final I beat Maria Bueno in three sets. In 1967, while Margaret Smith was taking a sabbatical from tennis and falling in love with yachtsman Barry Court, I won Wimbledon and the United States championship, beating Britain's Ann Haydon Jones in both finals.

I won those titles in 1967 while playing with Wilson's revolutionary T-2000 racket, the forerunner of the sophisticated graphite rackets in use today. Rosie Casals and I were the first women to bring the T-2000 to the public. The radically new racket, designed by former French star René Lacoste, featured a circular frame made of steel and was lighter and more maneuverable than the wooden rackets. It worked like a trampoline: if I hit a shot perfectly, the ball streaked over the net; if my timing was off, the ball flew into the fence. The racket had some flaws in it, to be sure, but it was the start of something new—the use of modern technology to generate unheard-of power.

For me as a player, the years leading up to 1968 were exciting yet frustrating. Tournament promoters used us as cheap labor. The most under-the-table money I ever made was $7,000 in 1967. I could have earned more if I had been allowed to play more European tournaments, which offered players twice as much money as the American tournaments, but I was not free to decide where I played. The USLTA's International Play Committee decided which American players, male and female, were eligible to compete in an overseas tournament.

Nancy Richey always wore an expression of steely resolve on the court. "I guess if looks could kill, I would have killed a number of people," she later mused.

For example, early in my career I did not want to come back to the United States after Wimbledon and play grass-court tournaments. I wanted to practice on the red clay in Europe in order to improve and round out my game. Unfortunately, the USLTA needed me to help draw crowds at their grass-court events, and I had to play in them. The USLTA did not allow me to play in the French championships until I was twenty-two years old and the top-ranked player in the world. I should have been playing in Paris four years before that. If I had, maybe I would have more than one French title to my name.

Ironically, lower-ranked Americans who were not considered drawing cards had more freedom than the stars. They played more in Europe than I did and made more money, too.

The system was infuriating and riddled with hypocrisy. The same officials who made the rules about amateurism literally bribed us to play in their tournaments. I remember the head of the International Play Committee telling my husband, Larry, "If Billie Jean will come back and play at the Merion Cricket Club during the summer, I will allow her to stay in Europe." In other words, if I entered his tournament he would authorize me to play a few additional European events, where I could make more under-the-table money.

Nancy Richey, an outstanding baseline player who ranked among America's top four from 1963 through 1976, recalled that tournaments "treated the players like dirt and then raked in the money." Nancy remembered the time she played with Maria Bueno in the women's national doubles championships at the Longwood Cricket Club. The tournament director had guaranteed her in writing a per diem of twenty-six dollars. When Nancy went to collect, however, the official tried to back out of the obligation. "You can't have the money because you're playing doubles with a foreigner," the official said, looking at Nancy as though she had committed a sin against her country. After recovering from her shock, Nancy opened her purse and whipped out the letter promising her a per diem. The official hemmed and hawed, then grudgingly gave her the money.

Nancy said that on another equally embarrassing occasion, a high-ranking tournament official discreetly led her into a cluster of bushes to present her with her under-the-table cash, and then tried to kiss her.

The final blows to "shamateurism" were delivered in 1967. Lance Tingay, the distinguished British tennis writer, has said that an incident involving Britain's Roger Taylor was the catalyst that forced Britain's Lawn Tennis Association to conclude that amateur tennis was out of control. When Taylor reneged on a promise to play in Austria for a secret guarantee in order to take advantage of a more lucrative guarantee at a Canadian tournament, the Austrian federation asked the LTA to punish Taylor for failing to uphold a non-amateur agreement. The LTA was infuriated by the hypocrisy of Austria's request.

The Roger Taylor incident was, however, only one reason for the LTA's concern. By the autumn of 1967 rumors were swirling that all of the remaining top amateurs, including Wimbledon champion John Newcombe, were preparing to turn professional. Lamar Hunt of Dallas, an oil tycoon and sports entrepreneur who had founded the American Football League in 1959, was known to be starting a professional circuit for men.

LTA officials, fearful that amateur tennis could soon become a sport without stars, decided to open Britain's tournaments to professionals, whether the rest of the world was ready or not. Derek Hardwick, vice-chairman of the LTA and brother of Mary Hardwick Hare, helped lead the way, and in October 1967, the policy-making LTA Council voted, 61–1, to present a proposal abolishing the distinction between amateurs and professionals at the LTA's general meeting in December.

In endorsing open tennis, the LTA Council was counting on support from the USLTA, then headed by Bob Kelleher. Bob, an attorney who later became a federal judge, was logical and fair. He had been lobbying the geographical sections within the USLTA to convince them that open tennis was in the best interests of the game. His politics paid off with the USLTA members agreeing to a resolution that said, in essence, if the ILTF did not open up the game, the USLTA might join the LTA and "break away" from the ILTF. By saying merely that it "might" join the LTA, however, the USLTA allowed the British to lead the way—which they soon did.

In the meantime, Lamar Hunt confirmed rumors by announcing the formation of his professional tour, World Championship Tennis, and by signing John Newcombe and four other top amateurs.

At the LTA's general meeting on December 14, by a nearly unanimous vote, the full LTA officially abolished the distinction between professionals and amateurs. Britain's tournaments would be open to all, beginning with the hard-court championships at Bournemouth in April 1968. Although the British risked expulsion by the ILTF in theory, the

ILTF had even more to lose: If the ILTF suspended Britain, it would have to carry on without the greatest tournament and without the greatest players in the world. Forty-seven member federations of the ILTF met on March 30, 1968, and voted unanimously for open tennis.

That was the beginning of tennis as we know it today. Major tournaments throughout the world began offering legitimate prize money, and one had only to look at other professional sports, including golf, to realize that the prize money would escalate steadily.

For women tennis players, however, a new kind of struggle was beginning. When Wimbledon announced the prize money breakdown for its first open tournament, every woman in the draw was destined to be a loser. While the men's champion was slated to earn £2,000, the women's winner—one Billie Jean King—would have to settle for £750. The men's total purse would be £14,800, the women's £5,680. The ratio was 2½ to 1.

Confusion reigned during the first two years of open tennis. No one knew how many open tournaments there would be. The major international tournaments were going to offer prize money, but officials of many of the smaller tournaments were not sure what to do. Eventually, those that did not want to get into the business of professional tennis simply vanished from the calendar. The eastern grass-court circuit, with its traditional stops at the Merion Cricket Club and Essex County Club, faded into oblivion.

I coped with the uncertainty by joining a traveling troupe of players as a contract professional. I was hired by George MacCall's National Tennis League (NTL), a commercial organization that kept us playing week in and week out. Within the NTL, we played in established tournaments like Wimbledon and the U.S. Open, and we also staged tournaments of our own. We spent two months playing our own tour in the south of France. The men in our troupe were Ken Rosewall, Roy Emerson, Fred Stolle, Pancho Gonzales, Rod Laver, and Andres Gimeno. The other women were Ann Jones, my doubles partner Rosie Casals, and Françoise Durr, the last Frenchwoman to win the French championship. I was guaranteed $40,000 a year, Ann was guaranteed $25,000, and Rosie and Frankie were guaranteed $20,000 each. The men were paid more; I know that at least one of them made $70,000.

We had a difficult life, traveling during the day and playing at night. Fortunately, we were friends; we had dinner together every night, went dancing together, and always kept our sense of humor. We also sat around and philosophized about the future of the game.

The amateur-professional question was supposed to have been resolved once and for all in 1968, but it was not. The ILTF, after voting for open tennis, promptly introduced special rules pertaining to contract professionals like those of us in George MacCall's NTL. As a result, Ann, Rosie, and I were not allowed to play in the Wightman Cup matches in 1968 and 1969. The USLTA also refused to include Rosie and me in the national rankings those two years.

Rosemary Casals and I were an established doubles team by the time open tennis arrived in 1968. We had won the Wimbledon and national doubles titles in 1967. Rosie, who learned to play at San Francisco's Golden Gate Park, was truly gifted. Sportswriters, dazzled by her shot selection, said she was the next Maureen Connolly and the most ex-

Ann Haydon Jones was the most underrated woman player of the 1960s. Here we are together before our 1969 Wimbledon final, which Ann won.

ANN HAYDON JONES

"We didn't play each other as much as they do today, which was an asset, because the result was less certain. There was not a pecking order developed in quite the same way as there is now. The circuit today grinds on and on, and if you're not careful, it grinds the players down with it.

"I found Billie Jean hard to play because her personality was ebullient and strong. It was difficult to play the ball and not Billie Jean, and it took me quite a long time to learn how to do that. Lots of champions are the same; Margaret Court was like that, for instance. They all try to draw attention to themselves—to how good they are—with various mannerisms. When they make a good shot they make you feel, '*That's* how well I can play and I'm going to continue to do that and what are you going to do about it?' But that's part of the makeup of the sport. A champion always attaches to herself an aura of ascendency. In many instances it's worth a point a game to them. They're confident and you're not; they're at home and you're not. They like to give you the feeling that they are in control and it's up to you to do something about it. And as I was often on the other end of that, never having been a supreme Number 1, I was often the one having to do something about it. And frequently I could and did. But sometimes by their strength of personality they get on top of you.

"I think in many ways I came up through more enjoyable times. We saw amateur tennis and we saw the beginnings of professional tennis and we saw team tennis develop, and we've seen enormous commercialism brought into the game. In many ways, it was probably the most interesting time.

"You can't say I wish I'd played now or I wish I'd been born in another era. Hoping for something you can't have is the biggest way to an ulcer or a sour temperament.

"Obviously, for a British girl to win Wimbledon is the apex of one's career. It was wonderful to win it, but I didn't realize at the time how much more strength it gave to your opinions afterward. It establishes you in the tennis world, and you're free to give your opinions, whether they're asked for or not, on a variety of tennis topics.

"Someone who had won Wimbledon more than once probably would feel differently, but I think the first time you win it, especially after so many attempts, you have a feeling of relief and disbelief. I remember standing there and holding the trophy, which seemed very heavy. The All England Club let me take it home for a few days. It was the first time it had been out of their hands. I was terrified somebody would steal it and I'd get absolutely decapitated."

---

citing player since Helen Wills. When Rosie was eighteen, Harry Hopman called her the best junior prospect in the world. "Everything came easily to me," Rosie said. "I was a good athlete; I moved quickly. Tennis was not work because I had a lot of talent."

Because Rosie was only five feet two, she needed to work *very* hard to reach the top. In order to beat players like Margaret Court, who was five feet eleven, she could not afford to give away any points through carelessness or poor footwork. Regrettably, little Rosie lacked discipline. She had the will to win, but she did not always have the drive to prepare.

Rosie's career record is an impressive one; it is also the story of "almost." Rosie made four Wimbledon semifinals, two United States finals, and two United States semifinals. In doubles she won nine Grand Slam titles, five of them at Wimbledon. She was the best player of her era who did not win a major singles title.

Adrianne Shirley Haydon Jones, better known as Ann, was another story altogether. Ann was a brilliant and underrated player who reached the Wimbledon semifinals seven times between 1958 and 1968 and finally won the championship in 1969.

Ann, who spent most of her career in the

shadow of more popular English players—first Christine Truman and later Virginia Wade—was solid but unsensational. She had no weaknesses in her game, but she had no outstanding strengths either. Her greatest assets were her resolve and her ability to maneuver an opponent around the court. She never disappointed the British fans with a terrible, early-round defeat, but she rarely lifted the crowd to its feet. Ann simply did not have the intangible star qualities of Christine and Virginia. Fortunately, she was content to have the attention showered on others. "I was quite happy playing on court ninety-two somewhere, with only half a dozen spectators," she said.

Ann, who came from a lower middle-class family, grew up on the outskirts of King's Heath in Birmingham. Both parents were table-tennis champions; her father, Adrian, was a former world semifinalist. Ann followed her father's path in table tennis and in 1957, at eighteen, she was runner-up in the World Table Tennis Championships. She began playing tennis at age twelve but did not devote herself completely to the game until she was nineteen.

Ann chose tennis over table tennis because it offered a better life. "The sunshine life is more interesting than the late nights and electric lights," she said. "It was a nicer life, a more genteel life. Table tennis was third class in the train. I wanted to see the world."

As a table-tennis player, Ann once came within two points of winning the world title. In tennis, too, she always seemed to be only a point or two away from the top. When she played me in her first Wimbledon final in 1967, losing, 6–3, 6–4, she had fifteen break points against my serve but won only one of them. "This had been the story of my Wimbledon life," Ann said later. "I had never been able to produce the necessary extra little bit. . . . When it came to the crunch I didn't have that little something more."

Being part of our NTL helped Ann immensely. She thrived in the atmosphere of tough competition and daily practice sessions against top men and women. She practiced extensively with Ken Rosewall, and that made her sharper. She was thirty years old and playing the best tennis of her life when her big moment came at Wimbledon in 1969.

That year everyone in England was talking about twenty-three-year-old Virginia Wade, who had won the first U.S. Open the previous summer. Virginia, Britain's new heroine, was a dramatic player whose classic serve was universally acknowledged to be the best in women's tennis. Tall and graceful, she was a joy to watch when she was playing well. Stubbornness, anger, and pressure occasionally got the better of her, however, and in the 1969 Wimbledon she blew a big lead against an unseeded player and lost in an early round.

Ann Jones, meanwhile, advanced to the Wimbledon semifinals for the eighth time in her career and then reached her second Wimbledon final by beating Margaret Smith Court in a spectacular match. In the other semifinal I easily beat Rosie Casals.

Ann beat me, 3–6, 6–3, 6–2, in a final that I cannot claim among my best. The crowd was pulling so mightily for Ann, calling balls in or out before the linesmen did, that at one point I turned around and gave them a little sarcastic curtsy, a gesture that did not help me in the least. Though bitterly disappointed (I had been going for my fourth successive championship), I was happy that Ann had finally won.

Ann Haydon Jones never played again at Wimbledon, but she did not retire from tennis. She was destined to be an important part of the new era that was about to begin.

Shamateurism had ended during the 1960s, but a new and equally difficult problem had arisen: now tennis had to answer the question, what were women worth? The rulers of tennis apparently were not impressed by the ballet of Maria Bueno, the athleticism of Margaret Smith Court, or the crowd-pleasing Wimbledon finals played by Angela Mortimer, Christine Truman, and Ann Haydon Jones. The precedent of grossly unequal prize money, established at the first open Wimbledon in 1968, had been accepted as gospel by the men who controlled the game. The women accepted it, too, but they were not going to accept it forever.

Chapter 6

Birth of a Tour

1970-1973

Birth of a Tour

Women tennis players made greater gains in the three years between 1970 and 1973 than in the thirty previous years combined. For the first time in tennis history, we stood up and fought for respect and decent pay. To accomplish what we wanted, we had to start a tour for women only.

The arrival of our own tour was a reflection of the times. The age of rebellion and liberal thinking that began in the 1960s reached a feverish pitch in the early 1970s. The issues of the previous decade—the Vietnam war, racial prejudice, the environment, and women's rights—were more a part of our consciousness than ever.

The women's liberation movement made us keenly aware of the inequities in our sport, but not everyone on our tour saw herself as a feminist or a radical. Gladys Heldman, the shrewd and well-connected founder, editor, and publisher of *World Tennis* magazine who helped found our tour, never claimed we were a part of the women's movement. When people asked her about "women's lib," she would smile and say, "It's Women's Lob." We were fighting for our own cause, for fairness, recognition, and the right to control our destinies, not some greater principle of women's rights within society. Nor were we actually fighting for strict equality in tennis; those who said we did were not listening. When we were demanding $18,000 in prize money for a field of thirty-two women, the men were asking for $50,000—plus expenses. Only at Grand Slam tournaments like the U.S. Open, where men and women still competed together, did we demand equal pay. Eventually, we won on virtually all counts.

A team of individuals made it happen: Gladys, of course; the powerful Joseph F. Cullman 3d, chief executive officer of Philip Morris; the adventurous promoters who stood to lose money on an unproven product, and a small group of women tennis players who were willing to risk everything in an effort to achieve greater status for women in tennis. We players and Gladys worked to exhaustion, but we succeeded in lifting women's tennis to new heights.

Overleaf, change was the common denominator in women's tennis in the early 1970s. I helped found a tour for women, while a couple of teenagers, Chris Evert, bottom, and Evonne Goolagong, right, emerged as superstars.

After our initial struggles, our sport achieved an even wider audience with the help of two upcoming young superstars, Chris Evert and Evonne Goolagong. Ultimately, we women players became household names because of a chauvinistic former champion named Bobby Riggs.

When the decade opened, tennis was expanding everywhere in the world. New sponsors were coming into the game, and prize money was on the rise. Tournaments were making more money. Promoters were making more money. Male tennis players were making more money. Everybody was making more money except the women, who were actually losing ground. In 1968, when open tennis began, the national tournaments' prize-money ratios had been about $2^1/_2$ to 1 in favor of the men, and they had stayed that way into the 1970s. At the less prestigious tournaments, however, the disparity in prizes was widening at an alarming rate. Ratios of 5 to 1 had been common in 1969, and they soared to 8 to 1 and 12 to 1 in 1970.

The women were being squeezed financially because they had no control in a male-dominated sport. Men owned, ran, and promoted the tournaments, and because many of them were former players themselves, their sympathies lay with the male players, who argued vociferously that most of the money should be theirs. Back in 1967, when we all knew open tennis was going to become a reality, my husband had predicted this would happen. Larry had theorized that the men would demand more and more of the money until the promoters reached the conclusion, "Why have the women at all?"

The reasoning among the old-boy network was based on three assumptions. They argued first of all that men played best-of-five sets in the Australian, French, Wimbledon, and United States championships while women played only best-of-three. Obviously, they did not understand that entertainers do not punch time clocks. As Bud Collins, long-time tennis critic for *The Boston Globe* and the NBC television network, has always said, "Sometimes a shorter opera is much better than a long one."

The male players further maintained that because they could beat us, they deserved most of the money. This argument also completely ignored the female tennis star's role as an entertainer. Sugar Ray Leonard probably could not have beaten heavyweights when he was the Number 1 middleweight, but he was still thrilling to watch. "I know women don't run as fast or hit as hard," Collins said, "but I don't think that has anything to do with it. It's the drama that you're looking for. The entertainment."

Finally, the men said we deserved less because few people came to watch us play. "It wasn't that the promoters disliked or disapproved of the ladies," said Bob Kelleher, the USLTA's president in 1967 and 1968. "They sincerely believed that if you put on a tournament with men and women playing in it, the people came primarily to see the men. And the only way to get the men to enter was to give them most of the prize money."

If we women were seemingly powerless in the first years of open tennis, we were blessed with an important ally in Gladys Medalie Heldman, a forward-thinking woman who had always believed that women could work and have careers if they wanted them.

Gladys, originally from New York City, was an intellectual who came from a brilliant family. Her father, George Z. Medalie, was a famous lawyer, her mother, Carrie, a Latin and Greek scholar. Gladys herself earned her bachelor's degree and Phi Beta Kappa key from Stanford University in only three years.

Gladys became interested in tennis after marrying Julius Heldman, who entered UCLA at fifteen, played the tennis circuit until he was nineteen, earned a Ph.D. in physical chemistry at twenty-two, worked on the Manhattan Project (which developed the atomic bomb) during World War II, and later, as a weekend tennis player, beat many a former champion, including Jack Kramer, Ted Schroeder, and Herbert Flam. Gladys began playing tennis after her second child was born and became proficient enough to earn the Number 1 ranking in Texas in the early 1950s and a berth in the Wimbledon draw in 1954. Her Wimbledon debut ended in a first-round defeat on a back court, 6–0, 6–0. "It's all right, I still love you," Julius shouted, as Gladys wept. "Only not as much."

Gladys's real achievements came off the court. When the USLTA voted not to hold the 1959 National Indoor Championships, which had always lost money, Gladys agreed to underwrite the losses and then turned an $8,000 profit for the event. In 1962, concerned by a decrease in the number of foreign entries at Forest Hills, she raised $18,000 to charter a plane to bring eighty-five overseas players to New York. Gladys and nine of her friends each donated $1,800. Gladys then enlisted scores of other friends, who paid $125 each to underwrite the foreign players' living expenses during the tournament.

Her founding of *World Tennis* in 1953 brought her the most renown. The magazine lost money at first, but as Stephanie DeFina, one of the early touring professionals, said, "Gladys did it for tennis. She loved tennis." By the middle 1960s, *World Tennis* had become a winner. With a circulation of 43,000, it was the biggest tennis magazine in the world.

From her forum, Gladys made enemies—hundreds of them. She edited every word in her magazine, and every month she and her staff blasted the governing officials of tennis for their archaic and self-serving rules. The male hierarchy disliked her intensely; they wanted tennis to stay the same, and Gladys represented change.

Gladys trumpeted the cause of open tennis for many years before it became a reality. Then she focused on the plight of the underpaid female tennis professional, documenting the unbalanced prize-money ratios at important tournaments. When a women's singles champion received less money than the men's doubles winners, for example, as was the case in the 1970 Australian Open, she registered her disapproval forcefully in the magazine.

Gladys's interest in women's tennis went beyond her conscientious editorializing. During the winter of 1969, she was responsible for staging three tournaments just for women: a $5,000 event in Philadelphia, a $5,000 event at the Vanderbilt Club in New York, and a tournament without prize money in Dallas.

Meanwhile, against the backdrop of mounting discrimination against women tennis players, Margaret Court, in 1970, was going about the business of winning a Grand Slam. It had been a goal that was always on her mind. Three times before she had won three of the four majors in one year. "I knew I had the ability to do it, and I was disappointed that I had gotten so close," she said.

Margaret started her slam by winning the Australian championships for the ninth time in her career, beating fellow Australian Kerry Melville in the final. She won the French Open with a victory over Helga Niessen of West Germany, and she won Wimbledon by beating me, 14–12, 11–9, in our most unforgettable match.

Margaret later said the match was one of the best she ever played at Wimbledon. My recollection is that neither of us was in top form. Margaret was playing with a painkilling injection in her ankle (she had had injections from the quarterfinals on), and I was playing with an injured knee that caused my leg to cramp. Toward the end of the match, I could no longer follow my serve in to the net because of the cramp. I underwent knee surgery three days later.

The match was unquestionably suspenseful, and it is always included in lists of the greatest matches ever played. The first set alone lasted eighty-eight minutes. Bellamy of *The Times* of London wrote, "It had a thrilling beauty that chilled the blood and, in retrospect, still chills the blood. . . . This was majestic and powerful tennis, the right stuff for a King and a Court to play before a crowd including three princesses and the prime minister. At the heart of the struggle lay each player's superb qualities as a competitor. They never gave an inch."

"I always remember the crowd," Margaret said later. "It was electrifying and explosive on that Centre Court, and it was a battle of fitness and a battle of nerves. To me it was exciting because of the atmosphere and the pressure. It got so that every point was like a match point. When I think about my most memorable match, this is the one I remember. I could say winning my first Wimbledon was the most memorable; I could point to matches I may have played a lot better in. I could say the last leg of the Grand Slam was the best. But it wasn't. The 1970 Wimbledon final is the one that always stands out in my mind."

Margaret Smith Court holds the U.S. Open trophy after beating Rosie Casals to win the final leg of the Grand Slam in 1970.

Margaret's victory gave her the first three legs of the Grand Slam for the first time in her career. She had only to win the U.S. Open, the final leg of the slam. This she did with the loss of only twenty-two games, beating Rosie Casals, 6–2, 2–6, 6–1, in the final. The initial euphoria Margaret felt—"I thought, praise God it's all over"—soon gave way to feelings of emptiness. "I was as flat as anything," Margaret recalled. "I think for about three months after I won it, I played terribly. I had been keyed up for so long preparing for it. It was like winning a gold medal and then being wiped out."

From the time Don Budge established the concept of a Grand Slam in 1937 until 1982, all four major titles had to be won in the same calendar year. In 1982, however, the International Tennis Federation ruled that a player who won four successive big-four titles, whether they were in one calendar year or two, was the winner of a Grand Slam – and a $1 million bonus. I think the slam is more difficult to accomplish today, because all of the great players enter every major tournament, whereas in Margaret's day, not everyone played in the French and Australian championships every year. I consider Martina Navratilova's string of six successive big-four titles in 1983 and 1984 a more impressive feat than Margaret's Grand Slam of 1970.

Nevertheless, Margaret's quest to win all four majors in one calendar year had its own special burdens. "You couldn't lose one and then try to win the next four in a row," Margaret pointed out. "You had to wait until the following year before you could start again. It's difficult to stay built up and be ready in each major tournament."

Margaret earned only $15,000 in prize money for winning the Grand Slam, but no one heard her complain about the disgraceful financial situation in women's tennis. She, like other top players, continued to earn money under the table. Margaret was apparently satisfied with this state of affairs and perhaps did not realize that she was still vastly underpaid. But she was a traditionalist, not a rebel. "I'm a happily married woman and I've no wish to wear the pants," she once said, and she wanted no part of our movement. "I am perfectly happy as an independent player and I see no reason why I should change my views."

While Margaret was making history and headlines on the tennis court, others of us were making history behind the scenes. Our revolt had begun. The catalyst was an ominous piece of news that had come to us several weeks before the 1970 U.S. Open: Jack Kramer, promoter of the Pacific Southwest tournament, which came a few weeks after the Open, was offering prize money slanted in favor of the men by an unprecedented ratio of 12 to 1. The men's winner would receive $12,500, the women's winner a meager $1,500. The women who failed to reach the quarterfinals would not get a cent.

Shortly before the Open, Rosie Casals and I were so angry with Kramer that we approached Gladys Heldman and proposed an outright boycott of the Pacific Southwest tournament. Gladys advised against a boycott but said she would try to persuade Jack to increase the women's purse. She twice approached Jack without success.

"Jack was intransigent," Gladys recalled. "He wasn't going to raise the prize money. He expected Billie Jean and Margaret Court and the rest to fly out to California and pay their own way. 'If they don't like it,' he said, 'I won't give them *any* prize money.' "

Then Gladys had a brainstorm. If the women were not going to be treated decently at Kramer's tournament, they would have their own tournament. Gladys picked Houston as the site, because she and her family were about to move there. Gladys immediately called the Houston Tennis Association, the Texas Lawn Tennis Association, and the Houston Racquet Club, and within three days she had arranged a $5,000 tournament for eight women. The money would come from ticket sales to members of women's groups associated with tennis in Houston.

Unaware of Gladys's negotiations, the women professionals held a meeting in the women's locker room at the West Side Tennis Club in Forest Hills and argued heatedly about whether to boycott the Pacific Southwest. The idealists among us thought it imperative that we make a point immediately, before 12-to-1 ratios became the norm. Some, however, wanted no part of any rebellion. Just when it looked as though we were getting nowhere, who should stride into the locker room but Gladys. A playwright could not have staged it better. There was no need for a boycott, Gladys said, beaming. Those who wanted to play in Kramer's event could do so; for eight others, there would be an alternative: the $5,000 Houston Women's Invitation.

Another noteworthy incident occurred during that U.S. Open at Forest Hills. Ceci Martinez, a professional tennis player from San Francisco, punched a hole in the myth that nobody came to tennis tournaments to see women play.

Ceci was typical of many young women in America in the early 1970s. She was a college graduate, she subscribed to *Ms.* magazine, she read books like *Sexual Politics* by Kate Millett, and she believed in equal rights for women. She came to the U.S. Open inspired by a demonstration in Washington, D.C., where thousands of women had marched to demand equality. She also came to the Open angry.

Ceci had hoped to make a good living playing professional tennis, but her dream was being trampled by the Jack Kramers of the world. "If they had given the women half of what they gave the men, I think we probably would have accepted it," Ceci told me. "But we felt the men were taking over."

Ceci had never believed the tennis establishment's contention that spectators did not come to see the women play, and she decided to put it to the test. She devised a one-page questionnaire that sought to determine how much spectators enjoyed watching women's tennis. Among her questions: Would you pay to watch a tournament with only women players? Which do you enjoy watching more—a men's match or a women's match, or both equally well?

"I had taken a class in psychology on how to write surveys," Ceci explained. "I had this feeling that people were interested in watching women play, but it was just a feeling. I had observed it, but I wanted to know scientifically."

On September 7, 1970, Ceci and her doubles partner, Esme Emanuel, stood under the main scoreboard and handed out copies of the questionnaire. They collected responses from 94 women and 184 men, about 2 percent of the 13,000 spectators in attendance.

The results, when taken in the context of that era, were stunning. One-third of the men and one-half of the women liked watching men's and women's tennis equally well; one-third of the men and one-half of the women thought prize money allocations should be equal, and more than one-half of the men and two-thirds of the women said they would pay to watch a tournament with only women players. "If you had these results today it would be awful," Ceci said in 1987. "But in 1970 it was promising, considering that we weren't getting the publicity the men were; we weren't put on the grandstand or center court; we just weren't given the respect."

Neil Amdur, the tennis writer for *The New York Times*, learned of Ceci's survey and wrote an article that appeared in the newspaper the following day. Amdur also invited Ceci and other women professionals to express their views at a meeting of the Lawn Tennis Writers Association. Amdur's gestures, though small, were representative of sentiment that existed from New York to Houston. Society had become sensitive to the issue of women's rights, and if the women tennis players spoke up and said they were being cheated, people were going to listen.

When Gladys Heldman told Jack Kramer that eight women would compete in Houston September 23–26, the same week as the Pacific Southwest, the male establishment began fighting back. To run her tournament in accordance with established rules, Gladys needed a sanction from the USLTA. Jack at first said he would not oppose a sanction because "I'm not that kind of guy."

However, once he had talked it over with his friends in the USLTA, including Stan Malless, chairman of the USLTA's scheduling committee, Kramer and the old-boy network decided they *would* oppose a sanction. They had neither precedent nor legitimate grounds

Ceci Martinez circulated a unique questionnaire in 1970 and proved that women's tennis was far more popular than the male promoters and tournament directors suspected.

for such action. They simply wanted to control us. They even tried to pin the blame for the decision to withhold a sanction on Perry Jones, the president of the Southern California Tennis Association, who at the time was hospitalized and in a coma. A telegram protesting our tournament was sent to Gladys, supposedly signed by Perry. Perry died twenty-four hours later.

Two days before the Houston tournament was to begin, we received an ultimatum from Alastair Martin, president of the USLTA: If we played in Houston, the USLTA would suspend us. Suspension meant we could not be ranked and could not play for the Wightman or Federation Cup teams. Our future in tournaments like the U.S. Open and Wimbledon would be uncertain.

These were strong threats, but we did not flinch. "At that point I didn't care if I never played Wimbledon again," Nancy Richey said later, her eyes blazing at the memory. "The USLTA had treated us so badly for so long that it didn't bother me if I never saw another major tournament. We were getting such raw deals that we decided to throw caution to the wind."

At the same time that Martin was trying to intimidate us, Gladys was working on another coup. She was negotiating with her friend Joe Cullman, of Philip Morris, to bring sponsorship money into the tournament.

Cullman was already deeply involved in tennis, both as a player and a sponsor. He had served as chairman of the United States championships and later the U.S. Open, and under his direction, Marlboro, a Philip Morris product, had become the Open's first sponsor. Although Cullman's previous tennis connections had been mostly with the men's game—he had hired players like Arthur Ashe, Manuel Santana, and Roy Emerson to represent Philip Morris in publicity roles—he also looked favorably upon the women's game. "I enjoyed watching women's tennis," Cullman recalled. "I felt women's tennis deserved better recognition from the viewing public."

Cullman was known as a champion of women and minorities. He was an early activist in the National Urban League, and in 1970 he thought "the women's liberation movement was long overdue."

In Gladys's request for money, Cullman saw the possibility of merging a cause he believed in with a successful business venture. He viewed the renegade tournament as a perfect vehicle for marketing Virginia Slims, a new cigarette designed primarily for women and identified with the slogan "You've Come a Long Way, Baby." Said Cullman: "I had no trouble convincing my associates at Philip Morris that the modest expenditure would be money well spent."

Cullman gave Gladys the use of the Virginia Slims name, and his company contributed $2,500 in prize money, which raised the purse to $7,500. The tournament was renamed the Virginia Slims Invitation.

Twenty-four hours before the historic event, the contestants arrived. In addition to Nancy Richey, Rosie Casals, and me, there were five others who competed: Valerie Ziegenfuss, Judy Tegart Dalton, Jane "Peaches" Bartkowicz, Kerry Melville, and Kristy Pigeon. Julie Heldman, Gladys's daughter, attended but could not compete because of an injury. I will never forget any of them.

During her career Valerie was ranked in America's top ten on four different occasions. Judy, an Australian, ultimately won seven Grand Slam doubles titles while working six months each year as an accountant. Peaches, a native of Hamtramck, Michigan, had won the national girls' eighteen-and-under title three straight times, equaling Sarah Palfrey's record. Kerry, another Australian, would go on to win the Australian Open in 1977 and the Wimbledon doubles with Wendy Turnbull in 1978. Kristy, the national junior champion in 1968, was ranked among the top ten women in the United States in 1969, and Julie was ranked among the top four.

Patti Hogan, another ranking American player, was supposed to play, but she decided at the last minute that she did not want to take the risk. Margaret Court also withdrew. Still drained from her Grand Slam, she had just suffered a discouraging loss to fifteen-year-old Chris Evert.

Shortly before the Virginia Slims Invitation began, Stan Malless of the USLTA called to

The women's tour began when nine players signed one-dollar contracts with Gladys Heldman in September 1970. Standing from left are Valerie Ziegenfuss, myself, Nancy Richey, and Peaches Bartkowicz. Seated are Judy Dalton, Kerry Melville, Rosie Casals, Gladys Heldman, and Kristy Pigeon. Not pictured is Gladys's daughter, Julie.

offer us one last chance and a tempting piece of bait. Stan said we could have a sanction for an amateur tournament with no prize money. If we played as amateurs for $7,500 in money under the table, we could stay in good standing with the USLTA, which meant, of course, that we would remain under their control. If we played for $7,500 in honest prize money, we would be suspended. We voted to take the latter route.

We also decided to sign one-week contracts with Gladys in order to protect the Houston Racquet Club from reprisals. Under the murky new rules of open tennis, which distinguished independent professionals under the jurisdiction of their national associations from those under contract to a promoter, the Houston club was allowed to hold an unsanctioned tournament only if the contestants were contract professionals outside the associations' jurisdiction.

With the tournament's start less than one hour away and the contracts still unsigned, I called USLTA president Martin on a pay telephone from the Houston Racquet Club. It was my turn to give *him* one last chance. "We do not want to do this," I told him, "but you have given us no choice."

Martin said he wanted us to play for the USLTA and the love of the game. He said he did not want the women to sign with Gladys, but he offered no assurance that the prize-money distribution would be more balanced in the future. Furthermore, he said the USLTA could guarantee only two tournaments for women the following year, the National Indoor Championships and the U.S. Open. I hung up the phone, walked about twenty yards, and joined the other women in signing a one-week contract for one dollar.

We knew we were gambling. Several of the men players said we were fools and would never succeed. We had no proof that we would be able to establish a series of tournaments beyond the initial tournament in Houston. We faced humiliation if we failed.

Our timing, however, was excellent. Society was ready for us, as was the press. Moments after we signed with Gladys, we held up our one-dollar bills for the photographers.

The next day the USLTA suspended us and we were front-page news.

Gladys and the "Original Nine," as we called ourselves, met frequently during the tournament to discuss our future. One evening we met in Gladys's enormous bedroom at her home. Some of us sat in chairs against the wall, others on the floor. I told everyone that if we were going to make a tour work, we had to find out how much money we needed to survive. That meant we all had to admit how much money we made under the table, because if we had our own tour, we would be playing for prize money supplied by sponsors and gate receipts, not secret guarantees. Although I was one of the few who benefited from the secret-guarantee system, I thought it was grossly unfair. A star with a guarantee could lose in the first round and still make more money than the woman who won the tournament.

Everyone was honest about what she made. I told how much I made under the table—$1,500 to $2,000 a week at that time. Nancy Richey said what she made. Val Ziegenfuss said she was lucky if she got enough to pay her expenses. After adding up the secret guarantees plus the expenses incurred by women who earned no guarantees, we figured that a total purse of $10,000 would be enough to support a tournament of sixteen women, and we established that as the minimum standard for our tournaments of the future. For tournaments with a thirty-two draw, $18,000 would be the minimum. In every case we wanted to make sure that first-round losers earned enough to cover their expenses.

Meanwhile, our revolution was already paying dividends. During our tournament Barry MacKay, chairman of the Pacific Coast Championships, which followed Kramer's Pacific Southwest, called Gladys with an offer: After seeing how much publicity we generated in Houston, he had decided to increase the women's purse from $2,000 to $4,400 for a draw of thirty-two (compared with $25,000 for the men). Gladys replied that members of the Original Nine would be happy to play for a purse of $11,000. Barry called Gladys the next day; the women's purse would be $11,000.

The winner of our first Virginia Slims Invitation was Rosie Casals, who defeated Judy Tegart Dalton to win the $1,500 first prize. But in another sense we had all won that week. Women's tennis would never be the same.

After the tournament had ended, we met at Gladys's home once again. By that time we were committed to having a circuit of our own in 1971, and only one question remained: Who would run it? The women voted to have Gladys run the tour. She had money and power, and she had Joe Cullman.

Cullman was delighted with the enormous amount of publicity generated by the Houston tournament. I think women's tennis received more media coverage in that one week than it had in the entire previous year. "If it hadn't been for people like Jack Kramer, the Virginia Slims tour never would have gotten that early recognition," Gladys said later. "When people ask me who founded the tour, I always say Jack Kramer."

Joe Cullman's $2,500 contribution to the purse at Houston was probably the best advertising investment his company had ever made. Within days, Cullman agreed that Virginia Slims would sponsor eight sixteen-women tournaments. The tour was born.

The number of women under contract to Gladys Heldman quickly grew beyond the Original Nine. Ann Jones and Françoise Durr, my friends from the days of George MacCall's National Tennis League in 1968 and 1969, became two of our biggest stars. Another mainstay was Betty Stove, a tall, strong woman from the Netherlands.

Margaret Court, Virginia Wade, and Evonne Goolagong did not sign with Gladys. They played in some of our events during the first few years, but they never were a part of our effort to build up the women's game. While we played mostly in the United States, they split their time between the United States, Europe, Australia, and South Africa. In America they continued to play the tournaments sanctioned by the USLTA, winning small amounts of prize money and larger under-the-table guarantees. "They just went where there was money for them and no competition, while we struggled,'' Rosie Casals said bitterly.

The traditionalists had their reasons for not joining. Some of them did not like Gladys. Others preferred the status quo. Margaret Court, for one, did not like the idea of a tour for women only. She later told me, ''Most of my friends at the time were the Australian guys; I couldn't bear the thought of women's tournaments and men's tournaments.''

Fortunately, we survived without them. In 1971 Virginia Slims broadened and extended its sponsorship, giving us a $250,000 tour with twenty-four tournaments. Other sponsors also helped: British Motor Cars, K mart, BioStrath, and the Ford Motor Company were among the first to come forward.

Gladys herself was a sponsor. She guessed many years later that she probably funneled about $100,000 into the tour.

''I had a slush fund for the women who couldn't quite make it on the qualifying circuit,'' Gladys recalled. ''I think I gave away about $30,000 to help players. I kept five black players on the circuit one year. They weren't good enough to get into the tournaments, and they had no money, so I kept them going in the qualifying events. I also added money to tournaments when I couldn't get enough from other places. In 1972 I put $20,000 into our first $100,000 tournament, in Boca Raton, Florida. And I put $10,000 into the Family Circle tournament to bring the purse to $100,000.'' In addition, Gladys worked without compensation and her magazine gave us free advertising.

Virginia Slims spent many thousands of additional dollars polishing the tour's image. They purchased scoreboards, produced a program, and even dressed us. In those days only a few top players had contracts with clothing manufacturers, and not everyone had the money to dress in a crisp outfit every day. Joe Cullman, appalled by the way some of the women looked, hired designer Ted Tinling, who supplied us with all the clothes we needed for several years.

Val Ziegenfuss recalled in 1987 that she still had about 100 of Tinling's dresses hanging in her closet. ''Those dresses are special,'' she said. ''I have a dress in which the whole skirt is white sequins. Talk about heavy! But when it picked up the light, it was like the color of the rainbow. I also have a beautiful halter dress. The top was black velvet and the skirt was silver lamé. Can you imagine sweating and playing tennis in velvet? But we were putting on a show. We were trying to put people in the stands.''

Pam Teeguarden, another tour regular, also kept her dresses. ''They're like new,'' she said. ''They were so much fun. Everybody looked a lot better than the players do now. The clothes today are nice, but they're like a uniform: skirt and shirt. They have some class, but they're not nearly as pretty or feminine as what we wore.''

Pam reminisced about the time she wore black for the first time in a tournament in Japan. ''When I came out the crowd went berserk. I had even dyed my shoes black, and I was wearing black socks. I got the dress from a lady in Houston who wanted to do something for me. She went into her closet and took out a $300 floor-length Adolfo evening gown with rhinestones. She cut it off and made it into a tennis dress for me.

''I also had a dress I called my 'Star Wars' dress. It was made of silver lamé, and it had a silver belt around the waist. When I took my sweater off I'd get standing ovations.''

It was in publicity that I made some of my greatest contributions. Because I was the Number 1 player on our tour and because I was never at a loss for something to say, everyone wanted to talk to me. I worked endlessly to meet their demands. I gave interviews on the 6:00 A.M. radio shows, even after playing tennis late into the night.

At our $100,000 tournament in Boca Raton, fans and sportswriters stopped me thirty times before I reached the court, according to Gladys. ''There was no way of guarding her in those days,'' Gladys said. ''At Forest Hills she couldn't walk from the marquee to the stadium without being surrounded and pestered and stopped. She was the star, and everyone wanted to talk to her.''

I remember that I was always exhausted. I know my tennis suffered, but my personal success was not as important to me as the success of our tour. I played about thirty tournaments a year during the early years of the

Ann Jones, bottom left, Rosie Casals, right, and I were mainstays of the young Virginia Slims tour. We played week in and week out and also spent long hours on promotion.

Birth of a Tour

PEACHY KELLMEYER

"Gladys Heldman was my first boss. She and Virginia Slims hired me as tour director in 1973. Gladys was a leader. She was one of the people, like Billie Jean, who had vision and could see ahead. Sometimes you think their ideas are off the wall, but they're idea people, which I'm not. I'm just a normal, everyday, trying-to-get-the-job-done type of person. Gladys is a fantastic woman.

"Gladys fought the USLTA tooth and nail the first year I worked on the circuit. The USLTA would not allow its officials to officiate our tournaments. They threatened that we couldn't play at clubs that had USLTA tournaments. Gladys fought that.

"It was difficult when Gladys was bargained out of the sport, and I know she must have felt hurt. She devoted her life to the women's tour. She was the editor of *World Tennis* at that time. I saw how hard she worked. Not only was she putting out a magazine once a month, but the tour was a twenty-four-hour-a-day job.

"Because I was new and didn't know anything, I wanted somebody to tell me what to do. But Gladys never did that. She let you make your own mistakes, and she was always supportive. Her daughter Julie was on the tour then, and I probably did some things that were not in Julie's best interests. I can't remember what they were exactly—maybe they had to do with interpreting the rules or scheduling—but never did her mother ever say a word to me. She gave you confidence, and she was always positive. It was a great experience being around her.

"Was there universal love for Gladys? No, I don't think anybody who is a real leader or doer is going to be universally loved. I mean Billie Jean is a good example. Leaders make decisions. When Billie Jean was on the circuit you had to be on your toes, and that was good. If the banners weren't right in the back of the court, she would tell you. If there was no water at the changeover, she would tell you. She wanted things right. People like that are not universally loved. They can't afford to be.

"When I first started as tour director we really didn't have any rules. We literally made them up as we went along. We had player meetings every now and then, and the players would decide what they were going to do about this rule and that rule. We had draws of sixteen, and we did the seedings based on how the players did the previous week.

"One week, just to show you how much more professional it has become, the tournament director didn't have enough linespeople, and when a guy came in to install the Xerox machine, they put him on a line. He had never seen a tennis match. He had never played tennis. They put the lines down on the court an hour before we were going to play. And when we finally got the court down, there were no tennis balls.

"It was a crazy life, but it was fun. Everybody knew everybody. If someone was sick or had a problem in her family, everyone knew about it. It was a close group of people trying to survive and build something.

"To me those were the good days, when the players really, really cared. Every player. I can remember Nancy Richey playing a match in Denver and she was so sick that she was gargling scotch to try to keep herself going. I think she had had a root canal done. But she played. She was so professional. She gave her best every time."

---

tour, including virtually every Slims event on our schedule. I felt I had to play week in and week out to make the tour a success.

I was not the only one who worked hard; everyone contributed. We stomped and politicked at the grass-roots level. "I remember trying to give tickets away at a K mart," recounted Betty Stove. "We said, 'Do you want to come to the tennis?' And they said, 'What tennis?' People had no idea what tennis was about." We also gave clinics, visited with spectators in the stands, and attended every cocktail party our sponsors gave.

Ann Jones's husband, Philip (Pip), a retired businessman, was our first tour director. One of his responsibilities was our lone tennis court, which was made of SportEze, a hard, vinyl-coated fabric that resembled a carpet. ''He had the problem of getting it to the next venue,'' Ann said. ''Renting American trucking companies to do it for us wasn't easy at the time.''

Our crowds were much smaller than they are today, but they were much bigger than what we had been used to. We frequently drew a few thousand at the final. The tennis establishment must have been shocked.

That first year we played mostly in country clubs or small arenas, where conditions were not always the best. ''I remember playing in gyms where there wasn't enough room for a swingback,'' Ann Jones recalled. ''The semifinals and finals tended to be in different venues from the earlier rounds. Sometimes we played outdoors until the semifinals and then moved indoors into an arena.''

The worst place we ever played was in a field house in Chattanooga. Ellen Merlo, who helped run the tour and later became vice-president of marketing services at Philip Morris, described the place and the scene: ''It was near a club, but not a very nice club, and we had to walk through a field to get to it. Nancy Richey walked in and was obviously disappointed. 'I guess it'll be all right when they put the lights on,' she said. Well, the lights *were* on. So we strung up bare bulbs in order to get more light, and we used chartreuse balls, because it was too dark to see the white balls. The day of the finals, all of the players and staff went out on the road with placards that said *Women's Tennis Here!* Billie Jean was out there, and she was in the finals. I think we got about a thousand people.''

Even playing in a tin shack, we were at least earning a decent living. The Virginia Slims Invitational of Chattanooga offered $10,000 in prize money, enough for every woman in the draw to make her expenses and more. We were winning.

The USLTA must have realized this, because in February of 1971 they tried to woo us back. We agreed under one condition: They could not force us to play in tournaments that did not meet our minimum prize-money standards. In return the USLTA made us promise to play all USLTA events that did meet our standards. The USLTA also demanded a piece of the pie, charging our tournaments stiff fees in return for USLTA sanctions.

It was an uneasy truce, however, and it did not last long; nothing had really changed within the USLTA. For example, while our tour was offering purses of $40,000 and $20,000 at two summer tournaments in 1971, during the very same weeks the USLTA was offering women purses of $7,500 and $2,700.

We celebrated our first birthday with that $40,000 event, the Virginia Slims International at the glamorous Hofheinz Pavilion at the University of Houston. I came away with the $10,000 first prize, the largest ever awarded to a woman tennis player until that time. Our advance ticket sales of $25,000 set another record for women. Margaret Court had planned to play in the tournament, but she withdrew when she discovered she was pregnant. As a courtesy to Gladys, Margaret attended the tournament and called lines.

We were winning, but we still had many battles ahead. Nineteen-year-old Evonne Goolagong had already emerged as a new superstar of women's tennis by winning the French and Wimbledon championships of 1971. Sixteen-year-old Chris Evert was about to burst forth as the star of the Wightman Cup matches and the darling of Forest Hills. Their luck could not have been better. When they strode onto the center courts of Wimbledon and Forest Hills, we had the spotlight shining and in place. Our luck could not have been worse. Evonne and Chrissie did not want to join our tour.

Evonne Fay Goolagong will be remembered as one of the loveliest tennis players of all time. She walked onto the court with a smile on her face, and it was apparent to all that, win or lose, tennis was a sheer joy for her. ''She's the nicest champion you'll ever want to meet,'' Chris Evert has said. Evonne was graceful and effortless, in the manner of Ma-

Winning never consumed Evonne Goolagong. She played tennis as though simply being on the court was the greatest joy in the world.

ria Bueno and Suzanne Lenglen, and she seemed to float rather than run over the court. Her backhand, which she usually sliced low over the net, was a breathtaking shot. Her only weakness was her forehand—the ball had a tendency to fly out of the court.

Evonne took her tennis seriously but never allowed it to rule her life. "Whatever I do, I like to stop and sniff the flowers," she said several years after her competitive days had ended. "I can get very determined when I'm playing, even though to a lot of people I don't look that way. But I never wanted tennis to be everything."

She took her victories in stride and rarely felt bitter after a defeat. When she lost to me in the long, hard U.S. Open final in 1974, Evonne said the match would be tougher to get over than most. "It may take me until tomorrow to forget about it," she said, in all earnestness. I could only shake my head. My worst losses haunted me for weeks.

"Evonne is one of a kind," said her husband, Roger Cawley. "She rolls through life as easily as she sweats around a tennis court. She doesn't allow unimportant things that can bother you or me to get anywhere near her. She's quite capable of getting upset. But somehow it's kept right in its place."

When Evonne became pregnant at age twenty-five, she was at the height of her powers, but she had no trouble pushing her tennis aside. "When you become pregnant," she said later, "the motherly instincts take over completely."

Evonne returned to the tour after the birth of her daughter, Kelly. With Kelly, Roger, and a nanny in tow, she was more popular than ever. Female fans could identify with her: Evonne did more than hit spectacular backhands on the run; she changed diapers, too.

"A lot of women feel they have something in common with me," Evonne said. "It's always the mothers who come up and start chatting. It's easy for them to approach me, and it's easy for me to approach them. They don't feel awkward about not asking tennis questions. They ask about the children, and I'd *rather* talk about the children."

Evonne's victory at Wimbledon in 1980 was a singular triumph. Not since Dorothea Lambert Chambers won Wimbledon in 1914 had a mother won the biggest title in tennis.

Because tennis did not totally dominate Evonne's thoughts, her mind occasionally wandered during competition, and she consequently lost matches that she probably should have won. Evonne was especially vulnerable if she grew bored. "My success," she wrote in her memoir, *Evonne! On the Move,* "seems to depend on the skill of my opponent, and I like it when she makes me run because that keeps my interest up. For me the most fun is catching up with and hitting a ball that looks impossible to reach. If there's not enough prodding from my opponent, if she's not challenging, the Goolagong fog descends and I vanish in a haze of inattention."

Evonne's coach, Vic Edwards, called her lapses "walkabouts," borrowing a word for the nomadic life-styles of Evonne's ancestors, the Australian Aborigines. Evonne once mentioned the word walkabout in a press conference. "I'm sorry I did," she said later. "I was getting tired of interviews and people asking, 'And *why* did you lose your concentration at this stage?' And I said, 'I just went walkabout.' Everybody laughed." It was a great joke at the time, but it became a label that Evonne could never shake.

The word "Goolagong" is an ancient Aboriginal name, and Evonne was proud of her heritage. The dark-skinned tribal Aborigines were the first inhabitants of Australia. They hunted on foot, felling their prey with spears, nets, traps, and boomerangs. Thousands of Aborigines perished when the European settlers arrived in 1788 and began taking over the most desirable lands. Modern Australia tried to assimilate the remaining Aborigines, but they remained an underprivileged economic class and were frequently subjected to prejudice and discrimination. Few Aborigines had ever had the chance to make it as Evonne did.

Evonne grew up in the Australian outback, in the tiny town of Barellan, a wheat-farming community with 900 inhabitants in New South Wales, about 400 miles southwest of Sydney. Evonne, the third of eight children, lived with her parents and siblings in a run-down tin shack on the edge of town. Her father was a sheep shearer.

Rabbit stew was her favorite dish. Fishing was her passion. "It is still my favorite pastime," Evonne said. "It's so peaceful and relaxing. Growing up, I can remember camping on the river, fishing, and swimming. I'd fish all day if I could, every day. It was fun even if you didn't catch anything."

Evonne's first baby toys included some old tennis balls her father found in a used Chevrolet he had bought. Later, her father borrowed a racket belonging to his employer's wife, and Evonne spent many happy hours hitting balls against the side wall of the butcher's shop. Her hobby came to a temporary halt when her younger sister burned the racket for firewood. "I was crying," Evonne recalled. "Dad had to take money out of his paycheck to pay for it."

The opportunities to play tennis in Australia were great in the 1950s, and Evonne was soon playing again, this time on the four clay courts at the War Memorial Tennis Club, next door to her home. Evonne became part of a junior program run by Bill Kurtzman, a retired grazier with a keen interest in tennis. Kurtzman, who thought she was one of the best tennis prospects he had ever seen, telephoned Vic Edwards, then a renowned teaching professional from Sydney, and Edwards came to see her play. Evonne was only nine.

"I didn't know he was watching me," Evonne recalled. "After he left, the townspeople were told to keep an eye on me to see whether I stayed interested in tennis." Edwards had been impressed.

When Evonne was eleven, she went to Sydney to work with Edwards for a couple of weeks. For the first time, she found herself self-conscious about her cultural background. "I felt I was a little showpiece," she said. "The writers' headlines were, 'Aborigine Yvonne Plays.' They never spelled my name right. They always spelled Evonne with a Y."

Two years later, Edwards thought it was time for her to work with him full-time. With her parents' approval, Evonne moved in with the Edwards family. Several of Barellan's wealthier residents bought her a suitcase and clothes and agreed to underwrite her living expenses in Sydney. Edwards became her legal guardian.

Evonne Goolagong won her Wimbledon singles titles in 1971 and 1980. The nine-year gap between victories was matched by only one other player in history, Bill Tilden.

Evonne's ability to leave her family and to cope with the attention focused on her race were the first examples of the reservoir of strength and self-assurance that lay hidden behind her placid exterior. "I got very homesick and cried every night," Evonne remembered. "But I never told anyone. I knew that if I told somebody that I was homesick I'd be back in Barellan. If I was able to handle that, I must have been tough in other ways, too."

Evonne had already accepted tennis stardom as her destiny. "It was drummed into my head that one day I would go to Sydney," she explained. "Then when I went to Sydney, it was drummed into my head that one day I would go overseas and play. It was something I knew from a very early age."

Evonne won all of the Australian national junior titles at age sixteen, and two years later, in 1970, made her international debut. The crowds latched on to her instantly. At Wimbledon she won her first match with ease, and there was so much talk about her that her next match, against Peaches Bartkowicz, was scheduled for the Centre Court. While Peaches pounded her ground strokes with authority, Evonne played uncertainly and lost, 6–4, 6–0. Most observers thought Evonne was a few years away from winning a major title.

But Evonne surprised them. Seven months later, in January 1971, she nearly defeated Margaret Court in the final of the Australian Open. Then in May she beat Australian Helen Gourlay in the final of the French Open to become the first woman since Althea Gibson to win at Roland Garros on her first try.

Evonne came to Wimbledon as the Number 3 seed and played magnificently. Even her forehand was impeccable. She beat me in straight sets in the semifinals and beat Margaret in the final with the loss of only five games. Walter Bingham, writing for *Sports Illustrated,* said that while playing Margaret, Evonne "gave a vivid demonstration of how wide and how long a tennis court can be" with her explosive passing shots, which traveled "an inch over the net and maybe an inch inside the line."

Margaret looked paralyzed; she could do nothing to counter Evonne's wonderful shots. "I had no coordination – my arms and legs seemed to be going the wrong way," Margaret said. "I even made a couple of air shots,

Evonne Goolagong shocked an erratic–and pregnant–Margaret Court in the 1971 Wimbledon final, 6–4, 6–1.

swinging and missing the ball completely.''

Pregnancy can do that to a woman. Margaret discovered she was pregnant a few days after the match, and Danny Court was born eight months later.

Evonne Goolagong, the French Open and Wimbledon champion at nineteen, went home to Sydney to a ticker-tape parade. ''It was a big thrill for everyone, but at the time I did not appreciate it as much as I really should have,'' she said. ''I didn't realize how important winning Wimbledon was. I was just having a good time; I had nothing to lose against these players. I was ready to go for everything, and everything seemed to come off.''

Despite her fast start, Evonne never won as many tournaments as the all-time greats. She simply did not have the intensity or the desire. Yet she said her career was a fulfilling one. She won the Australian Open four times during the 1970s. At the U.S. Open, she reached the final four successive times, twice on grass and twice on clay, between 1973 and 1976. She reached the Wimbledon final three times before she finally won again in 1980, three years after the birth of daughter Kelly and nine years after her initial success.

Two months after Evonne Goolagong's first victory at Wimbledon in 1971, an even bigger star surfaced in women's tennis: Chris Evert. She was an entirely different kind of champion from Evonne. Chris would no sooner have gone walkabout than she would have served into the wrong court; and while Evonne never cried over her losses, Chris took her defeats hard. In the spring of 1972, shortly after the two women had been introduced to each other, Evonne was astonished to find Chris sobbing in the dressing room after losing to me in the quarterfinals of a tournament in Dallas. Evonne could not believe anyone could be that upset after a defeat.

Winning meant everything to Chris, the most competitive person I have known and one of the toughest competitors ever. From the time she was sixteen she was likened to Helen Wills because of her steely, unsmiling expression on the court. Like Helen and Maureen Connolly, Chris had the ability to concentrate at all times.

The elfin Chris Evert had impeccable concentration and ground strokes when she reached the 1971 U.S. Open semifinals at sixteen. She is shown here in her first-round match, against Edda Buding.

Her unwavering focus, combined with her great, natural coordination and her father's marvelous training, made Chris Evert one of the giants of the game. Through 1987 she had won more than 1,200 matches and 150 tournament titles, figures approached only by Martina Navratilova, who dominated women's tennis in the early and mid-1980s. Through 1987 Chris had won eighteen singles titles in Grand Slam tournaments: a record seven in the French, six in the U.S. Open, three at Wimbledon, and two in the Australian Open. The only women to win more were Margaret Court, who won twenty-six, and Helen Wills, who won nineteen. Martina Navratilova had won seventeen by the end of 1987.

Chris Evert's consistency, unsurpassed in the annals of the game, is reflected in her three most important records. She reached at least the semifinals of every Grand Slam tournament she entered—thirty-four tournaments in all, beginning with the U.S. Open in 1971 and ending with the French Open of 1983. She won at least one singles title in a Grand Slam tournament for thirteen straight years, from 1974 through 1986. And on clay, the surface on which she won ten of her eighteen big-four titles, she won a record 125 successive matches between August of 1973 and May of 1979. No other player in modern times has come close to establishing such a long winning streak on a single surface.

Chris was first in one other respect. She was the first woman tennis player since Suzanne Lenglen, Helen Wills, and Maureen Connolly to spend her entire career as an international celebrity.

The public embraced Chris for reasons other than her excellent tennis. Chris was the ultimate professional, always a model sportswoman. She rarely questioned a call, and she never did anything that interfered with her opponent's ability to concentrate or perform.

Crowds also liked Chris because of her all-American looks. Chris considered herself more feminine than most of the women playing professional tennis when she became a star, and she cultivated her image as America's sweetheart, right down to her mascara, hair ribbons, and brightly polished fingernails.

Christine Marie Evert was born in Fort Lauderdale, Florida, the second of five children. Her mother, Colette, grew up in a well-to-do family in New York's Westchester County. Chris's father, Jimmy, came from a poor family in Chicago. Jimmy Evert, an excellent tennis player, attended the University of Notre Dame on a tennis scholarship, competed at Forest Hills five times, and was ranked as high as eleventh in the country in 1943. He left the amateur circuit to teach tennis in Fort Lauderdale.

Jimmy Evert was always thankful for the opportunities tennis had given him. Because he wanted his children to enjoy the same opportunities, he started bringing them to the courts when they were very young. Eventually, all five Evert children reached the final round of a national championship. Jeanne Evert, Chris's younger sister, appeared for a while to have as much potential as Chris. When Jeanne was only thirteen, she beat tour regular Rosie Casals; at fifteen she was beating seventeen-year-old Chris regularly in practice. Jeanne played professionally for a few years and was ranked as high as ninth in the United States in 1974.

Jimmy Evert began teaching Chris to play when she was five and a half years old. He taught her to keep both hands on the racket when she hit her backhand, because she was too small and weak to execute the stroke with one hand.

Chrissie, as she liked to be called, and her father have given varying accounts on the subject of how hard he pushed her in the game. Jimmy Evert has described those days as some of the happiest of his life. "I'd like to live them over again," he said. "There were very few unpleasant moments." Jimmy acknowledged that Chris was not allowed to swim as much as her friends or to attend slumber parties on Friday nights, because Saturday was always an important day for practice. Still, Jimmy did not think Chris was overwhelmed with work. "She didn't play nearly as much tennis as the kids play today," he said. "During the winter months after school, she played two forty-minute sessions. She would play with Laurie Fleming, a top junior player, three or four days a week, and I think the two of them talked half the time. They were great friends."

In contrast, Chris's memories were of long, tedious workouts. "It was always work," she said. "My father was a strict disciplinarian, and he didn't hand out compliments too easily. He was a tough, demanding teacher. I get on him for it now, because he was very critical of my play. I didn't have much fun working. What made me happy was the satisfaction of winning a tournament and seeing my parents happy."

Nevertheless, Chris acknowledged that her father's discipline was "probably what made me a champion." Even as a slightly built child, Chris rarely missed. She did not hit the ball hard, but she hit it perfectly, in the center

Jimmy Evert

"We didn't know too much about the two-handed backhand when Chris started playing tennis. There weren't too many people around who used it. Jimmy Connors was one of the first, but I hadn't seen him at that stage. It was a controversial stroke at the time, and some people said Chris would never be a good player with the two-handed backhand. But Chris just couldn't swing the racket with one hand. That's all there was to it.

"At that time we didn't think about how good she was going to be. We weren't thinking of today and tomorrow and next week. We weren't thinking about two years from now and three years from now and turning pro. I just wanted her to play the game.

"From time to time in later years I did try to change her to a one-handed backhand. I'd hit with her for half an hour with the one-handed backhand, and the next day I'd see her out on the court playing with someone and she was using the two-handed. So we just left it at that. In her case, it turned out to be her best weapon.

"I'd hit with Chris and her sister Jeanne for a couple of hours a week, but that was about it. I'm not as gung-ho on instruction as some people are. I think some people have the impression that a good coach is all you need, but the bottom line is how much talent a child has.

"I could see from the beginning that Chris was doing a lot of things very well. She seemed to have a good head for the game right from the beginning. She was a bright person. She was competitive. She had good feet. She moved well. She had quick hands. She had good anticipation. If she were lacking in any one of those areas—if she didn't move her feet well, for instance—she would not have become the player she is. You have to have all those things. She's a better athlete than she gives herself credit for.

"I have a little ten-year-old I'm working with now who comes to the net quite a bit. Sometimes Chris needles me and says, 'Dad, why didn't you teach me to come to the net when I was ten?' I tell her, 'We're really learning from your mistakes.' But it really wasn't a mistake. Chris at that time was playing mostly on clay. It's hard to get in to the net on clay. The kids were hitting those high, loopy balls. When I was a youngster growing up in Chicago, we played indoors on board courts in the wintertime—they had eight indoor courts in all of Chicago; now they have 800—and those board courts were lightning fast. If you didn't go in to the net on every shot, you were lost. But on clay, it's an entirely different game. The tendency is to stay back and play the baseline. Chris seemed to be more comfortable back there. Her serve was always adequate but never great, so she never thought much about serving and volleying. Had we concentrated more on the net and spent more time working on it, I just don't think she would have been the player she was. I don't think she had the weapons to play that style of game.

Jimmy Evert competed at Forest Hills and later helped his daughter Chris become a champion.

"I remember Margaret Court came here one day. Chris might have been thirteen or fourteen at the time. I was watching Margaret practice with one of her fellow Australians, and she was hitting the ball *so hard* that I thought Chris at that stage couldn't have won a *game* from her. In those early years I thought playing from the baseline was the only way Chris could become a good player."

of the racket and nearly always from the same position: knees bent, racket parallel to the ground, head down, and eyes on the ball. Invariably, the ball floated back over the net to within a foot of the baseline.

Her forehand was excellent and her two-handed backhand became a weapon that would topple champions. Chris, with her hands close together on the handle of the racket, could hit the ball well out in front of her body, with both arms extended for maximum power. She could also hit her backhand several different ways. She could hit the ball flat, with topspin, or with slice. Because a last-minute flick of her wrists was all she needed to direct the ball, her opponents never knew where she was going to hit it.

Chris also mastered two other shots: the drop shot and lob. She became so skillful with her four-shot arsenal that, early in her career, she could beat top players, even without a potent serve, volley, or overhead.

Chris was about fifteen when she began to gain notoriety within tennis circles. Nancy Richey was one of the first professionals to discover her. Nancy, then in her mid-twenties and one of the top two players in the United States, lost a set to her. ''I had to fight for my life,'' Nancy recalled. ''I couldn't believe a girl that young could play like that.''

A few more professionals learned the same thing when they met fifteen-year-old Chris in the Carolinas International Tennis Classic, a small event sandwiched between the 1970 U.S. Open and our inaugural Virginia Slims Invitation in Houston.

The Carolinas International, a clay-court tournament held in Charlotte, North Carolina, was unique in several ways. It featured draws of only six men and six women, and it had a $10,000 purse that was divided evenly among the men and women. The tournament promoter, Cliff Turner, offered equal money to the women—a move unheard of at the time—in order to draw top female players. The idea worked, and he got commitments from Margaret Court, Nancy Richey, Virginia Wade, and Françoise Durr. To round out the field, he took a gamble and invited two promising amateurs, Chris Evert and her friend Laurie Fleming. ''I got a lot of criticism for doing that,'' Turner said at the time.

Turner, however, wound up looking like a genius. Laurie lost to Virginia Wade in two close sets, 6–4, 6–4, and then Chris upset Françoise Durr, 6–1, 6–1. It was Chris's first important victory in women's competition. ''Françoise was ranked Number 4 in the world, and it was a big shock,'' Chris remarked later. ''I killed her. It was so easy.''

An even bigger thrill followed the next day, when Chrissie, then a five-foot-three-inch, ninety-eight-pound high school sophomore, met Margaret Court, who had just won the Grand Slam a few weeks before. Chris's name was incorrectly spelled ''Everet'' on the scoreboard, but within a couple of hours, everyone in Charlotte knew her name.

Margaret played nervously throughout the match, double-faulting fourteen times, while Chris could not have looked calmer. To the amazement of all who watched, Chris won, 7–6, 7–6. She won the first set in a nine-point tiebreaker, 5–1, and then won the second-set tiebreaker, 5–4.

''I was a cool cookie back then,'' Chris admitted. ''That girl is a stranger to me now, because I'd be a nervous wreck if I beat Martina Navratilova, 7–6, 7–6. But back then I just played and didn't really think or feel much during a match.''

Chris felt plenty of emotion *after* beating Margaret, however. She has referred to that victory many times as the most exciting of her life. ''It makes everything worthwhile in my tennis career when I think about how I felt afterwards,'' she told me. ''I was there alone, and I rushed to the phone and called my dad. He couldn't believe it. It's unbelievable for a fifteen-year-old to beat the Number 1 player in the world.''

Chris could not beat the best clay-court player in the United States that year, however. Nancy Richey, who has said she was never nervous playing against teenagers, pounded away at Chris's weak serve in the final and triumphed, 6–4, 6–1.

But with Chris's help, women's tennis had made an impression on Charlotte. The women received a standing ovation from the 3,500 spectators after the match. *The Charlotte Observer* noted, ''A bigger crowd turned out

In an almost mirror image of the point played by Maureen Connolly and Shirley Fry (shown on page 86), I slice a backhand down the line against Chris Evert in the 1971 U.S. Open semifinals.

Sunday to see Chrissie than watched the Davis Cup match between the United States and Ecuador in the Charlotte Coliseum two years ago.''

Chris Evert continued to compete in junior tournaments as a sixteen-year-old, but every time she entered a senior event, she knocked off somebody new. In April 1971 she won the St. Petersburg Masters, a professional tournament that had appeared to be doomed until Virginia Slims stepped in with sponsorship money at the last minute. Chris had victories over Françoise Durr, Julie Heldman, and me.

In August Chris became the youngest woman ever to play for the American Wightman Cup team. She won both of her matches, beating Winnie Shaw, 6–0, 6–4, and Virginia Wade, 6–1, 6–1. She was ready for Forest Hills.

Forest Hills, in turn, was ready for Chris Evert. In 1971 the U.S. Open was desperately in need of a star. Several of the top men who were contract professionals under Lamar Hunt bypassed the tournament in order to rest up for one of Hunt's more lucrative events. Missing among the women were Margaret Court, who was pregnant; Evonne Goolagong, who had stayed home in Sydney; and Virginia Wade, who was injured.

Tournament chairman Bill Talbert, sensing that Chrissie Evert was among the most appealing in the draw, scheduled her first-round match for the stadium court. ''Tennis is show business and you have to create excitement,'' he said years later. ''Chrissie *was* excitement. She was cute and attractive and everything you wanted a tennis player to be.''

At the time, Chris said she was petrified at the thought of walking out onto the center court in front of 9,000 people. Once she started winning, however, she loved it. She beat her first-round opponent, Edda Buding of West Germany, 6–1, 6–0.

The crowd enjoyed Chris's match so much that Talbert decided to put her second-round match against Mary Ann Eisel in the stadium court as well. Mary Ann, a good grass-court player who had been ranked as high as eighth in the world, won the first set, 6–4. She broke Chris's serve for a 6–5 lead in the second set and then raced to a 40–love lead and triple match point.

The moments that followed launched Chris Evert toward stardom. Chris staved off the first two match points by lashing out with the boldness and spontaneity of a champion. She hit two clean winners off Mary Ann's serve, one a backhand down the line, the other a

I have just beaten Chris in the 1971 U.S. Open, but the photographers are far more interested in the blossoming young champion than they are in me. (I am by the umpire's stand.)

forehand crosscourt. Mary Ann, shaken, then double-faulted to bring the score to deuce. Mary Ann had three more match points in that game but won none of them. Chris finally won the game to even the set at 6–all. She won the tiebreaker easily and then crushed Mary Ann in the final set, 6–1.

"Miss Evert left the court to a roaring ovation," wrote Herbert Warren Wind, the distinguished tennis writer for *The New Yorker* magazine. "She had captured the imagination of the spectators—and the millions watching over national television—as no other young American player had in years. From that moment on, she was the tournament. I cannot remember attending a major tennis event where there was so little conversation about the men players."

After the match, the press asked Chrissie what she was thinking when she faced triple match point. "I was trying to decide how I should walk off the court," she answered. "Would I smile at the crowd or would I look dignified and serious? But each time Mary Ann served I seemed to see the ball bigger and bigger. I decided to hit for certain spots on her side to make winners, and they just went in each time."

While attention was being showered on Chris by spectators, tennis officials, journalists, and television crews, jealousy was raging behind the women's locker-room door. Many of the seasoned professionals who had toiled for a measure of respect were outraged that a sixteen-year-old amateur could appear from nowhere and take away their publicity. Chris said later that when she walked into the locker room, only two or three of the women spoke to her.

I gathered the players together one day and tried to make them understand that Chris was good for tennis. I explained that she was going to be an all-time great and we were lucky to have her. Because of her, everyone was talking about women's tennis. This was exactly what we wanted, was it not? Unfortunately, some of the players remained bitter; they said they were upset because the crowd was pulling for Chris to beat them. I told the women that the crowd always pulls for the underdog and that Chris would have her problems eventually, too—which she did.

Out on the stadium court, meanwhile, Chris seemed to be getting better and more confident with every match in the 1971 Open. Her passing shots, accurate and well disguised, more than made up for her powderpuff serve and her overhead, which was barely proficient by professional standards.

Chris beat Frankie Durr in the third round, once again coming from behind to win in three sets, 2–6, 6–2, 6–3, and she came from behind to defeat Australian Lesley Hunt in the quarterfinals, 4–6, 6–2, 6–3. Her victories brought her to the semifinals, where she met me.

I knew I had to beat Chris Evert for the sake of our fledgling tour. Everyone assumed that Chris would shun the Virginia Slims circuit in favor of the traditional USLTA tournaments, and if she defeated me, the Slims' top player, our tour would be in trouble.

The crowd of 13,647 nearly filled the stadium, and most of them were pulling for Chris and another upset. But I was primed. I varied my spins to keep her from developing a rhythm from the backcourt; I was nearly flawless at the net, and I crushed Little Miss Chris, 6-3, 6-2. I then beat Rosie Casals in the final to win my second United States singles title. Chris went back to being a sophomore at St. Thomas Aquinas High School in Fort Lauderdale.

I finished 1971 by becoming the first woman athlete to win $100,000 in prize money in a single year. I played more tournaments than I would have liked in order to reach that figure, but I thought it was important for the visibility of the women's game to have a $100,000 winner. After passing the historic mark with a victory over Rosie Casals in the Virginia Slims Thunderbird championships in Phoenix, the fans cheered for ten minutes. Rosie and I doused each other with champagne, in the tradition of World Series champions.

In February of 1972 the USLTA and Gladys Heldman arrived at another truce, and this time Gladys was asked to become the USLTA's coordinator of women's tennis. But a few months later, the USLTA went back on its word and announced that it would stage its own women's tour, starring Evonne and Chrissie. A longtime USLTA official, Edy McGoldrick, was named to administer it. At the same time the USLTA renewed its threats of suspension for anyone who played on our tour.

By that time, however, the USLTA could not hope to control us on its own terms. We had come too far, and our backing from our sponsors was too strong. The Original Nine had grown to sixty, and our prize money had swelled to $660,000. Still, the USLTA's "Evonne and Chrissie show" hurt, especially when Chris won our first $100,000 tournament in Boca Raton.

The Slims players generally forgave Chris Evert for supporting the USLTA when it was trying to undermine our tour, because she was only seventeen. Her father, who did not like Gladys, had made the decision for her. Gladys said that Chris's mother wanted her to join the Slims tour. "But her father would not allow it. He is very conservative. This is a little tough to say—he's a man of great dignity, great teaching ability, and great humanity—but he would have been a Tory in the American Revolution."

"My dad felt an allegiance to the USLTA because they had helped me as a junior," Chris explained later. "But you know what? Looking back, maybe it wasn't such a horrible thing. Both tours did well. Both tours had superstars. I don't think you can blame the women for breaking away, but I don't think you can blame us for sticking with the establishment, either. The Virginia Slims tour was still a risk." Chris added that she thought the younger players were a bit frightened of me, because I was "so aggressive and so much of a leader in a radical way."

I won Wimbledon in 1972, but Chris and Evonne were the stars of the tournament. People had been waiting to see the "dream match" between Chris and Evonne for nearly a year, and the two stars finally met for the first time in the Wimbledon semifinals. The buildup was enormous.

When Chris and Evonne walked onto the court together and curtsied, each wearing a white dress trimmed in red, it was one of those special moments in tennis history. Evonne trailed, 4-6, 0-3, but rallied to win the last two sets, 6-3, 6-4. The crowd honored both women with a prolonged standing ovation.

"It wasn't a terrific match," Bud Collins commented, "but it was terrifically exciting, and it was a wonderful occasion. It was the start of a wonderful rivalry." From the crowd's perspective, my 6-3, 6-3 victory over Evonne in the final was anticlimactic.

When we arrived at Forest Hills two months later, the women professionals were in the midst of yet another battle. Although a woman—Chris Evert—had saved the U.S. Open a year earlier, the prize-money ratio in 1972 still favored the men by more than 2 to 1. A month before the Open the women on our tour had voted to withdraw, if chairman Bill Talbert did not bring the women's purse into line with the men's; Gladys, however, had told us that such a threat would be unfair to Bill, who could not be expected to raise $50,000 that fast.

Instead of withdrawing in 1972, we decided to put Bill on notice. I met several times with him and said something *had* to be done. After winning the tournament and accepting my $10,000 prize, which was $15,000 less than what Ilie Nastase earned for winning the men's title, I gave an ultimatum in an interview with the press: "If it isn't equal next year, I won't play, and I don't think the other women will either." Talbert took the cue.

The year 1973 was a momentous one for every woman in tennis. It began with a final outbreak of fighting between the establishment on one side and Gladys Heldman and our tour—which by then included Margaret Court—on the other.

The uproar stemmed largely from two incidents: our decision to sign contracts with Gladys that called for the founding of a Women's International Tennis Federation, and Gladys's lawsuit, which I later joined, seeking an injunction to prevent the USLTA from disrupting our tournaments. We reached a crisis in April, when the ILTF declared that we must either submit to our national associations or be banned from the Grand Slam tournaments forever. Less than a week later, Gladys and I lost our lawsuit.

At that point, Philip Morris officials, deeply concerned about the ILTF's threat and the escalation of negative publicity, stepped in and virtually ordered the divided parties to straighten out the mess once and for all. John Granville, head of the Virginia Slims division at Philip Morris, negotiated a genuine truce by May 1.

As of autumn 1973, both tours would be merged into one, with Virgina Slims remaining as our major sponsor. The sacrificial lamb, if she could ever be thought of as a lamb, was Gladys. The tennis establishment, which could not tolerate her, did not want her running the women's tour. "I was out, but the war was over, and that was the most important thing," Gladys recalled. "Instead of having two tours and constant fighting, it ended absolutely wonderfully in that the women players still had the support of Virginia Slims, and for the first time the USLTA was working with them instead of fighting them."

I believe Gladys could have remained in women's tennis in another capacity, however. I offered her the position of executive director of the Women's Tennis Association (WTA), which we finally established during the 1973 Wimbledon. I wanted Gladys to be our figurehead, our symbol of power. Years later, Gladys said she did not recall my offering her the position, but I am certain that I did. I remember being dismayed when she declined. We reluctantly said good-bye to Gladys and hired Martin Carmichael, a New York attorney, as our first executive director.

The founding of the WTA in a packed conference room at the Gloucester Hotel in London was a historic moment for all of us. I had wanted an organization like it since 1964, and I had begun selling the idea to the players in 1968, with the help of Rosie Casals, Ann Jones, and Frankie Durr. It is hard to believe, but in 1973 many women professionals still did not want, or think we needed, a union; they thought that because the women were going to be together on one tour, all the issues facing us had been settled. Still, that unity did not guarantee us a voice in our future. I did not want the USLTA and the ILTF making decisions about women's tennis without our input.

I decided to hold one last meeting to try to convince the women that we needed our own organization. I was exhausted, having been up half the previous night with the flu. When sixty-three women had gathered in the Gloucester conference room, I told Betty Stove to stand in front of the door and not allow anyone to leave. "We're either going to have the association or we're not," I told the women. "I'm totally burned out. I'm not going to waste one more breath of air."

Hours later, we had our association. I was elected president; Betty Stove was elected treasurer. Betty, who had to collect the dues, had perhaps the most thankless job of all. "I had to approach all of the players." she remembered. "I felt that every time I went into a room, people would walk out because they were afraid they had to pay me. We had no mailbox, so I had to collect in person."

A few days after the WTA was founded, I beat Chris Evert, 6–0, 7–5, to win my fifth

Wimbledon singles title. I beat Chris from the backcourt in the first set for the only time in my life, but I was lucky to win the second set, because I was tiring. I brought Chris in to the net and gave her very little pace. A few months later, I would play a man named Bobby Riggs the same way.

Bobby Riggs played an important role in women's tennis in 1973. Riggs was an egotistical, chauvinistic, bandy-legged man of fifty-five, who had won the triple crown at Wimbledon the same year as Alice Marble, nearly a quarter of a century earlier. With Bobby's unwitting help, we took women's tennis to the masses. The man on the street, the woman in the office, the sports fan in the bar—all had heard of women's tennis by the end of 1973. Declared Rosie Casals, unequivocally, "I've always said that Bobby Riggs did more for women's tennis than anybody."

This photograph epitomizes the match between Bobby Riggs and Margaret Court. Bobby, in total control, has his feet planted comfortably, while Margaret is lunging, fighting to save the point.

It was in late February that Riggs challenged me to a $5,000 match, winner take all. He wanted to play me—and beat me, presumably—to prove a point. Bobby had been trumpeting that because women tennis players were not as good as men, they did not deserve to get as much prize money. He was also upset that the women professionals were making more money than older men, like himself, who played on the senior tour.

I knew a match with Riggs would have appeal, because Bobby was a showman and a con artist—the ultimate hustler. He had become well known in tennis circles for his ability to defeat lesser opponents while subjecting himself to great handicaps. He would offer to play some unsuspecting club member while holding a suitcase in one hand or a dog on a leash, make a huge bet, and then win and collect.

I turned Bobby down, however, because at that moment I did not want to deal with a sideshow. I wanted to protect women's tennis, not jeopardize it, and although I thought I could beat Bobby, I was not sure.

Riggs then challenged Margaret Court, and she accepted. I think she was enticed by the money, a guaranteed $10,000. Margaret said at the time that playing Riggs would be like taking a stroll in the park. She was dead wrong, of course. The match, played during the height of the women's movement and promoted by Riggs's endless chauvinistic blather, took on political overtones that made it bigger than any women's match had ever been. Margaret, who hated women's liberation and embraced everything gracious and traditional in tennis, had unwittingly walked into a circus carrying the banner of women's rights. To make matters worse, Margaret, who did not relish undue pressure, had everything to lose. As one columnist put it, "Can a woman beat even a very old man? It's not a very promising argument for the women."

Indeed, Rosie Casals told *Sports Illustrated* at the time that she saw no reason why women should have to justify themselves against "an old, obnoxious has-been like Riggs, who can't hear, can't see, walks like a duck, and is an idiot besides."

We *did* have to prove ourselves, however: Margaret had been hustled, and women the world over were counting on her; the tour was counting on her. "Margaret," we told her, "you've *got* to win."

Margaret was at the top of her game as she prepared for the match with Riggs. After a twelve-month layoff following the birth of her first child, Danny, she was fitter and more at ease than ever when she returned to competition in 1973. "I played about twenty-eight tournaments and I think I won twenty-seven of them," Margaret recalled. She also became the first woman athlete to win $200,000 in one year.

Nevertheless, her success in the legitimate and dignified arenas of tennis could in no way prepare her psychologically for what she faced on Mother's Day 1973, in a secluded resort complex near San Diego. Journalists had come from thousands of miles away, and CBS was going to televise the match nationally. Australians would rise at 6:00 A.M. to see the match live. In the midst of the commotion, Bobby Riggs talked endlessly about his fitness program and the 415 vitamin pills he took each day.

The day began badly for Margaret when Danny dropped one of her tennis shoes in the toilet. When she walked onto the court, Riggs tried to rattle her by giving her a Mother's Day bouquet. Margaret curtsied and from that moment was in the palm of Riggs's hand. Riggs destroyed her, not with speed and power, but with junk shots—dinks, lobs, and spins.

"I didn't expect so many soft shots," Margaret said afterward. "We girls don't play like that."

Margaret remembered the match as a nightmare. "It was a mistake that I ever did it," she said. "I'd never been in anything like that before. It was show biz, and here I was coming off the sedate courts of Wimbledon and the U.S. Open. I never got into it. I thought what in heaven's name am I doing out here? It was as though I was on the court and I was off the court, and that was it. I thought, did I ever really play?"

I did not see the match, because I was in Japan. I was boarding a plane when I turned on my radio. There was static, but I could make out the words, "Bobby Riggs has just annihilated Margaret Court . . ." Walking down the aisle to my seat, teeth clenched, I could not imagine what had happened to Margaret. Now I would have to play him. When Bobby called to challenge me a few days later, I accepted. I had no choice.

During the next few months the showdown was arranged by Jerry Perenchio, a big-time promoter whose résumé included a $5 million fight between Muhammad Ali and Joe Frazier. Bobby and I were to play September 20 at the Houston Astrodome, not for $10,000 in prize money but for $100,000, winner take all. In addition, the winner would get $200,000 in fees from television rights, the loser $100,000.

Before I played Riggs, however, another milestone in women's tennis occurred. At the 1973 U.S. Open, for the first time in a major tournament, women played for a purse equal to the men's. Tournament chairman Bill Talbert raised the money from a new sponsor, Bristol-Myers. Although Talbert had not considered the old prize-money ratios unfair, he nevertheless saw the prize-money issue as a vehicle for bringing more female fans into the stadium and for generating more headlines.

Not everyone agreed with Talbert's move; most of the male players felt the additional dollars should be theirs. In an attempt to soothe their egos, Talbert met with members of the men's union, the Association of Tennis Professionals, and argued that equal purses would make the entire tournament seem more important and that everyone would benefit from the publicity.

Margaret Court won the historic U.S. Open and the $25,000 first prize, a 150-percent increase over the $10,000 I had won the previous year. Runner-up Evonne Goolagong received $12,000.

For me, the Open was a disaster. It was one of a long line of hurdles leading up to my showdown with Bobby Riggs. I had withdrawn from a couple of tournaments before the Open because of poor health, and I was taking penicillin when the Open began. I was also suffering from hypoglycemia. I advanced as far as the third round and then retired, because I became ill during my match against Julie Heldman.

My next tournament was two weeks later in Houston, the very week of my match with Riggs. I had entered the tournament before the Riggs match was scheduled, and I felt I had to play. I played my second-round match the day before I faced Bobby, and I played my third-round match the day after. I lost the latter contest quickly, because I had nothing left to give. At the time Peachy Kellmeyer, who helped run the Houston tournament, was upset with me for appearing not to care, but years later, she came to realize that in the long run the Houston tournament was less important than my match with Riggs.

The truth is—and I am sad to say it—my showdown with Riggs was the biggest match in the history of tennis. No match since has received as much exposure. People still come up to me and tell me where they were that night.

The night before I played Bobby at the Astrodome, I met with Dennis Van der Meer, a longtime friend and business associate and one of the best coaches I know. I wanted him to help me prepare. We watched a replay of Margaret's match with Riggs, and we noticed that Margaret was so tense that she could not swing her arm freely. I felt sorry for her, because all champions have been in that position at one time or another. I thought, "Please, God, don't let this happen to me tomorrow."

I had an advantage, however, that Margaret did not have. Dennis pointed out an important error Margaret had made. Bobby hit short, and Margaret always backed up instead of following her returns in to the net. She ran forward to hit a short ball and then ran back. She was totally unaware of her positioning; by the end of the match she was exhausted.

My plan was not to play fast and furiously and not to hit my serve too hard. I wanted Bobby to generate all the pace, and I wanted to hit plenty of balls to his backhand. I also decided to stay in the backcourt and prolong the rallies to test his conditioning, even when I had a chance to put the ball away. He had been insistent about playing three out of five sets, so I said to myself, "That's fine, macho boy, let's see how you do. You're big talk, in great shape, take 500,000 vitamin pills a day, and a woman athlete couldn't come close to you. Let's find out." I had trained hard for this; I could have gone ten sets if necessary.

Two hours before the match, I was so nervous that I felt sick. My mouth was dry, and I was nauseated. I was in the visitors' dressing room at the Astrodome, pacing, when the trainer pointed out the cubicle my brother, Randy Moffitt, used when his baseball team, the San Francisco Giants, visited the Houston Astros. I went over and stood next to his cubicle for a long time. I wanted to feel connected to something secure.

A hundred thoughts flashed through my mind. I thought about my career and my dreams as a child. I thought about women and low self-esteem, and I thought about athletics and acceptance. My brain was going a mile a minute. I was at top throttle as I awaited the biggest match of my life.

Then, when I finally went out onto the court—I was carried out like a royal princess on an Egyptian litter, Bobby in a Chinese rickshaw—I felt exhilarated. This was what I had always wanted: arenas, sequins, and nighttime tennis. I was wearing a white dress with blue trim and rhinestones, a blue sweatband, and bright blue tennis shoes. Bobby gave me an enormous caramel sucker in a gesture of goodwill; I gave him a pig wearing a pink bow. A crowd of 30,472 watched from the stands. Away from the dome, fifty million more were watching on television, and many were seeing tennis for the first time.

When I led, 2–1, in the first set I knew I would win. I could see that Bobby was sweating profusely and hyperventilating, and I could tell that he had underestimated me. I played him just as I had planned: I did not hit my hardest, I did not rush the net at every opportunity, and I did not always end the point when I had the chance. I moved him from side to side, played his backhand, and gave him plenty of junk, which forced him to generate the pace. When I did put the ball away, I smashed away his lobs and angled away volleys he could only watch and admire. I won the set, 6–4, and breezed through the rest of the match, 6–3, 6–3.

What did I prove? I knew that as an athlete my victory over a man twenty-six years my senior was no great feat. Yet if I had done nothing sensational in beating Riggs, I had shown thousands of people who had never taken an interest in women's sports that women were skillful, entertaining, and capable of coming through in the clutch. The match legitimized women's tennis. It was the culmination of an era, the noisy conclusion to the noisiest three years in the history of the women's game.

The symmetry of those years was impossible to escape. We began our quest in Houston in 1970, rebels with a cause and an uncertain future. And we came back to Houston in 1973 after proving that we could make it on our own. We began our quest in Houston in 1970 because a man, Jack Kramer, underestimated our value as athletes and entertainers. And we came back to Houston in 1973 because another man, Bobby Riggs, dared to make the same mistake. "You've come a long way, baby," was our slogan in 1970. Three years later, when I shook hands with a defeated and tired-looking man, we had come a very long way, indeed.

Chapter 7

Growing Pleasures, Growing Pains

1974-1981

Growing Pleasures, Growing Pains

The sport of tennis, 100 years old but shimmering with excitement and newness, attracted thousands of participants and spectators during the 1970s. The growth was greatest in the United States, where people had leisure time and money to spend on a relatively new concern: fitness. My match with Bobby Riggs fueled this "tennis boom," which had been gaining momentum since the beginning of open tennis in 1968. Increased television exposure and the rise of Chris Evert and her male counterpart, Jimmy Connors, propelled it further.

For tennis professionals, it was a boom time as well. Purses skyrocketed, and endorsement opportunities mushroomed as corporations scrambled to link their products to the increasingly popular game. Colgate-Palmolive joined Virginia Slims as a major sponsor of women's tennis in 1977, and Avon Products replaced Virginia Slims in 1979 with the most extensive corporate sponsorship yet. Tennis also was a godsend for attorneys and agents, who found lucrative careers managing the income and endorsements of suddenly wealthy and famous tennis players.

The influx of money caused radical changes in the sport. More and more athletes pursued the game, and the competition became fiercer. Equipment improved and the players' mechanics—everything from footwork to service motions—improved.

These improvements helped spawn another significant change: the replacement of the historic grass courts at the West Side Tennis Club in Forest Hills in 1975. In previous eras, the grass had remained relatively green and lush through the tournament finals, but the new tennis shoes, with soles designed to grip and avoid skidding, and the harder, more powerful play chewed up the courts more quickly than ever. The result was an uneven surface, bad bounces, and endless player complaints. The USLTA, keenly aware of the problem, plowed under the famous courts and replaced them with Har-Tru, a surface of crushed, natural green stone, often referred to as clay. Har-Tru is faster than real clay, the red dirt used at Roland Garros and other European tournaments, and it is slower than asphalt. Like both red clay and asphalt, Har-Tru produces consistently true bounces.

Overleaf, Chris Evert, left, dominated women's tennis in the mid-1970s. She was a major beneficiary of—and contributor to—the tennis boom. Martina Navratilova, center, who defected from Czechoslovakia in 1975, adjusted to life in the United States and became a leading contender for the major titles. In 1977 Virginia Wade said she had the "will-power and guts" to win Wimbledon, and she was right. It was her sixteenth try.

Wimbledon and the Australian Open also suffered chewed-up grass, but no changes were made. The Australians finally switched to asphalt in 1988, but I think true lawn tennis will always be played at Wimbledon.

Women's tennis changed rapidly during the middle and late 1970s, probably too rapidly. Along with the arrival of our first millionaires, we had our first casualty, the gifted young Tracy Austin. In hindsight we realized that she and many other young women like her had become part of a frenetic and physically demanding style of life before they were strong enough to handle it. The sad result was a series of injuries and emotional setbacks among promising young athletes.

In 1974, however, women's tennis was in better shape than it had ever been. With Chris Evert, Evonne Goolagong, Margaret Court, Virginia Wade, and me, we had five players capable of winning major championships. Women's tennis has not been so rich in talent at the top since.

Day in and day out, the best of the group was Chris. Between 1974 and 1977 she won Wimbledon twice, the U.S. Open three times, the French Open twice, and the Italian Open twice. All told, she won fifty-five of seventy-six tournaments and 339 of 361 matches. "If she gets her volley down," Bud Collins said at the time, "they can close the tournaments." In 1974 Chris won a record $261,500 in prize money; in 1975 she won $413,000.

Chris's dominance was enhanced by the switch to Har-Tru at Forest Hills. Chris, the greatest female clay-court player in history, won all three U.S. Open singles titles played on Har-Tru, from 1975 through 1977. The strengths of Chris's game—her consistency and concentration—made her virtually unbeatable on the slow surface. Chris said that on clay, "I can do whatever I want with the tennis ball. I can handle any situation and don't feel threatened by anyone." (Of course, Chris was superb on faster surfaces as well: She won three more Open titles on asphalt, after the tournament moved to Flushing Meadow in 1978. Through 1987 she had also won five big-four titles on grass.)

The Chris Evert who ruled women's tennis

Chris Evert and Jimmy Connors, engaged to be married in 1974, fueled the tennis boom and charmed the tennis world with a "love double" at Wimbledon.

in the 1970s had tremendous endurance, the result of long hours of practice in hot and humid Florida. I cannot recall ever seeing her tire in a match.

Nevertheless, Chrissie was plump and soft compared with the lean, muscled athlete she became in the 1980s. Nautilus was not yet a regular part of her routine. She said she would *never* lift weights. Chris still saw a conflict between athleticism and femininity, and she wanted the public to understand that even if she *was* athletically inclined, she was unquestionably feminine, too. In her late teens she made statements like, "No point is worth falling down over," and "Too long a tennis career can harden a girl." When Chris trained away from the tennis court, she did not push herself to the limits of fatigue. "When other players train, like the Aussies, they kill themselves," Chris said. "I've always been consistent with myself. Once you feel pain, you should stop."

In those days, Chris was not alone in such sentiments. The weight-training methods pioneered by Margaret Court had not caught on with the other players. Of course, Margaret was not exactly promoting the idea. As fellow Australian Wendy Turnbull, a U.S. Open finalist in 1977, observed: "Margaret didn't let anything out of the bag. She did most of her training in Australia."

I knew Margaret was benefiting from her workouts, and I started experimenting with weights on my own after my knee operations during the late 1960s and early 1970s. Unfortunately, I never had any systematic coaching in weight training. Margaret had her own trainer, but until the 1980s, none of the other women had that luxury.

Chris Evert came to symbolize women's tennis even before she earned the Number 1 world ranking for the first time in 1974. The timing was undeniably perfect. Television brought her to America's living rooms just as tennis was beginning to take off. Maureen Connolly, who had exploded on the tennis scene even faster than Chris, did not receive half the exposure Chris did. Players had rarely been quoted in newspapers and magazines; Chris was quoted from the time she electrified the U.S. Open in 1971.

Thus the world watched her grow up, and people came to feel as though they knew her. They saw how she changed, and they read about the loves and personal crises in her life. They liked her, because even under the glare of celebrity, she remained the girl next door. It did not matter that she told the press she wanted to be considered sexy or that she dated macho men like Jimmy Connors and movie star Burt Reynolds. Chris conveyed a wholesomeness that was not threatening to men or women.

Chris's image was that of a private person. Although in later years she talked openly about her personal struggles, in the 1970s she was guarded in public. In that respect she had some of the remoteness of Helen Wills. "Sometimes I wish I could be more outgoing and express myself on the court, but most of the time I'm glad to keep it inside," she said. "I don't want too many people taking a piece of me, knowing me too well."

The story of Chris as America's sweetheart reached fairy-tale proportions in 1974, when she and her then fiancé, Jimmy Connors, became Princess and Prince of Wimbledon. Chris had a big scare in the second round of the tournament when she nearly lost to Australia's Lesley Hunt. With the score tied at 9–all

Growing Pleasures, Growing Pains

CHRIS EVERT

"To be a top tennis player you have to have a tough streak in you. I was ruthless and determined, and I'm sure my friends and family all got pushed aside at times, because I really wanted to win. It's good for women to have a tough streak, just like it's important for a guy to be sensitive. I guess toughness is supposed to be a masculine quality, but I don't know; roles don't come into effect in my life as much anymore. I'm thirty-two years old and I don't have three kids around me and I'm not in the kitchen.

"The day of a match I'm pretty moody. Not that I'm snapping at everybody, but I'm pretty introspective and I'm really thinking a lot about my match. I'm visualizing certain points and my opponent's weaknesses and strengths. I'm thinking, not chitchatting about what beautiful weather we're having or what's the political situation in Afghanistan right now. I'm trying to be single-minded, especially if it's a big match. And the people who are close to me sense the mood and they know not to chatter on endlessly.

"When I was younger, I concentrated better. I was able to block out everything. That's still a trademark that I have, but I'm probably more easily distracted now because I think more, feel more, and have more things in my life. It's not like you can shut out 15,000 people. It's obvious that they're rooting for somebody. You hope it's for you and it kind of hurts when they're not for you, but I always try to concentrate and think about playing well. I focus on my game more than my opponent's game. I take my time and don't show a lot of emotion on the court, because I don't want to waste energy and I don't want my opponents to see how I really feel. I look at my mom, my dad, my boyfriend, or my coach for support. When I've played my best I just surge forward. I try to play aggressively, and nerves don't enter into it at all.

"I'm so glad I came along when I did, as opposed to when Billie Jean and Margaret Court came along and as opposed to now. I came along at the perfect time. The tennis boom and prize money came in the 1970s. I feel the players who came before me were cheated out of the prize money.

"I'll also be happy to get out of the game because it's so different now. There's more pressure, it's more demanding, and there are more people trying to get a piece of you. I think the tennis players will burn out at a younger age. I don't think you'll see them playing into their thirties.

"I'm just starting to learn about my achievements, because I never paid much attention to them. I'd win a tournament and then I'd go on to the next one. Now when they give my introduction, I listen—eighteen Grand Slam singles titles, the most tournaments won, the most matches won—and I'm getting more of a feel for my place in tennis history."

---

in the third set, darkness brought the match to a halt. The next day Chris practiced with Jimmy and then won two straight games to take the match, 8-6, 7-5, 11-9. Her biggest challenge of the tournament was behind her. In the final she defeated Olga Morozova of the Soviet Union, 6-0, 6-4, to win the women's championship for the first time. When Jimmy won the men's title, Wimbledon celebrated a "Love Double."

Famous and attractive, Chris Evert helped lure thousands of youngsters into the game. The number of boys and girls registered in the USLTA nearly doubled between 1968 and 1974, from 26,690 to 50,004. By 1977 the number had swelled to 65,791. Chrissie also spawned a generation of girls who yearned to play tennis the way she did. The two-handed backhand, once the exception, became the rule among American girls and women and became popular in other parts of the world as well. During the 1970s and early 1980s, a parade of two-fisted baseline players emerged. A few were successful enough to challenge Chris, but most were only imitators.

Not all of the new challengers were in

Olga Morozova of the Soviet Union beat me to reach the 1974 Wimbledon final against Chris Evert. In the 1980s she would coach a rising Soviet women's team.

Chris's likeness, however. Thousands of miles from Florida, behind the Iron Curtain, another champion was developing quite differently. This woman, who became Chris's most enduring rival, did not like to play safely from the baseline; instead she followed the path traveled by Suzanne Lenglen, Alice Marble, Margaret Court, and me. Martina Navratilova attacked the net.

Martina won her first Wimbledon titles in 1978 and 1979 and during the next decade became one of the greatest women tennis players in history. She achieved the two longest winning streaks of modern times and through 1987 had won seventeen Grand Slam titles, a feat surpassed only by Margaret Court, Helen Wills, and Chris Evert. Martina won six straight Grand Slam singles titles during 1983 and 1984, and she won three modern Grand Slams in doubles with Pam Shriver of Lutherville, Maryland, between 1984 and 1987. Martina's most dazzling records, however, were achieved at Wimbledon. By 1987, she had won her sixth successive Wimbledon singles title and her eighth overall.

Although the Martina we first knew was only a distant cousin of the superior athlete she later became, she showed enormous potential from the moment she set foot in the United States in 1973. When she played her first matches against Chris Evert and Evonne Goolagong on the tour run that year by the USLTA, Martina's major goal was to make her opponents remember her. Chris beat her, 6–3, 7–6; Evonne beat her, 6–4, 6–4. And yes, they remembered her.

Martina came from Czechoslovakia, a nation of 15 million people with a 100 percent literacy rate and a proud history in tennis. Czechoslovakia celebrated its first Wimbledon champion in 1954, when the bespectacled, thirty-three-year-old Jaroslav Drobney beat the teenage Ken Rosewall in the men's singles final. Jan Kodes, another Czechoslovak, won the French men's championships in 1970 and 1971 and captured the Wimbledon title in 1973. Vera Sukova, the first female star from Czechoslovakia, reached the Wimbledon final in 1962.

Martina was born on October 10, 1956, into a sportsminded family. Her mother, Jana, was an avid tennis player and a fine skier; her grandmother had ranked as high as Number 2 among Czechoslovak women tennis players before World War II.

Martina's parents were divorced when she was three, and her mother subsequently moved to Revnice, a village of 5,000, near Prague. There Jana met and married Mirek Navratil, who was also an accomplished tennis player. (Navratilova is the feminine form of Navratil.) Martina's natural father died when she was nine; many years later Martina learned that he had committed suicide.

When Martina was six, her stepfather, whom she always referred to as her father, began teaching her to play tennis. Like me, she wanted to be the best in the world from the time she was a child. "At the time I didn't know how big the world was," Martina said later. "I didn't realize what an undertaking it would be. Now it overwhelms me. I wish I knew where that drive comes from. My parents were intelligent people and good athletes, but they were not overachievers in any way. My father, in fact, was an underachiever. He was talented, but he was happy with whatever was happening to him. My mother was a good athlete. She put herself down, saying she didn't have much talent when she *did* have talent. Then I came along and I knew I was better than all the other kids. I thought I was smarter, faster, and quicker. Things came easily to me. I knew that one day I was going to be the best tennis player in the world. I've had that in me ever since I can remember.''

Martina entered her first tournament, an event for girls twelve and under, at age eight. The tournament organizers tried to reject her entry, arguing that she was too small, but they eventually relented and allowed her to play. Little Martina surprised everyone by reaching the semifinals.

Like Chris Evert, Martina grew up playing on clay. But unlike Chris, she found playing from the baseline dull. She liked to rush the net even as a child.

''My first coach, George Parma, was an excellent teacher,'' Martina said. ''He taught me the mechanics of the game correctly. He saw from the start that I was an attacking player, so he let me be that. He wasn't trying to mold me into anything. My father was also interested in my game being an all-around game, which is one thing that's lacking today. Kids are just hitting ground strokes; they forget that there is a volley, an overhead, and a serve.''

Life was not all play for young Martina. At age eleven, on August 20, 1968, she was introduced to the complexities of life, when 600,000 Soviet troops swept into Czechoslovakia. Their purpose was to subdue the rise in independent thinking among Czechoslovaks, a byproduct of the political reform movement known as Prague Spring. Martina, who was competing in a tournament in Pilsen, forty miles from Revnice, was staying at the home of her doubles partner when the troops arrived during the night. She and her friend awoke in the morning to see Soviet tanks in the street. Later that day, Martina's father rode to Pilsen on his motor bike and took Martina home.

Martina was deeply affected by her nation's upheaval. Her coach, George Parma, who was in Austria with his family during the invasion, defected and never returned to Czechoslovakia. Her cousin, Martin, also defected.

A year or two after the invasion, Martina played in a doubles match against two girls from the Soviet Union. Afterward, when one of the defeated Soviets tapped Martina's hand instead of shaking it, Martina blurted: ''You need a tank to beat me.''

In her memoir, *Martina,* she described her disillusionment and that of her people. ''When I was twelve or thirteen, I saw my country lose its verve, lose its productivity, lose its soul. For someone with a skill, a career, an aspiration, there was only one thing to do: get out.''

In spite of her discontent, Martina continued to play tournament tennis, and at fourteen she won the national girls' fourteen-and-under title. A year later, in 1972, she became the Czechoslovak women's national champion; in 1973 she made her debut in the United States. Martina did little of note on the USLTA tour that year, but she became extremely popular with the players and the crowds. She learned English quickly and developed a taste for American freedoms and a passion for American foods.

As a result of her love affair with American junk food, Martina gained twenty-five pounds in two months. On one occasion, when players kidded her about being the tour's ''pancake champ,'' she paused between bites of a hamburger, grinned, and rattled off the theme of a popular television commercial: ''I can't believe I ate the whole thing.'' She could be funny in English, even though it was a new language for her. In the late 1980s, spicing her English with idioms, slang, and turns of phrase, she was wittier than ever.

Martina won the 1973 Wimbledon junior championship (a tournament inaugurated in 1948) and showed vast improvement in the spring of 1974 by finishing second at the Italian and German opens. In September, just shy of her eighteenth birthday, she won her first important tournament, a tour event in Orlando, Florida. A few months later she beat Margaret Court in the quarterfinals of the Australian Open. In 1975 she beat Chris Evert

Françoise "Frankie" Durr, the French champion in 1967, had some of the most unusual strokes ever seen in tennis. But no matter how unorthodox her wind-up and grip on the handle, her racket was almost always in perfect position when she made contact with the ball.

Maria Bueno, right, won fame and major titles during her peak years, between 1959 and 1966. Only wealth was missing. "I don't think it would be a bad idea," she later said, "to do what you like and get paid millions."

At right, Bobby and I entertain members of the press. George Foreman, the boxer, is at my right.

My showdown with Bobby Riggs in 1973 was part prizefight, part circus. Below, I am carried into the Houston Astrodome's arena on an Egyptian litter, loving every minute.

I did not hit as hard as I could have against Bobby. I kept the ball in play and let him run, run, run.

One could never predict how Evonne Goolagong would play, recalled John Parsons, veteran tennis writer for the London Daily Telegraph. *"But you knew it would be interesting, sometimes outrageous, usually exciting, and sometimes absolutely awful. You didn't dare take your eye off her for a second."*

Rosie Casals, right, shows off one of the eye-catching tennis dresses worn on the early Virginia Slims tour. The women were accustomed to playing in sequins, lamé, and velvet.

After her spectacular career, Margaret Court, left, focused her life on raising four children. She also became a minister. "My life is very full these days," she said in 1987.

Great Britain's Virginia Wade, left, played in 100 Federation Cup matches and 56 Wightman Cup matches, more than any other woman.

Chris Evert, Tracy Austin, and Martina Navratilova pose for the camera early in their championship careers. The threesome monopolized the Number 1 computer ranking from November 1975 until August 1987.

Chris Evert's two-handed backhand, shown at left, changed the look of women's tennis. This 1981 photo captures her flawless preparation and the extension of her arms to the maximum.

Tracy Austin, above, reached two Grand Slam finals during her career, at the U.S. Open, and won both. She reached the Wimbledon semifinals twice.

Martina Navratilova enjoyed a wide range of interests outside of tennis. She followed politics and was a strong supporter of the arts and charities benefiting children.

In 1981 Kathy Rinaldi, at right, set records for precociousness. Only fourteen, she became the youngest quarterfinalist in the history of the French Open and the youngest player to win a match at Wimbledon.

Although injuries brought a premature end to her career, Andrea Jaeger did not think she began playing tennis too soon. "I was lucky to compete when I was young," she said.

I am holding the Maud Watson trophy at Maud's old club, the Edgbaston Priory Club, in Birmingham, England. Maud, the first woman to win Wimbledon, won this trophy in the 1880s.

Martina Navratilova and Chris Evert, above, will be remembered for their triumphs and their friendship. Here, Martina embraces Chris after losing to her in the 1985 French Open final.

Anne White, left, stirred up memories of Gussy Moran's lace panties when she appeared in a controversial body suit during the 1985 Wimbledon championships.

Chris Evert and Martina Navratilova, above, leave the court after a Wimbledon final. Women finalists have carried their bouquets of flowers onto the court ever since 1946, when Pauline Betz and Louise Brough decided the All England Club's prematch gifts were too lovely to leave behind in the locker room.

Chris Evert, right, was in perfect form as she defeated Martina Navratilova, 2–6, 6–3, 6–3, in the final of the 1986 French Open.

Afterward, Chris held the silver Coupe Suzanne Lenglen for the seventh time. No other player has won seven French titles. The great Suzanne won six.

West Germany's sensational Steffi Graf, above, could hit a forehand drive as fast as some men.

When Hana Mandlikova, right, played her best tennis, there was no one more exciting to watch.

Above, Martina Navratilova savors a special moment with American teammates Zina Garrison, far left, and Chris Evert during a ceremony at the 1986 Federation Cup championships in Prague.

Chris Evert was nowhere more at home than on slow clay courts. Her 125-match winning streak on clay was one of her most memorable achievements.

Gabriela Sabatini, left, lost her first eleven matches against fellow teenager Steffi Graf. After improving her stamina and adding variety to her game, Gaby began 1988 by beating Steffi twice.

At left, this prize-winning photograph of Martina Navratilova says volumes about one of the greatest grass-court players of all time. Even in the air, she is a portrait in fluidity, balance, and power.

Steffi Graf, above, in 1987 became the youngest woman ever to win the French championship. She was eight days shy of her eighteenth birthday.

Is Martina reading the names on the Wimbledon salver? If so, she may be eyeing her own. The names of the early champions appear on the interior of the plate. Martina's appears on the exterior.

Although thirty-year-old Martina Navratilova, above, lost the Number 1 ranking to Steffi Graf in 1987, the aging champion was still able to win Wimbledon and the U.S. Open.

Lori McNeil, a superb athlete, was one of the top American prospects in women's tennis in the mid-1980s.

Gabriela Sabatini, left, a woman of few words, was nevertheless one of the most colorful players in tennis in 1987 and 1988. She dazzled audiences with her beauty and style.

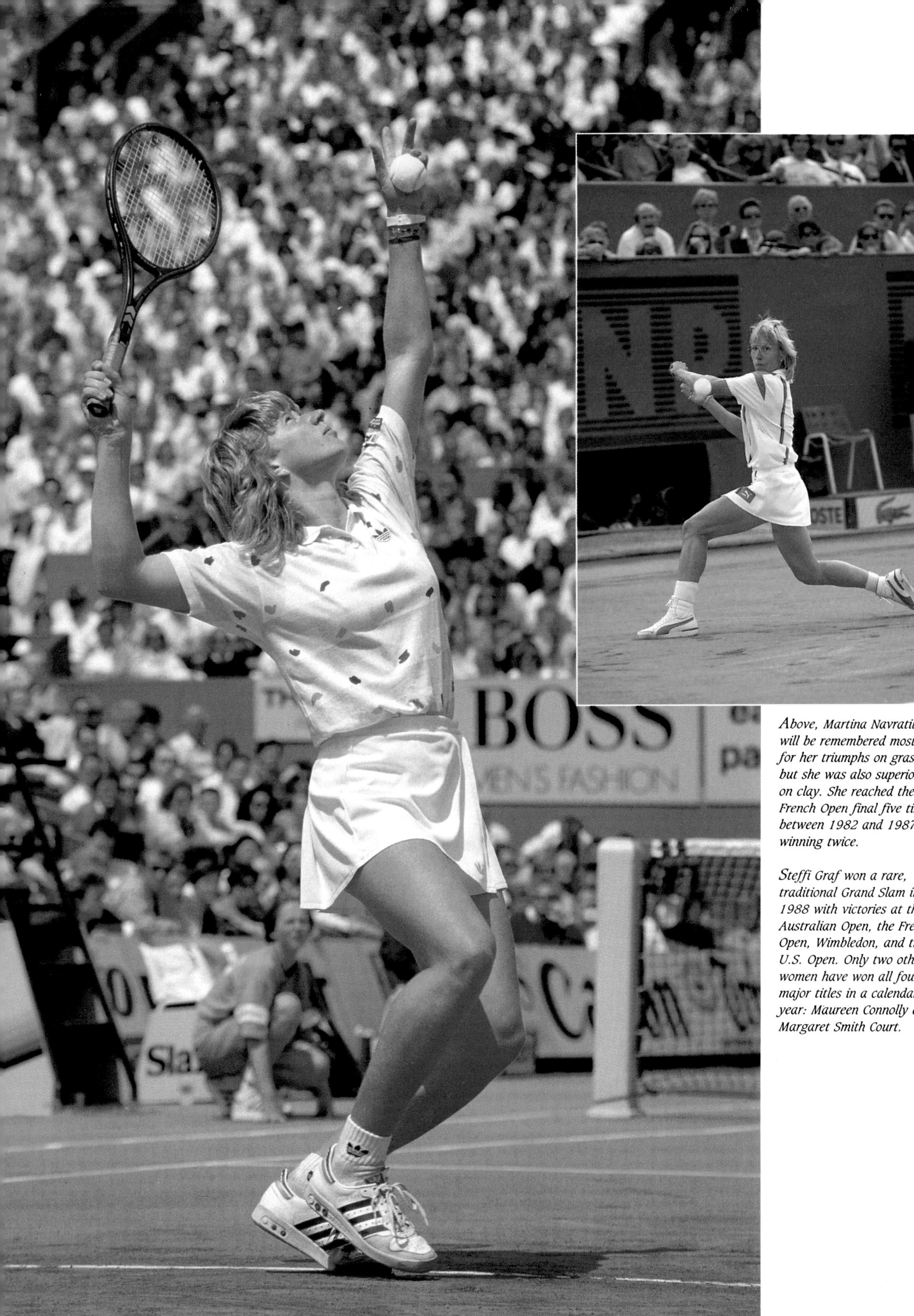

Above, Martina Navratilova will be remembered most for her triumphs on grass, but she was also superior on clay. She reached the French Open final five times between 1982 and 1987, winning twice.

Steffi Graf won a rare, traditional Grand Slam in 1988 with victories at the Australian Open, the French Open, Wimbledon, and the U.S. Open. Only two other women have won all four major titles in a calendar year: Maureen Connolly and Margaret Smith Court.

The storied rivalry between Chris Evert and Martina Navratilova began with this match in Akron in 1973. Chris is about to hit—not a classic forehand—but an Elizabeth Ryan chop.

for the first time and led Czechoslovakia to its first victory ever in Federation Cup play. Martina was doing better financially, too. The Czechoslovak Tennis Federation, which previously had taken all of her prize money, giving her only $17 a day, now allowed her to keep 80 percent of her winnings.

Nevertheless, Martina was unhappy. Officials within the Czechoslovak Federation were criticizing her for becoming "too Americanized" and were threatening to restrict her travel. Martina began to wonder whether she should defect. She worried that if she did defect, she might not see her family again. She also feared that her government might withhold opportunities from her younger sister, Jana. On the other hand, she believed she would never achieve her goals in tennis if she remained in Czechoslovakia. She wanted to be Number 1, and to do that she knew she had to compete consistently in the United States, where "the big tennis" was. When the federation nearly prevented her from playing in the 1975 U.S. Open, Martina decided she would not return.

During that tournament, a few hours after losing in the semifinals, Martina requested political asylum in the United States. Months of turmoil loomed for her, but so did the accomplishments she craved.

In 1974 a special man became part of women's tennis: Jerry Diamond. Jerry, a quick-thinking, tough-talking New Yorker, was working in public relations at a major car dealership in San Francisco, when I asked him to take over the WTA helm. Martin Carmichael, our first executive director, had not been cut out for the job; already we were $35,000 in debt. I knew our organization could not survive unless it was financially sound.

I called Jerry and told him I was coming to see him on important business. We met at a coffee shop. "The WTA needs a good leader and you're a good businessman," I told Jerry. "I want you to take it over."

"There's absolutely no way," Jerry replied. "It's too much work."

I reminded him that he owed me a favor. I had introduced him to tennis a few years earlier, and since then he had done well as a promoter.

Jerry started to bend. "OK," he said, "I'll tell you what. I'll take it on under two conditions: First, I have no contract. I work from month to month. And second, anytime you and I get into a fight over policy and I lose, I

Chris and Martina became friends soon after they met. They shared the women's doubles trophy at Wimbledon in 1976.

Growing Pleasures, Growing Pains

JERRY DIAMOND

"The Women's Tennis Association (WTA) became the focal point of my life for seven or eight years. It was almost like creating a piece of artistic work, starting with nothing, and creating something.

"I remember going to England with Billie in January or February of 1975 to argue with the All England Club for equal prize money. At that time the women were getting 60 percent of what the men were making. The press swarmed us at the airport. Naturally, the British press is very pro–All England Club. 'What are you trying to do?' they said. 'You've got your nerve.'

"An important figure in the process was the attorney for the WTA, Larry Aufmuth. He helped put together in legal form the strategy I had figured might win us a decision at the meeting. We prepared a contract for the women to sign that stated they would play in another tournament during Wimbledon the following year, if the women's prize money at Wimbledon was not comparable to the men's.

"About 80 or 90 percent of the women signed it. Almost every major player in the world agreed to play in a tournament during Wimbledon of 1976, on grass, to be arranged at a later date. Our goal was to go to the Hall of Fame at Newport, Rhode Island, and establish a grass-court tournament there. I had a sponsor lined up that was prepared to put up some pretty big money. I knew that Wimbledon, like the U.S. Open, would never throw the women out, because they would lose their lucrative television contract.

"So we met with about twenty members of the All England Club Committee, right in the Directors Room, and basically told them in nice language that either they raised the prize money or the women would not play the event. They snickered and said let's wait and see what happens when the time comes. And I said, 'No, you don't seem to understand: It's not an emotional issue anymore. The women have signed a contract to play in another tournament, and if they decide they want to play in your tournament we'll legally prevent them from doing so. They have no choice, and you have no choice.' We eventually settled for 80 percent of the men's total purse, with the women's champion receiving 90 percent of what the men's champion received."

---

quit. If you agree to those terms, I'll come on as the executive director."

Jerry came aboard with one employee and worked for six months without pay. He knew he would get paid eventually, but he did not take home a check until after he had sold a couple of endorsements and a television package to CBS. That was only the beginning. Under Jerry's leadership, both the WTA and the tour prospered. The WTA staff added more than two dozen employees, including tour referees, public relations directors, and trainers, while prize money rose from about $1 million in 1974 to $14.2 million in 1986, the year Jerry left.

Hiring Jerry Diamond was one of my last big achievements. Winning the 1974 U.S. Open and the 1975 Wimbledon were two others. My game had started to go downhill, but in the Open I was able to defeat Evonne Goolagong in a tremendous, three-set final. I think it was the best match the two of us ever

Here I am winning my sixth and last Wimbledon singles title in 1975. I was in top form that year and beat Evonne Goolagong in the final, 6–0, 6–1.

played. At Wimbledon the following summer, I survived a dramatic semifinal against Chris Evert, rallying from an 0-3 deficit in the third set. Then I beat Evonne, 6-0, 6-1, for my sixth and last Wimbledon singles title.

One of my regrets is that I made my original decision to retire in 1975, one year too soon. Had I played at Wimbledon in 1976, I think I could have won a seventh singles title. I practiced with Chris and Martina at Wimbledon that year and beat them routinely, even though I usually do not play well in practice. In the tournament Chris beat Martina in a close, three-set semifinal and then overcame Evonne in the final, 6-3, 4-6, 8-6. I made a comeback in 1977, following my third knee operation, but by then I was thirty-three and my time had run out. I lost to Chris for the first time on grass in the quarterfinals of Wimbledon, 6-1, 6-2, in forty-eight minutes.

Nevertheless, I remember the 1977 Wimbledon as a joyous one. It was the year Virginia Wade finally won. Less than two weeks shy of her thirty-second birthday, "Our Ginny" won the elusive title on her sixteenth attempt. Even more thrilling, she triumphed in the year of the Centenary, Wimbledon's 100th birthday, and the year Queen Elizabeth celebrated her silver anniversary as monarch. As I watched Virginia close out the match I told Marjorie Fraser, the women's locker-room attendant, "This script was written in heaven."

Virginia had ranked in the world's top ten since 1967 and had won two Grand Slam titles, but until 1977 she had never reached a Wimbledon final. She had reached the semifinals only twice. Frequently, she had lost in an early round to a lesser opponent. Virginia was an emotional player to begin with, and the majesty and tradition of her country's championship apparently overwhelmed her.

Ann Haydon Jones, the 1969 Wimbledon winner and the last British champion before Virginia, described the crowd's enthusiasm for the English players as a double-edged sword. If an Englishwoman was playing well, the crowd's enthusiasm gave her an emotional boost, and she was likely to play even better. If she was playing poorly, the crowd's disappointment—the audible groans after every lost point—made her even more self-conscious and frustrated than she was.

Because Virginia carried herself with a regal air, many members of the British sportswriting profession found her easy prey when she failed. They had sympathy for the sweet and unassuming Christine Truman in the 1950s and 1960s but not for the "imperious" Virginia Wade. Not all of the London newspapers lambasted her, of course; traditional papers like *The Times* of London and *The Daily Telegraph* were invariably fair to all the athletes. The tabloids, on the other hand, produced some of the most tasteless headlines I have read anywhere in the world. "Ginny Fizz" was one of their favorites. When Virginia blew a big lead and lost to unseeded Pat Walkden of Rhodesia in the 1969 Wimbledon, the tabloids trumpeted: "What a Flop, Ginny," and "She Looked Like a Tigress—Then Went Out Like a Tabby."

How did any of the British players win Wimbledon while playing under such scrutiny? Christine Truman said she never read anything written about herself. Angela Mortimer said she developed an immunity by growing up with it.

Either Virginia finally learned how to endure Britain's expectations, or she simply outlasted them. Her triumph occurred under circumstances remarkably like those of Angela Mortimer in 1961 and Ann Jones in 1969. Angela and Ann triumphed at Wimbledon late in their careers and only after shedding the burden of being Britain's greatest hope. Similarly, Virginia was considered past her prime when she made her successful run for the title in 1977. By then the Brits were touting a new star, Sue Barker, whose photograph appeared on the cover of the British Broadcasting Company's program guide for the 1977 Wimbledon.

Virginia, the daughter of an Anglican vicar, was born in Bournemouth on the southern coast of England on July 10, 1945, but spent most of her childhood in Durban, South Africa. The family's home was next to the Durban Lawn Tennis Club, where Virginia and her older siblings learned the game. The Wades moved back to England when Virginia was sixteen.

Throughout her adolescence and young adulthood, Virginia was more than a tennis player; she earned good marks in school, played the piano, and enjoyed the ballet and theater. She studied mathematics and physics at the University of Sussex and as of 1987 was the last college graduate to win a Wimbledon singles title.

Like many of the women professionals, Virginia benefited from World Team Tennis, a professional league comprising sixteen American-based teams, including the Boston Lobsters, the Detroit Loves, and the Phoenix Racquets. World Team Tennis, spawned in 1974 by the tennis boom, gave men and women players a lucrative salary in addition to the prize money they earned by competing in tournaments. The league disbanded in 1978 because of infighting among the owners.

Virginia played on the same team I did, the New York Sets, which later became the New York Apples. During the season, which ran from May through August, we women practiced with our male teammates daily, received constructive coaching, and improved our games technically. We also became stronger mentally because of World Team Tennis's unorthodox format, which was designed to create excitement for the spectators and pressure for the players. Our matches consisted of one six-game set, with no-ad scoring: When the score reached deuce, it was sudden death, and the winner of the next point won the game. Furthermore, because the matches were played in an arena, players had the sensation of being on center court every night.

Before the 1977 Wimbledon, Virginia made some technical adjustments in her forehand and serve. Her advisers were Hamilton Richardson, an American star in the 1950s, and Jerry Teeguarden, a well-known teaching professional and the father of Pam Teeguarden, one of the first Virginia Slims regulars. Virginia came into Wimbledon feeling like a new woman; for the first time in her life, she believed she could win.

In the quarterfinals Virginia faced the acrobatic Rosie Casals, always a difficult opponent for her, and won in straight sets. In the

Britain's Virginia Wade, shown serving to Betty Stove in the 1977 Wimbledon final, won the championship on the anniversary of the 100th Wimbledon.

Queen Elizabeth II, making a rare appearance at the All England Lawn Tennis and Croquet Club, presented Virginia "Our Ginny" Wade with the Wimbledon trophy in 1977.

semifinals she met Chris Evert, the defending champion. Chris, after playing so well against me in the quarterfinals, came out flat, while Virginia came out with fire in her eyes. She was confident, controlled, and aggressive; she served and volleyed sensationally, hit winners on the run, and won the match, 6–2, 4–6, 6–1. That left one more hurdle for Virginia: Betty Stove, the tall, sturdy Dutchwoman who had played an important role in the formation of the original women's tour.

Virginia prepared herself during the hours before the final by smothering her telephone with a pillow and playing Rachmaninoff's Second Symphony loudly on her stereo. When a small battalion of photographers knocked on her door, Virginia's first thought was to send them away. Then she paused. "What am I doing?" she asked herself. "Why be so prickly today of all days?" She allowed the photographers to enter and take pictures.

At Wimbledon a few hours later, a military band played "God Save the Queen" as Queen Elizabeth II arrived. Many miles away in the Netherlands, members of the Dutch Parliament were glued to a television set. What everyone saw was wonderful theater. Virginia, after a ragged start, emerged triumphant, 4–6, 6–3, 6–1. She accepted the gilded salver from Queen Elizabeth and heard her say above the noise, "Well played. It must have been hard work." Virginia held the trophy high, and the crowd spontaneously began to sing "For She's a Jolly Good Fellow."

"The result means everything to me," Virginia said afterward. "Everyone thought I was past it and couldn't do it. I wanted to prove I deserved to be out there among the champions. I felt I belonged—that I was the best player who hadn't won Wimbledon so far."

The 1977 Wimbledon was memorable for another match, one that took place in the second round on Centre Court. The match featured twenty-two-year-old Chris Evert and fourteen-year-old Tracy Austin, who had beaten Elly Vessies-Appel of the Netherlands in the first round. In the locker room before their match, Chris taught Tracy how to curtsy to members of royalty seated in the Royal Box, a courtesy women players traditionally show while entering and exiting from Centre Court. (Male players must bow.) Chris walked onto the court feeling sick from nerves. She was so jittery that, during a point in the third game, she slipped and fell. Chris sat there, humiliated, but she recovered quickly. Although she whipped Tracy, 6–1, 6–1, Tracy showed her spunk by winning 38 percent of the points.

Tracy, who came from Rolling Hills Estates, California, was a disarming moppet in 1977. She was still small, weighing about ninety-five pounds. She had braces on her teeth, she wore her hair in pigtails, and she dressed in pinafores trimmed in gingham.

For Tracy's international debut in 1977, a sixteen-year minimum-age requirement for contestants, previously imposed by the International Tennis Federation, was waived. The age limit, which had never been tested in court, probably could not have sustained a legal challenge, and ITF officials technically did the right thing in abolishing it. In retrospect, however, the ITF had reason to be concerned about the age of the players, and Tracy herself was among the first to make them realize it. Sensible age limitations throughout the sport might have prevented a great deal of heartache, not to mention injuries to shoul-

Tracy Austin, a fourteen-year-old dynamo in braces, delighted the Wimbledon crowds during her 1977 debut.

ders, backs, legs, and feet. Several years later, the governing bodies of men's and women's tennis imposed limits on the number of professional tournaments youngsters could play in order to protect them from the physical grind and emotional trauma of a highly competitive adult world. The rules were sure to help the next generation of players, but they would come too late to help Tracy.

Martina Navratilova, during the months that followed her defection, was suffering from homesickness and loneliness. Telephone calls to her family were tearful. "I was eighteen years old, like a kid leaving home to go to college," she recalled. "But all of a sudden I was alone, four or five thousand miles from my family. I couldn't go back there, and they couldn't come see me. And I was doing it in front of the whole world. I think it would have been less turbulent had my life been more private, but that was impossible. Going through adolescence is a pretty scary trick for anybody, but this made it even more difficult for me to grow up."

Martina made her home in Palm Springs, California, and quickly grew accustomed to a life of excesses. Not only was she still the pancake champ, but she became a champion shopper as well. Young, wealthy, and free to do what she pleased for the first time in her life, she was like a kid let loose in the candy store. But instead of candy, she was buying designer clothes and luxury automobiles. "I get carried away in jewelry stores," she once said. "People are always asking if I am in the jewelry business." Sportswriters in every town critically noted her materialistic tendencies. Martina was deeply hurt but seemed incapable of changing her style of life.

Martina's immaturity was apparent on the tennis court as well, and she agonized over every failure, no matter how small. One bad line call could snap her concentration and send her to defeat.

The year 1976 marked a turning point for Martina. At the U.S. Open, where she was the Number 3 seed, her career was at a low ebb. She entered the tournament with little preparation, and her weight was at an all-time high, 167 pounds. She lost in the first round to American Janet Newberry and then sobbed uncontrollably as the cameras zoomed in on her. It was a portrait of desolation seen in living rooms throughout the United States.

Even as Martina wallowed in her misery, better days were already in sight. Early in the year she had gained a new friend and mentor in Sandra Haynie, an American women's golf champion known for her calm and businesslike approach to her game. Sandra, a member of the Ladies Professional Golf Association's Hall of Fame, knew little about the technicalities of tennis, but she understood the psychology of sports.

Sandra talked to Martina continually and started to accompany her to tournaments. "I watched her have some of her temper tantrums," Sandra recalled. "Martina expected an awful lot of herself, and she expected a lot from others, such as linesmen and officials. Chris Evert's attitude was always superior. If she got a bad call, she would just shrug her shoulders and turn away and go on and play the next point. That was something she had learned at a young age. It was something Martina had to learn later in life.''

With Sandra's help, Martina took a giant step toward maturity. She left the Southern California fast lane for a more temperate life in Dallas, lost twenty pounds, and began the 1977 tour more at ease with her new world. She was by then fluent in English and could beat native-born Americans in a word game called ''Boggle,'' a popular locker-room pastime. She won six tournaments in 1977, five more than she had won in 1976.

In 1978, at age twenty-one, Martina won her first Wimbledon. She triumphed not only with her powerful serve and exciting net play, but also with a mental resilience that her challengers could not match. Martina defeated Evonne Goolagong in the semifinals and in the final came from behind to beat Chris Evert. Martina's run had appeared finished when Chris broke her serve at love to take a 4–2 lead in the decisive third set, but Martina stood fast and broke Chris's serve, then held her own to tie the score at 4–all. Chris forged ahead, 5–4, but it was she who cracked, not Martina. As Chris sprayed her shots wildly, Martina won twelve of the next thirteen points to win the set and the match. ''She has been through a lot of hurt and loneliness,'' Chris said afterward. ''But she is tougher than I am at this point, this week.''

Janet Newberry comforts Martina Navratilova, the Number 3 seed, after upsetting her in the first round of the 1976 U.S. Open.

Martina's greatest accomplishment had a bittersweet quality. ''I don't know whether I should cry or scream or laugh,'' she said. Her family, whom she had not seen since her defection three years earlier, was not there to share her moment of triumph. The Czechoslovak newspapers, which had steadfastly referred to her as ''another woman player'' since her defection, did not report it.

A year later, however, when Martina strode onto Wimbledon's Centre Court for a rematch with the recently married Chris Evert Lloyd, her mother watched from the stands and cried tears of happiness and pride. The Czechoslovak government had issued Jana a two-week visa after she received a formal invitation from the All England Club. When Martina won the final point, Jana jumped up and danced around her seat with joy. In another departure from normal procedure, Czechoslovakia's national television station showed a tape of the final.

The next day, Martina and I teamed up against Betty Stove and Wendy Turnbull in a historic women's doubles final. A victory would give me my twentieth Wimbledon title and break the record I shared with Elizabeth Ryan, who won nineteen Wimbledon doubles championships between 1914 and 1934. Martina and I won the doubles match in three sets, but it was not a grand occasion for me, because I could not stop thinking of Elizabeth. She had suffered a stroke the day before the doubles final and had died en route to the hospital. She was eighty-eight.

Martina went on to be ranked Number 1 in the world for the second straight year and looked as though she had arrived. But she and Sandra Haynie went their separate ways in 1980, and Martina's personal life fell into disarray. Losing sight of her goals, she plunged into another slump.

Allan Nemiroff, a Los Angeles entrepreneur and longtime friend of Martina's, remembered an evening he and his wife spent with Martina during Wimbledon in 1980. After going to the theater, they stopped at a restaurant for dessert. ''Martina ate something like banana flambé,'' Nemiroff recalled. ''I couldn't believe it. She was going to play

Chris Evert in the semifinals the next day. After we ate—it was about 12:30 A.M.—I said, 'OK ladies, you stay here and I'll go out and get a taxi.' I was trying to wave down a taxi by Piccadilly and all of a sudden I saw Martina dart out into the middle of the street. She ran right in front of the taxi and hailed him down. I was thinking, there but for a few inches goes one of the greatest tennis players of all time. The point was that Martina did not fully appreciate how wonderful she was. She was so blessed, and she did not realize how far she could take her blessing.''

Martina lost to Chris the following day. When she woke up to her incredible potential a few years later, however, women's tennis would take a giant step forward.

Tracy Austin was a sixteen-year-old child in pigtails when she won the U.S. Open in 1979. She was five feet four inches tall and weighed a mere 110 pounds, but she played with a fearlessness and tenacity seldom seen in tennis. Chris summed it up by saying, ''The only person who has come close to my determination that I've seen was Tracy. She was tough. She had determination and control over situations. I could see it in her eyes.'' Martina's comment was: ''One cannot think of Tracy as a child. If you do, she will beat you.''

Tracy, the daughter of a nuclear physicist, was the youngest child by five years in a family of excellent tennis players. Her mother, Jeanne, was once a ranked player in southern California. Her sister, Pam, played on the women's circuit for a few years, and her brother John played on the men's circuit. (In 1980, Tracy and John became the first brother and sister to win the Wimbledon mixed doubles title.) Another brother, Jeff, played for UCLA.

Tracy first handled a tennis racket at two and a half. By age four she was enrolled in a special kiddies' program run by Vic Braden, a teaching professional and entrepreneur, at the Jack Kramer Tennis Club in Rolling Hills Estates. From that time forward, Tracy lived for tennis. She later came under the tutelage of teaching professional Robert Landsdorp, also at the Jack Kramer Tennis Club; her early achievements included twenty-five national junior titles.

''Tracy was always competitive,'' Jeff Austin recalled. ''She could focus in and concentrate at a very young age. She always wanted to win. In card games, she could memorize the cards when she was four or five years old. If she knew she had to go on a trip, she would sit down and crank out about three weeks of homework. I think those are the qualities that allowed her to do what she did at so young an age.''

Going into the 1979 U.S. Open, Tracy had already won one important title in historic fashion, the 1979 Italian Open. In the semifinals she had snapped Chris Evert's incredible clay-court winning streak at 125 matches. Nevertheless, Tracy was not expected to win the U.S. Open. Even after her hard-fought semifinal victory over Wimbledon champion Martina Navratilova, by a score of 7–5, 7–5, she was considered a long shot to beat Chris in the final. Tracy's coach, Robert Landsdorp, considered her chances so slim that he promised to quit smoking if she won.

In 1979 Tracy Austin conquered Chris Evert to become, at sixteen, the youngest female to win the United States singles championship.

Tracy would be dangerous, however, because she saw the Open final as just another match. She had won the national girls' twelve-and-under championships, the national fourteens, the national sixteens, and the national eighteens. "Well," she thought with her child's logic, "now it's time to win the U.S. Open."

"I can still remember driving in to the Open from Long Island for the final against Chris," Tracy recalled at twenty-five. "I was with my family and I was so relaxed. We were joking and laughing in the car, playing some silly word game with tongue twisters. I was laughing hysterically. And then I played Chrissie. I didn't know how important the Open was."

Tracy beat Chris at her own baseline game, 6–4, 6–3, to become the youngest female to win the United States title. (Maureen Connolly was three months older than Tracy when she triumphed in 1951.) In setting the record Tracy prevented another. She stopped Chris Evert's winning streak at four United States championships, a string matched only by Helen Jacobs and Molla Mallory.

I did not foresee that Tracy would have trouble with injuries, but I knew that she took her physical condition for granted. By 1979 most players still did not know that they should warm up properly before competing or working out. I told Tracy she should stretch, but she scoffed at me. Before leaving the locker room to play a match, Tracy caught my eye and then bent down and touched her knees—once. "There, Billie, I stretched," she said. I shouted at her in exasperation, and she laughed. Later, after she had injured her back, she said she wished she had listened.

But in 1979 Tracy was still in good health, and her future looked bright. The future of women's tennis looked bright, too. Only eight years after our tour had started, the total prize money for women reached another all-time high, $6.2 million, and the schedule featured a tournament somewhere in the world virtually every week of the year. Martina Navratilova, the leading prize-money winner that year, earned a record $691,198.

A good portion of our prize money came from a new sponsor, Avon. We had broken from Virginia Slims, our original sponsor, in 1979, because we were unable to reach an agreement on the format of the tour—specifically, the distribution of prize money and player commitments. Jerry Diamond and I (I was the WTA president at the time) wanted to redistribute the prize money at Slims tournaments, increasing it substantially at events in major markets. We reasoned that if we raised the purses to new highs at events on the Slims tour, which began in January and culminated with the Virginia Slims Championships in March, sponsors like Colgate and Family Circle, which had major tournaments later in the year; would raise their purses, too.

Virginia Slims, however, wanted identical purses throughout their three-month tour, with a jackpot reserved for the championships. They rejected our proposal for uneven purses, because they feared the top players would enter the lucrative events and skip the others, depriving the tour of any continuity. Already the stars were saying they wanted to compete in fewer Slims events. Chris Evert, a master at pacing herself, disliked playing in the winter, or on fast carpet, any more than she had to. Evonne Goolagong was playing less because she was having trouble with her legs on the carpet, a hard, unforgiving surface. I had cut back on my schedule because I was thirty-five years old.

Avon was only too happy to replace Virginia Slims. The new sponsor raised the prize money and fueled the Avon Futures circuit, a relatively new series of tournaments for second-tier professionals. The week-long 1979 Avon Championships at Madison Square Garden drew a record 59,225 spectators; the final drew 13,752, the largest crowd to watch a match at a women's tournament until that time..

Lured by the ever greater financial rewards, more and more young people—and their parents—began chasing the golden goose. Tracy Austin, who became a celebrity at fourteen at the 1977 Wimbledon, was only the first in a long line of child professionals, including Pam Shriver and Andrea Jaeger.

Pam, Tracy's rival on the junior circuit, turned professional at fifteen and the following year became the darling of the 1978 U.S. Open. Pam's "most glamorous moments," as she remembered them, came in the biggest arena in tennis: the United States Tennis Association's new National Tennis Center at Flushing Meadow, New York. The USTA (the word "Lawn" had been dropped in 1976) left the impossibly cramped West Side Tennis Club in 1978 and moved into the 1939–1940 New York World's Fair grounds. The highlight of the National Tennis Center—Louis Armstrong Stadium—looms eight stories high and seats 20,000.

Pam Shriver, a curly-haired, six-foot-tall, serve-and-volley stylist, blanketed the net with an unusual and significant new weapon: the oversize Prince racket. The aluminum racket, designed by Howard Head, a retired engineer and the inventor of metal skis, featured a circular face 60 percent larger than that of a conventional racket. It had a sweet spot—the hitting area in the center of the racket face—three times larger than normal. The larger sweet spot was forgiving and allowed players more room for error.

Some players ridiculed the Prince racket in the beginning because of its cumbersome appearance; some of Pam's friends called it a snowshoe, a trampoline, and an old duffer's racket. Nevertheless, midsize and oversize rackets proliferated in the late 1970s and early 1980s and revolutionized the game, evolving into powerful tools made of newer materials like graphite and boron. With these weapons, players were able to hit harder than ever, and one by one they abandoned their standard-size rackets. Pam's wise decision to embrace the Prince before others did may have contributed to her fast start.

Pam was still playing in sixteen-and-under tournaments when she came into the 1978 U.S. Open as the Number 16 seed. "I thought it was pretty neat to be seeded in my first Open," she said. "I took it all in with such a laid-back attitude. I was happy to be there. I was missing a few days of school."

Within days, Pam was feeling like Alice in Wonderland. One victory followed another. When she gained a semifinal berth opposite Martina Navratilova, Wimbledon champion and Number 1 seed, she had yet to lose a set. "Everyone thought that would be it," Pam said. Instead, she toppled Martina with the help of five serving aces, 7–6, 7–6.

Sixteen-year-old Pam Shriver was all arms, legs, and oversize Prince racket when she became the surprise U.S. Open finalist in 1978.

"I remember the emotions," Pam said. "I didn't go nuts because I felt kind of bad—a Wimbledon champion going out to a sixteen-year-old rookie."

The rookie came back down to earth in the final against twenty-three-year-old Chris Evert. Chris won, 7–5, 6–4. The following day, Pam was back in high school.

Tennis critics who predicted that Pam would be the next Helen Wills were wrong. She was stymied by chronic shoulder problems, and during a six-month period in 1979 she failed to win a match. At the 1979 U.S. Open, a year after her magical debut, she lost in the first round.

"Now I know why it happened," Pam said. "I was a tall, skinny kid. I was a weak child and I served too hard for my strength. If I had it to do over, I would have started on a weight program at fourteen."

In the nine years that followed the 1978 Open, Pam ranked consistently near the top of the game but failed to reach another Grand Slam final.

Tracy Austin and Pam Shriver were soon joined on the tour by another youngster, Andrea Jaeger. As an eighty-pound thirteen-year-old with long, swirling pigtails, Andrea won the girls' eighteen title at the international Orange Bowl tournament in Miami Beach. She turned professional at fourteen and became a tour regular. A few days before her fifteenth birthday, she reached the quarterfinals at Wimbledon.

Andrea typified the new generation of young Americans. She played backcourt tennis, hit a wicked two-handed backhand, and wanted passionately to win. She had no prejudice against the powerful new rackets, nor did she have any fears about not being feminine on the court. Andrea went all out; she even screamed at umpires and linesmen if she thought screaming would win her a point. For Andrea, tennis was never just a game.

Andrea was coached by her father, Roland Jaeger, a hard-working and ambitious man who grew up in Germany, near the Swiss border. Roland, who compiled a 66–3 record as an amateur boxer in Europe, worked as a bricklayer before he and his German wife, Ilse, moved to Lincolnshire, Illinois, a northwest Chicago suburb, in 1956. There Roland worked long hours managing a bar. He started to play tennis and later became a teaching professional.

The early days of Andrea's career were happy. Andrea's older sister, Susy, an excellent college player before injuries thwarted her, remembered, "The competition was intense, but we had a great time." Susy recalled accompanying Andrea, who was still an amateur, to one of her first tour events: "She beat Rosie Casals and Wendy Turnbull in Seattle. She was fourteen. She and I were also playing doubles. We stayed with a family and we baked cookies and cakes at their house. We ate huge lunches. I remember we gave interviews that were as far as possible from the truth."

Those happy-go-lucky days were short-lived, however. A year later, in 1980, after Andrea had won twice on Wimbledon's Centre Court, she admitted, "Now that I've turned pro, it's more of a profession. It's not like I go out to have fun. Whenever I'm on the court, in a match, I'm serious."

Andrea tried to hold on to her childhood. Later that summer, when she became the youngest semifinalist in the history of the U.S. Open, she took pride in scoring a record 884,000 points on the pinball machine in the women's locker room. "Next year I'll be sixteen," Andrea said. "But I'll still be playing pinball and Space Invaders."

Indeed, even at eighteen Andrea would delight in playing tag underneath the bleachers with the ball boys and ball girls. But by then the adult world would be closing in around her. She would earn millions in prize money and endorsements during her brief career—but for a price.

The youngsters stole much of the limelight in 1980, but the happiest story of all involved a twenty-eight-year-old veteran. Evonne Goolagong Cawley, mother of three-year-old Kelly, returned to peak form and captured the 1980 Wimbledon title, her first since 1971.

Evonne had been hampered by injuries since Kelly's birth in 1977. Her troubles began when an injection for pain hit her sciatic nerve. "I was numb from the buttock to the knee in my right leg for months after," Evonne recalled. "When I was playing I found I could no longer hit my beautiful topspin backhand that I had had for years. I found that I had to chip the ball and try not to put my right leg over my left as far."

Evonne performed well in the years that followed but never reached the heights of the early 1970s. For a while 1980 did not look promising, either. She suffered from anemia and could not win a tournament. Two weeks before Wimbledon, however, she came back from a six-week absence and reached the final of an English tournament. "I lost to Chris Evert in three sets," she remembered. "But I felt really good, and I felt quietly confident. I knew I was going to play better. I could feel it. By the time Wimbledon came, I couldn't *wait* to get out on the court."

Evonne had no walkabouts at this Wimbledon, only determination. She was down a set in the third round but won, and she trailed a gifted, eighteen-year-old Czechoslovak named Hana Mandlikova, 6–7, 1–3, in the fourth

Andrea Jaeger was yet another in a long line of teenage prodigies. Her career would be cut short by injuries.

round before winning. "I didn't say to myself, 'I'm going to win the tournament,' " Evonne explained. "I kept telling myself, 'I'm not going to lose this match.' " Evonne then survived a difficult semifinal against Tracy Austin, the Number 2 seed.

In the final Evonne met her old rival, Chris Evert, who had upset Martina Navratilova in the semifinals. Evonne, ever confident, raced through the first set, 6–1, as Chris struggled to find her rhythm. Evonne did not need her wonderful topspin backhand; her chipped backhand was working perfectly, staying low on the grass. Evonne led, 1–0, in the second set, when the rains came.

"We had to go off the court and I was cursing under my breath," Evonne recounted. "I was playing so well and she didn't start off too well, so naturally I wanted to keep going. But even after the break I felt good; I was eager to get back on. I even felt confident enough to stay on the baseline and rally, which against Chris is something you shouldn't do."

Evonne won the second set, 7–6, and was soon holding the Wimbledon salver for the second time in her life. Evonne did not return to defend her title in 1981. She was at home caring for Kelly and Kelly's new baby brother, Morgan.

Chris Evert, a few months after losing to Evonne at the 1980 Wimbledon, reasserted herself as the queen of women's tennis by winning her fifth U.S. Open in six years. Only three other women had won that many: Molla Mallory, Helen Wills, and Margaret Court. In the semifinals Chris ended a five-match losing streak against Tracy Austin, beating her with a bold assortment of drives, volleys, and overheads. In the final she met the teenage starlet Hana Mandlikova.

Chris beat Hana, 5–7, 6–1, 6–1, but not before Hana had reawakened memories of Lenglen and Bueno and Goolagong. Tall, slender, and graceful, she was another tennis ballerina. Not merely enchanting, she was spectacular—she was an all-court player, who could hit any shot from any position. "I can beat everybody," she claimed, and she looked as though she could. After the match Chris Evert's husband, John Lloyd, shook his head. "She's going to be dangerous," he said. "She's eighteen? It's frightening."

In 1977, at age fifteen, Hana came to the United States for the first time and won the girls' sixteen-and-under title at the Orange Bowl in Florida. A year later she was runner-up to Tracy Austin in the Wimbledon junior championships.

Although the Czechoslovak Tennis Federation nurtured Hana's career, Hana told me that the system did not provide her with everything she needed as a child. Her father, Vilem, a sportswriter and a former Olympic sprinter, spent a good deal of his own money on her training. After Hana became the world

Growing Pleasures, Growing Pains

EVONNE GOOLAGONG CAWLEY

"It was a big challenge for me to come back after having a child. I had a lot of injuries afterward, and I wasn't sure that I would come back. It was a big decision for me. Naturally, I wanted to bring Kelly up right and try to give her a stable life.

"As it turned out, she traveled to so many places and met so many people that today she is very outgoing. She likes people, and she is easy to get along with. Kelly was good for me, too, because I would go out and play my matches and then go home to her and forget everything. It was always a pleasure to do fun things with my family.

"Children bring out so many emotions you've never had. It actually makes me feel more comfortable with anything else I do. I guess children teach you to be less selfish. They also teach you a lot of patience. I've always had the motherly instinct because I came from a big family.

"I competed until I was four months pregnant. The only thing that stopped me from playing was the heat in Australia. After the first four months I played just to keep fit. Having been a competitor so long, I'd always run after the ball and hit it on the first bounce. It was natural for me to do that. The doctor suggested that I let it bounce a few times, but I couldn't. At seven months he said I definitely had to stop because I might have Kelly on the court. Then I did a lot of swimming. It seemed funny when I went into the hospital to have Kelly. They asked me whether I needed a wheelchair, and I said, no, I don't.

"I didn't think about tennis right away after Kelly was born. I was too busy worrying about whether I'd be a good mother.

"But after a few months I started to think that sooner or later I would have to start hitting a few balls to find out whether I wanted to go back. I started up again four months after Kelly was born, but it was too soon. After losing in the first round of a tournament in Toronto, I decided to train two more months and then try again.

"Before Kelly was born, I had kept fit by playing tournaments. After Kelly, I found my whole body had changed. For the first time in a long time I found myself lifting some weights and cycling to strengthen my legs. I felt I had to start all over again. It did strengthen my body, so I felt I was back to normal, except that I ended up having a lot of injuries in my legs. Margaret Court said that when she had her first child she had several leg injuries, too. Pregnancy seems to affect your legs more than any other part of your body. I think that's because your legs swell and you get varicose veins. If there are going to be more mothers who compete at a top level in sports, it would be nice if there were a doctor who could suggest special training for them."

---

junior champion, she thought she needed a coach to travel with her. "So we went to the Czech Federation and asked for a coach," she reported, "and they said, 'We have no money.' "

Nor did Hana have much money when she, accompanied by her father, came to the United States to try the professional tour in 1979. Betty Stove, who became Hana's coach in 1980, claimed that Hana had to win money in her first tournament in order to go on to the next one.

Hana withstood the pressure of having to win her meal money and more: she won five tournaments in 1979 and earned a reputation for being a brilliant, though occasionally erratic, player. In 1980, under Betty's guidance, she began to look like the next superstar in women's tennis. Her U.S. Open final was her first of four successive Grand Slam singles finals.

Less than a month after Hana's brilliant Open final, Tracy Austin felt a sharp pain in her right buttock, a harbinger of trouble that lay ahead for Tracy, Hana, and numerous other young women. Tracy's pain worsened, and eventually she was forced to stop playing tennis. Doctors diagnosed the injury as sci-

In 1980 Evonne Goolagong became the first mother to win Wimbledon since Dorothea Lambert Chambers in 1914.

atica, an inflammation of the sciatic nerve. For Tracy, it was the beginning of an eight-month ordeal, consisting of rest and painstaking rehabilitation. For women's tennis, it was the beginning of an ominous trend. The unrelenting intensity of the professional circuit would take a toll on the young and still-growing competitors. With few exceptions, the child stars of the late 1970s and early 1980s suffered injuries that scarred, and in some cases ruined, their careers.

Hana, following her appearance in the 1980 U.S. Open final, won the 1980 Australian Open, her first Grand Slam title, and several months later, the French Open as well. In the quarterfinals at Paris, Hana whipped the latest junior upstart, fourteen-year-old Floridian Kathy Rinaldi, the youngest player to compete in a Grand Slam tournament. In the semifinals Hana became the first woman since Margaret Court to beat Chris Evert at Roland Garros. After losing, 7–5, 6–4, Chris concluded, ''Hana has it all.'' In the final, Hana beat Sylvia Hanika, a twenty-one-year-old West German.

But Hana did not have it all. Midway through the French Open she had felt a severe spasm in her back. A month later at Wimbledon, she was able to reach her fourth successive Grand Slam final, but her back injury continued to nag her. Chris Evert, a losing finalist three years in a row, did not let the opportunity slip away. She overwhelmed Hana, 6–2, 6–2, to win the third, and possibly the last, Wimbledon championship of her career.

For Hana, the end of Wimbledon was the beginning of her own version of Tracy's nightmare. ''I could not play for four months,'' she said. ''The injury set me back, for sure. I lost my confidence. Every time I did some exercise I got a bad spasm. I didn't know whether I was going to come back. I didn't know if I would be able to play tennis again. I was nineteen and I was scared.''

Tracy Austin's comeback began with ''workouts'' in which someone hit a tennis ball directly to her for a period of seven minutes. It was a grim new beginning for a young woman who had never been acquainted with adversity. She began stretching her muscles diligently and gradually extended her workouts. Tracy returned to the circuit in the summer of 1981 and played well enough to reach the quarterfinals of Wimbledon. By the time the U.S. Open began in August, she had made a complete return to form. A favorable draw helped her breeze through to the final, where she met Martina Navratilova.

Martina, after playing aimlessly for two years, had finally regained the form she showed in winning Wimbledon in 1978 and 1979. She had a new coach in Renee Richards, a new trainer and mentor in basketball

Hana Mandlikova had the makings of a great champion at age nineteen. With effortless grace, she beat Wendy Turnbull in this quarter-final match in the 1981 Wimbledon.

star Nancy Lieberman, and a new identity: she had become a United States citizen in July. That same month, Martina had come under painful public scrutiny when details of her private life were published in a New York tabloid. She had, however, developed an inner strength in the wake of her courageous defection, and she came into the U.S. Open with a more positive self-image than she had ever had.

Martina played one of her greatest matches against Chris Evert in an emotional, seesawing semifinal and eked out the victory, 7–5, 4–6, 6–4. The next day, still a little worn, Martina took aim at Tracy and won the first set, 6–1, with a stunning display of power tennis. As Tracy sat in her chair at courtside during the changeover, her head in her towel, she told herself, "Let's gut this out; let's fight." Recalling the moment, she said later, "That's what I felt I had done all summer: struggle and fight to get back in shape. I remember thinking it was on national television and I just wanted to try to get some games because it was going so fast."

Martina, with a break point for a 5–4 lead in the second set, took a big swing at a shoulder-high forehand volley and slammed it into the net. Tracy went on to win the second and third sets, 7–6, 7–6. She took the third-set tiebreaker, 7–1, with a bold and perfectly executed change of strategy. She had hit her forehands crosscourt to Martina's backhand

Kathy Jordan, left, and Anne Smith won each of the four Grand Slam doubles titles once between 1980 and 1981.

TRACY AUSTIN

"I think many young players have learned and benefited from what happened to me, but they have also been hurt by the fact that I won the U.S. Open at sixteen. I think I started a belief that one *could* win the U.S. Open at sixteen, and therefore people started to put a lot of pressure on young players. And I think the young girls put pressure on themselves. They expected much more. And I *never* expected to win the U.S. Open at sixteen. It wasn't something that had crossed my mind before that. There wasn't any pressure. It just happened. Whereas now, it's possible. If a seventeen-year-old girl is only thirteenth in the world, the parents, the press, the agents, and the players start asking, 'What's taking you so long?'

"So that was a disservice to young girls. Chris Evert came along at sixteen, but that was eight years before me, and I don't think the circuit was as developed then. I had no one before me to show me what to do. I was new at it; the circuit was new at it. The tour didn't know how to deal with a fourteen-year-old. Now, there are tons of them out there. Those parents who are out there have seen a family do it before them, or maybe ten families. And they think, 'Oh that family or that little girl and her parents have done it well; let's take after them.' My family and I had to go through it blindly.

"I don't regret that it happened that way. I don't think I regret too many things, because that's the way it was and you take it for what it is. You can't change things. I enjoyed it. I enjoyed playing Chris for the first time on Centre Court when I was fourteen. I look back now, I was such a little girl. I weighed eighty-nine pounds; I was about four feet eleven. One thing that was hard was that the press kept harping on how little I was in my pinafores and my pigtails.

"They said my mom tried to make me look like a little girl. But I *was* a little girl. I didn't mature quickly, physically or emotionally. Some of these girls at fourteen wear makeup, are five feet eight, and have developed physically. That didn't happen to me. I wouldn't change that, either. I was basically unaffected. But instead of thinking of it as nice, people tried to cut it down.

Tracy Austin, Chris Evert once said, is "the only person who has come close to my determination."

"It was difficult at first because I think anybody going through adolescence has a tough time among their peers. And here I was growing up in front of the public, in front of the press, and the press was saying things that weren't true.

"I was very, very shy. Now I can talk to anybody and I can talk as long as you want. But back then I *was* shy. I found the press could be very hard. They asked me questions I had never thought about."

Martina Navratilova lost the 1981 U.S. Open final to Tracy Austin and then cried tears of happiness when the crowd thundered its approval of her effort—and of her.

all afternoon, but suddenly she riffled them down the line and caught the tiring Martina by surprise.

Tracy repeated her victory over Martina late in the year at the Toyota Championships, a major season-ending event held by an important new sponsor, and she finished 1981 as the second-ranked woman tennis player in the world. Unfortunately for her and for women's tennis, it was her last hurrah. Early in 1982 her back injury recurred. Although Tracy made several attempts to return to competition, she was never the same.

The awards ceremony at the 1981 U.S. Open was a joyous occasion not only for Tracy but also for Martina, who received a thunderous ovation from the fans. For the first time, an American crowd was embracing this muscular, aggressive athlete, who did not fit the stereotype of the traditionally feminine, all-American girl. It was a proud moment for all women athletes. When the crowd accepted Martina for who she was, it accepted all of us. Martina cupped her hands over her eyes and burst into tears.

That closing scene of the women's Open—Tracy smiling, Martina crying—in retrospect held a poignant irony. Tracy's best days were almost at an end, while Martina's were just beginning. Women's tennis was going to get tougher, more powerful, and less ladylike in the 1980s, and Martina was going to lead the way.

Chapter 8

Brave NewAthlete

1982 & Beyond

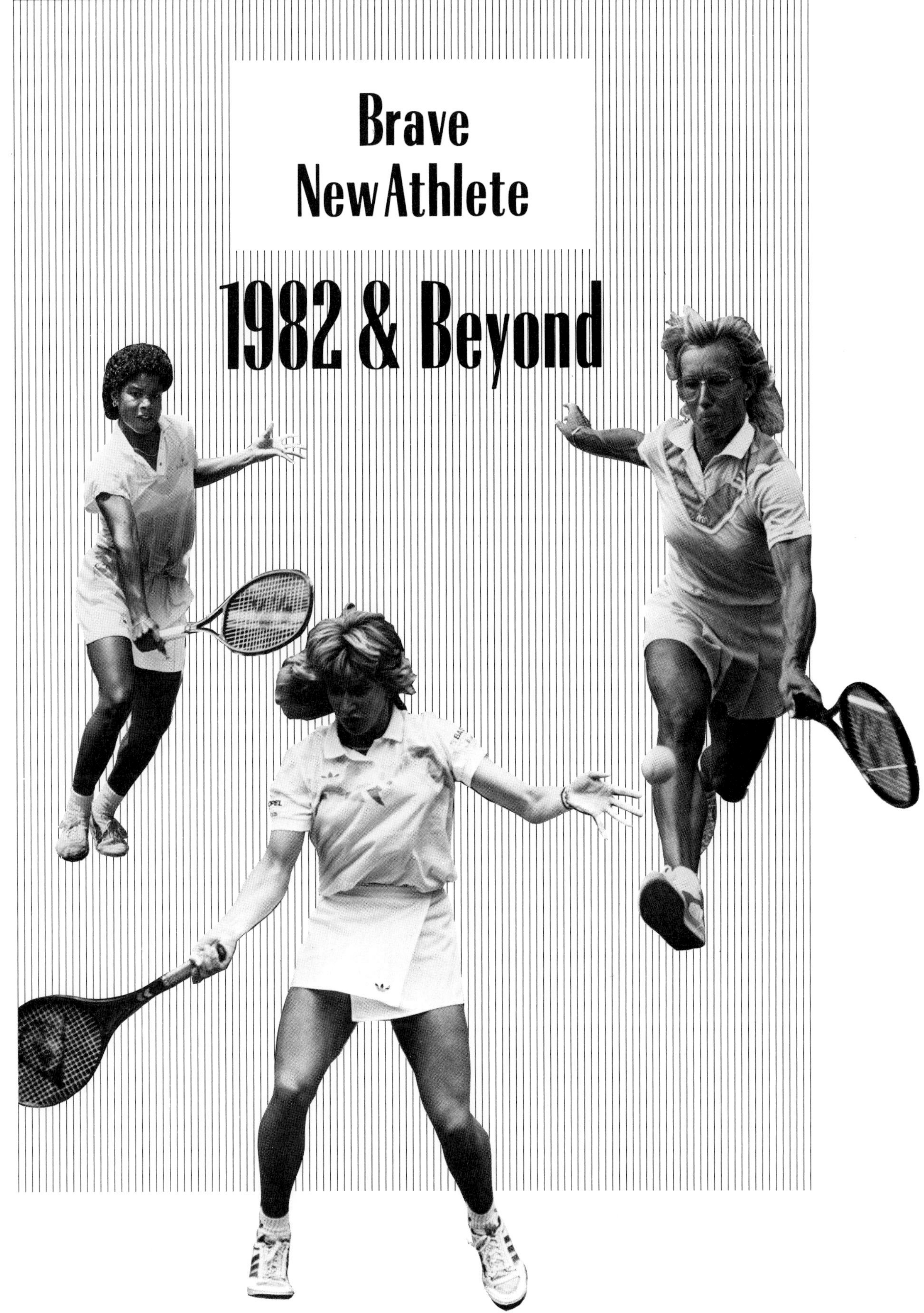

"Tennis is more than an amusement. It is a difficult sport which is constantly perfecting itself through new and interesting methods." Those words, written by Charles Lenglen, the father of Suzanne, have been true since the day they appeared in the London *Evening News* in 1926. In the 1920s Suzanne brought women's tennis closer to perfection than it had ever been. In the 1980s Martina Navratilova did the same.

Martina attacked the game on three fronts: the physical, the technical, and the intellectual. She achieved near perfection in all three areas and in so doing became the most dominating woman tennis champion since Suzanne Lenglen and Helen Wills. From 1982 through 1986, the years that will be remembered as her prime, Martina won twelve Grand Slam tournaments and compiled a stunning won-lost match record of 427–14.

Martina began her final climb to the pinnacle of women's tennis in 1981, when she was twenty-five years old. Until then she had won only three Grand Slam titles. She had a habit of losing matches she should have won, sometimes because she succumbed to tension and lost confidence in herself. Then she met Nancy Lieberman, a former collegiate and professional basketball star, and for a second time reached out for help outside tennis. Nancy watched in disbelief as Martina lost to Chris Evert, 6–0, 6–0, at a clay-court tournament at Amelia Island, Florida, in the spring of 1981. Nancy had trained fiercely in her sport, and she found Martina slothful by comparison. When Nancy told Martina she was throwing her talent away, Martina, for the first time, saw the sand running through the hourglass. "Nancy made me realize I didn't have all the time in the world, that I'd better get myself in gear," Martina said. "I think I wanted to do that, but I needed someone to push me along."

Overleaf, American Lori McNeil, left, met the new standards for strength, quickness, and versatility. West Germany's Steffi Graf, center, developed a perfect forehand and began a rapid rise to the top of the women's game. Martina Navratilova, right, ushered in an age of total fitness and all-court tennis.

With Nancy's help, Martina worked as no woman tennis player had before. She practiced and trained seven hours a day, lifting weights, running sprints, and performing agility exercises.

Diet was another of Martina's new concerns. She hired a nutritionist, Robert Haas, who prescribed a diet high in carbohydrates and low in fat. I shake my head when I remember our eating habits in the 1960s. We ate steak and eggs for breakfast, not because we were stupid but because we were ignorant. I occasionally grew dizzy toward the end of long matches but never knew why. Now I realize that I did not have enough energy-producing carbohydrates in my system.

Martina was no slouch technically when she won the 1978 and 1979 Wimbledon titles, but she had clear weaknesses in her game. She lacked consistency from the baseline; at the net she occasionally swung at her volleys instead of punching them with short, crisp strokes, and she hit her backhand only with slice, never topspin. Incredible as it sounds, Martina had not had a coach since her defection to the United States in 1973. That changed late in the summer of 1981, when she hired Renee Richards, a New York

When a conventional shot was not enough to save a point, the great Martina Navratilova invented a return.

ophthalmologist with a unique history in men's *and* women's tennis.

Renee was the former Richard Raskind, who had played for Yale University and had earned a high ranking in the East. Dr. Raskind was competing in men's thirty-five-and-over tournaments when, in the early 1970s, he underwent a sex-change operation and became Renee Richards. Renee was allowed to join the women's tour in 1976, despite protests from some of the women. Her success as a competitor was limited, but she became a splendid coach.

Under Renee's guidance, Martina eradicated her technical flaws and added power to her left-handed serve. (Renee was also left-handed.) Martina developed a ruthless infallibility at the net, and she became nearly as consistent from the baseline as the baseline queen herself, Chris Evert. Martina also added a significant backcourt weapon, a topspin backhand. That stroke would always be the most difficult for her, but she proved her courage by using it at crucial times in some of her most important matches.

Martina expanded the horizons of her sport by introducing the computer to tennis. Her nutritionist, Robert Haas, doubled as her scout, charting her opponents during their matches and plugging their winning and losing shots into a computer. In this way he detected players' subtle tendencies, enabling Martina to know her rivals better than they knew themselves.

Some people called Martina the "brave new athlete," an allusion to Aldous Huxley's *Brave New World* and its view of people of the future as machinelike and almost inhuman. But whereas Huxley's title was sardonic, Martina really *was* brave. In a society that viewed slender, lithe women as the ideal, Martina had to have enormous faith in herself to further build up her already muscular body. Photographs of the new Martina showed muscles rippling, veins clearly defined in her arms and legs. "She looks like a man" was the pejorative and frequently heard remark. Martina chose to believe in her own definition of femininity.

"I never found myself particularly attractive," she said in 1982. "I wasn't bad looking, but I had a strong face. My body was more like a boy's than a girl's. But I've been growing into it and the last few years I've felt more like a woman than ever before."

The final hurdle standing between Martina and greatness was not physical, technical, or intellectual. It was emotional. She had to learn to have utter confidence in herself. Even when she was ranked Number 1 in the world, her excellent results were not enough to make her rivals forget that she had collapsed in a few important tournaments. Martina had lost to Tracy Austin in both the 1981 Open and the 1981 Toyota Championships after building big leads, and she had lost to Sylvia Hanika, then West Germany's top player, in the 1982 Avon Championships after leading, 6–1, 3–1. Those matches earned Martina the unflattering label of a player who could engineer her own demise. Martina's rivals perpetuated the reputation. Chris Evert once suggested before a major final that Martina's nerves "might enter in." Or as Ted Tinling once said: "Martina goes from arrogance to panic with nothing in between."

Martina was vying for a "modern" Grand Slam (four successive major titles spread over two calendar years) at the 1982 U.S. Open, when her mental courage was questioned again. Martina, suffering from toxoplasmosis, came within two points of beating Pam Shriver in the quarterfinals but faded midway through and lost, 1–6, 7–6, 6–2. Martina had a good excuse for losing; her doctor confirmed the illness, explaining that her white blood count was elevated far above normal. Nevertheless, Martina found herself on the defensive. "It's not my nerves," Martina said, imploring the press to believe her. "I didn't choke. I don't want that label on me. I don't deserve it."

Chris Evert went on to win the Open, her sixth, trouncing Hana Mandlikova in the final. During the months that followed, while Martina recovered her health and put the finishing touches on her game, Chris enjoyed the last long streak of dominance of her career. Chris beat Martina in the final of the Australian Open and then won her fifth French title in the spring of 1983. Suddenly, she was in the same position Martina had been in less

MARTINA NAVRATILOVA

"Going onto Wimbledon's Centre Court is special every time, but it's more special on the opening day when you are the defending champion and the grass is all green. The defending champion gets to play the first match of the ladies' event, and that's like dessert after you've won it, even though it comes a year later. Nowhere else do they give you this honor. I think that might be what makes Wimbledon so much more special than anything else.

"When you walk out there for the final, that's what you've been sweating for all those years. I'm so excited that the nerves seem to disappear. Just being there overtakes everything else for me. All the anxiety is gone.

"You just soak it all up; you remember everything; you look at the whole stadium. You don't see the faces, really; you only see the people in the bottom rows. They vanish into the blackness because the stadium is very dark. And you look at the friends' box and the Royal Box and check out who is sitting there. And maybe you also look at the members' box to see all the past champions sitting there.

"The greatest thing about Centre Court is that you never lose sight of a ball, whereas in the U.S. Open stadium, or on any other court, you often lose the ball because of the lights or because the background is too light or the people sitting there have shirts that are too light. At Wimbledon the backdrop is very high and dark green. The only time you lose the ball is in the sun.

"When I think about tying Helen Wills Moody's record of eight Wimbledons, it overwhelms me, so I really don't think about it. If I did dwell on it, I'd think I was the greatest thing since popcorn. By one token the human race is very young and tennis is that much younger; tennis has only 100 years of history. When you put it into that kind of perspective, the record is peanuts. At the same time, 100 years is longer than most people's lifetime, and there are a whole lot of people playing tennis. So when you look at it that way, then it's an amazing achievement, hers and mine, and I'm just very happy to have done it.

"I would like to be remembered as a bright, talented athlete who did just about everything she could to bring that talent to fruition. In other words, I didn't leave any stone unturned. I never tanked a match in my life; I never gave up.

"I think my 'mental frailty' was exaggerated. I don't think I was ever as weak as they portrayed me to be. I certainly couldn't have made such a turnaround if I had been. It's hard to be winning Wimbledon and still be weak.

"I could be riding a forty-five match winning streak and people would say I wasn't mentally tough. I've felt for a long time that I was tougher mentally than Chris Evert and not getting credit for it, because people always wrote about my physical talents instead of my mental talents. I also think Chris hasn't gotten enough credit for her athletic ability, which she has plenty of. She would have been a great golfer or even a volleyball or basketball player. She's a great athlete. She can catch a ball; she can throw it, and she can hit a target. She would have been a good quarterback if she had been a man."

---

than a year before: She was one tournament away from a modern Grand Slam.

Through some perversity of fate, Chris was destined to lose her chance, just as Martina had lost hers, through illness. The night before her third-round match at Wimbledon, Chris became violently ill with a stomach ailment. She looked pale the next day when she went onto the court against Kathy Jordan of King of Prussia, Pennsylvania.

Kathy, a national collegiate champion while at Stanford University, was regarded as one of the grittiest players on the tour. She was best known for her doubles prowess (she had won all four Grand Slam doubles titles with Texan Anne Smith), and on her best days she was capable of beating anyone in singles. Kathy attacked the net routinely, and she hit an unorthodox sliced backhand, which stayed low on the grass. It was a bad combination of strengths for the ailing Chris. As Kathy marched toward a 6–1, 7–6 victory, the crowd watched in silence. Chris's attempt at a Grand Slam was ending, and so, too, was her incredible record of having reached the semifinals in thirty-four successive Grand Slam tournaments, every one she had played since her Cinderella debut at the U.S. Open in 1971. The streak was something few people had thought much about until it ended. Only then did we pause to appreciate how magnificent it was.

Even as Chris was bidding for her modern slam, Martina was emerging as the major force in women's tennis. She had lost only three of ninety-three matches in 1982, and in 1983 she lost only one of eighty-seven, that to a young American backcourt specialist, Kathleen Horvath, in the quarterfinals of the French Open. Afterward, Martina left Renee Richards, who had advised her to play conservatively against Kathleen, and found a new coach in Mike Estep, a men's touring professional whom she had met through World Team Tennis in the 1970s. Martina's victory in the 1983 Wimbledon was her first of six successive Grand Slam championships, a record equaled only by Maureen Connolly and Margaret Court.

Martina's dominance became complete when she won the only major title that had eluded her, the U.S. Open. Martina ravaged the field, losing only nineteen games in seven matches and crushing Chris Evert in the final, 6–1, 6–3. In the turning point of the match, Martina sprinted from the net to the baseline to retrieve one of Chris's perfect lobs. Getting there in time, Martina set her feet, whirled, and cracked a topspin backhand down the line for a winner.

In the year and a half that followed, no one could touch Martina. I remember thinking that her play bordered on the unreal, in part because of her unbelievable speed and power. She moved and placed her shots so quickly that her opponents had little time to prepare and were consistently rushed.

In April of 1984 Martina extended her reign to clay, the surface least suited to her game. At Amelia Island, on the same court where Chris had routed Martina three years earlier, 6–0, 6–0, Martina pummeled Chris, 6–2, 6–0.

Martina was seeking an unprecedented seventh successive Grand Slam title and a traditional Grand Slam at the 1984 Australian Open in December, when she encountered a young Czechoslovak, Helena Sukova, the daughter of Vera Sukova, who had been a Wimbledon finalist in 1962. Helena, nineteen years old and six feet two, was powerful and aggressive. She beat Martina, 1–6, 6–3, 7–5, thus ending Martina's winning streak at seventy-four matches, a modern record. In the final, Helena pressured a nervous but determined Chris Evert before losing in three sets.

Martina was by then treated like a superstar all over the world—everywhere, that is, but in her native Czechoslovakia, where she was still an outcast, her rare achievements written up in newspapers as though they were

The moment of victory was never sweeter than when Martina Navratilova, on her eleventh try, won the U.S. Open in 1983.

ordinary. Then, in August 1986, Martina went home again. In one of the most moving events of her career, she returned to Prague for the first time since her defection eleven years earlier and led the United States Federation Cup team to victory. The Czechoslovak government was forced to issue a visa to Martina in order to hold the event in their beautiful new Stvanice Tennis Stadium. The officials barely acknowledged her presence, but the fans gave her ovations befitting a great and much-admired champion. During her first match, which was played outside the stadium court, trains slowed down as they passed so that the passengers and crew could look out the windows and savor a few moments of history.

In a dramatic finish to a tournament in which forty-one nations had competed, the United States and Czechoslovakia met for the title. Chris Evert won the first match against Helena Sukova, and Martina clinched the victory when she beat her former countrywoman, Hana Mandlikova. During the closing ceremonies, Martina cried and told the crowd she hoped she would not have to wait eleven years to return. "The countryside was more beautiful than I remembered it," Martina later said. "Prague was more beautiful than I remembered it. Everyone was so friendly. It exceeded all my expectations."

Czechoslovakia's Helena Sukova, daughter of Vera Sukova, a former Wimbledon finalist, reached the final of the Australian Open in 1984 and the U.S. Open in 1986.

Chris Evert was among those who took Martina's training methods to heart. "Once you've been Number 1," she once said, "you can never be satisfied with less." To return to the top, Chris knew she had to make changes. She started working with weights in 1983, switched to a more powerful graphite racket in 1984, and began attacking more at the net. In early 1985 she ended a thirteen-match losing streak against Martina, and at the French Open a few months later, she beat Martina again in a suspenseful final that is remembered as one of their greatest matches. The score was 6–3, 6–7, 7–5.

Just as Martina had once lifted her game to Chris's level, now Chris lifted herself even with Martina, if not on grass and other fast surfaces, then most certainly on clay. "I made Martina more disciplined," Chris said. "She made me more physically fit." Chris said she probably would have retired had Martina not presented her with a new challenge. In meeting that challenge, Chris reached the peak of her career.

The seesawing nature of Chris's and Martina's rivalry made it the longest and greatest in women's tennis. They played seventy-five matches from March 1973 through the end of 1987. Chris dominated the early years of the rivalry, winning twenty of the first twenty-four through 1977. Between 1978 and 1984, Martina had the edge, winning twenty-seven out of thirty-seven. Then, from 1985 through 1987, the two achieved a kind of parity; while Martina won nine of the fourteen confrontations, Chris was nearly always in contention.

The rivalry worked because both women were ambitious and flexible and because they were nearly the same age. Chris was a year and a half older than Martina. My rivalry with Margaret Court, who was only a year older than I was, had also produced memorable matches. Regrettably, we did not play each other nearly as often as Chris and Martina; on clay we played each other only once.

Chris and Martina will remain forever linked in history because of the number of times they met in important matches and the special friendship they shared. They became friends soon after Martina arrived in the United States in 1973, and Chris was one of the few people who knew that Martina planned to defect.

Martina and Chris played doubles together for a while and won two Grand Slam titles, the 1975 French and the 1976 Wimbledon. The partnership ended, however, once Martina began to threaten Chris's supremacy. Later, when the end of their careers drew closer, the barriers came down again. ''Chris and I were never jealous of what the other one had,'' Martina said, ''maybe because we were so different in our style as well as our approach to the game.''

Chris liked to keep her distance during major championships, but she was still able to sit down and chat with Martina. After their matches, the two often found themselves side by side in the locker room. ''Sometimes we talk about the match; sometimes we don't say anything at all,'' Martina said. ''We know if the other one wants to talk about it or not, and the winner is always considerate of the loser. We've both been through so much on the positive side as well as the down side that we never gloat. We always were like that, actually. We never rubbed it in. When I was eighteen or nineteen we were always considerate of each other. Maybe we knew we were going to be around for a long time.''

Chris Evert conquered Martina Navratilova, 6–3, 6–7, 7–5, in the seesawing final of the 1985 French Open championship.

While Chris and Martina were providing the main story line in women's tennis, a variety of subplots continued to unfold. Among them were the stories of Andrea Jaeger and Tracy Austin. Andrea had one of her happiest moments in tennis when she clobbered me in the Wimbledon semifinals in 1983. As I walked off the Centre Court with Andrea, I turned around and looked at the stadium one last time. I knew I would not return. I was thirty-nine years old.

Andrea lost the Wimbledon final to Martina, 6–1, 6–3, and then Andrea, too, walked off the Centre Court for what was probably her last time. She was eighteen. She would end 1983 as the third-ranked woman in the world, but injuries were already tormenting her. Like Tracy Austin, Andrea was essentially finished by the time she was twenty.

According to conventional wisdom, Andrea was a victim of emotional burnout, Tracy a victim of injury. I think those explanations are too simple. Both players suffered from serious injuries and complex responses to them.

Tracy, after injuring herself the second time, made several attempts to come back, but complained of nagging pain. She played sparingly in 1983 and by 1984 was no longer competing. I think Tracy loved tennis but was afraid she would never be as good as she once was.

Tracy also had other reasons for wanting to leave the game. During her rehabilitation in 1982 she began to enjoy life away from the circuit, and the incredible single-mindedness that brought her two U.S. Open titles by age eighteen evaporated. While attending Wimbledon in 1987 as a correspondent for ABC television's *Good Morning America,* twenty-five-year-old Tracy admitted she missed the competition but added, "There's so much I don't miss. I love to travel, but I get homesick if I'm away for more than two or three weeks. For me there was a hollowness to tour life. Ever since I've been off the tour I've been able to see the other side of life. I've developed friends who never even saw me play tennis."

Tracy said that had she followed my advice and strengthened her body through stretching, she might still be playing. But she was quick to admit, "I might also be still going around on that merry-go-round and I might not be as happy as I am now. I might have been thirty years old and not a balanced person, like some of the others."

In contrast to Tracy, I thought Andrea stopped enjoying the game. She was happy enough when she was a little sprite of fifteen, but by the time she reached eighteen her outlook had changed. She began acting strangely, losing matches she could have won. I remember saying that if Andrea could get away from her father, she would quit.

Later Andrea told me her problems had been physical, not emotional, as many people believed. She was then working in the personnel department of Time Inc., and she said, "I would trade being president of *Time* magazine if I could still be playing tennis. It's not that I miss the glorious thoughts of professional life. I miss the competitiveness, of having someone come to the net and being able to pass them four different ways. I miss the exercise, the jumping, the laughing. I don't miss the part where you can order a limo. If God would come down now and grant me a miracle—I'm the type of person who would want my family's and friends' health to come before mine—but if He granted me *two* miracles, I would want to be playing tennis."

For reasons that are not entirely clear, Andrea apparently played on and on despite painful injuries to her feet, neck, shoulder, and pelvis. Her explanation was that she "never got good responses from doctors." However, Pam Shriver recalled that her own doctor examined Andrea in October 1982 and found severe trauma in her right shoulder. "I can remember him taking a reflex test," Pam said. "Her left arm reacted with a good, healthy jump; her right arm didn't react. My doctor told her she should take some time off, but her reaction was, 'I can't.' "

Susy Jaeger Davis, Andrea's sister, explained, "Andrea was Number 3 in the world and people were coming to her, asking her to play. Tennis needed her to play some of these events. It was tough for her to be put under that pressure at her age. She was not mature enough as an athlete to say, 'I'll take some time off.' She was using drugs that would mask the pain, but she wouldn't be able to sleep or eat. It made her feel terrible."

Unfortunately, Andrea's father did not urge her to rest. "I don't think my dad realized how much it hurt," Andrea said. Susy said their father was "from the old school" and did not believe in injuries. "You're supposed to grit your teeth and plow through it."

Andrea, who was much like her father, played through her pain. "If I didn't keep playing, I thought I'd be a quitter," she said.

Although Andrea felt she had no choice but to keep playing, Jerry Diamond, then executive director of the Women's Tennis Association, our players' union, said no player—Andrea included—ever was forced to play a tournament when injured. "The WTA had a full-time trainer almost from the beginning in 1973," Diamond said. "The problem with Andrea was that you never knew when she was injured or not. She had so many emotional problems on the tour."

Andrea finally faced reality at the Los Angeles Olympics in August 1984. Tennis, which

Gabriela Sabatini, a fifteen-year-old Argentine, in 1985 became the youngest semifinalist in the history of the French Open.

had not been an Olympic sport since 1924, was featured as a demonstration sport in the 1984 Games. Andrea struggled through her first match but afterward could not lift her arm above her head. The United States team doctor examined her and told her to default. "That was the first time a doctor had said I couldn't play," Andrea said. The doctor advised specific tests and therapy and told Andrea not to play for six months. Andrea put down her rackets and said she would play no more tennis in the foreseeable future.

While Andrea and Tracy both suffered great personal losses, the game suffered as well. Tracy and Andrea, along with Hana Mandlikova and Pam Shriver, were the backbone of the next generation. Their absence contributed to the seemingly endless dominance of Martina and Chris.

When Andrea left the game, Diamond voiced his concern over the game's loss of some of its most promising young women. Another teenage star, Hungary's Andrea Temesvari, was suffering from a back injury at the time. Meanwhile, more and more children were streaming into the game, lured by the prospect of earning millions from prize money and endorsements. Just a few weeks after Andrea stopped playing, a fourteen-year-old Argentine, Gabriela Sabatini, became the youngest female to win a match at the U.S. Open. Naturally, Gabriela already had an agent; at major junior tournaments agents hovered over players only twelve years old.

"There are a ton of players who are running into physical, emotional, and mental problems," Diamond said then. "The pro game is ruining a heck of a lot of good talent. The whole area requires review.

"Many of the young girls, because they're not emotionally and intellectually mature, find themselves unable to cope. There are tremendous pressures caused by agents, parents, and others. A parent goes to an agent, and the agent goes out and makes a shoe deal. Then the kid gets to the finals at Wimbledon. Or the semifinals. Others get involved, and suddenly the player is making $150,000 more than her prize money, in endorsements.

"Now you have a fifteen-year-old who has no financial problems in the world. She walks down the street and people ask for her autograph. People fawn over her. Suddenly, reality escapes that young child. She doesn't realize that the world is very fickle, that one day you're a star and the next day you're a bum. It's an incredibly complex problem."

Diamond in 1984 was already investigating the possibility of limiting the participation of children on the professional tour. Within a year, at the urging of Diamond and other members of the WTA, the Women's International Professional Tennis Council—a body consisting of three representatives each from the WTA, the International Tennis Federation, and the tournaments themselves—barred children under fourteen from competing in professional events and limited fifteen-year-olds to a reasonable schedule.

What happened to the rest of that struggling generation, Hana Mandlikova and Pam Shriver? Neither fulfilled her original promise, but both survived injury and pain to become mainstays on the women's tour.

Hana recovered from her back injury of 1981 with the help of special exercises. "I know that I have a very fragile body and am not as strong as someone like Martina," Hana said. "That's the way I was born. The back problem couldn't take all these matches and praticing. The doctor told me to do my exercises 100 times in the morning and 100 times at night. Since then I have had no problems with my back.'' Hana continued to have minor injuries, but nothing as serious as her back problem.

In 1985 she took her exercise program a step further, training harder than she ever had in her life. ''I started to work much more physically,'' she said. ''I spent three hours a day on physical fitness and one and a half hours on tennis. It didn't show at the French Open that year. I lost in the quarterfinals because I was tired physically. But then it paid off at the U.S. Open. I felt so strong mentally and physically that I felt nobody could beat me.''

Hana, twenty-three, stunned Chris Evert in the semifinals, then upset Martina in the final. No player since Tracy Austin in 1981 had beaten Martina and Chris back-to-back. ''I was really happy, flying in the clouds,'' Hana recalled. ''I enjoyed holding the cup for two, three minutes in my hands.''

Hana said she was equally proud of herself for continuing to play on the circuit and for

Czechoslovak Hana Mandlikova ranked among the top five women players in the world six times between 1980 and 1987.

Martina Navratilova and Pam Shriver embrace after one of their many doubles victories. Through the 1988 French Open, they had won seventy titles together, nineteen in Grand Slam events.

''trying to do much more'' than she already had. Surely Hana could have left the tour and lived comfortably, as Tracy did. She had won more than $3 million in prize money through 1987. ''I feel that somebody else would just give up with all the injuries that I've had,'' Hana said. ''I keep coming back; I feel I still have certain goals to achieve.'' Her biggest ambition—to win Wimbledon—had been a goal since she was nine years old.

As for Pam Shriver, despite periodic shoulder difficulties, she carved a place in the record books for herself as Martina's doubles partner. From 1981 through the French Open of 1988 she and Martina won seventy doubles tournaments, including nineteen Grand Slam titles, and $1.91 million in combined prize money. They also achieved the longest winning streak in women's doubles history: 109 matches from June 1983 through July 1985. The streak ended in the women's doubles final at Wimbledon, when they were defeated by Kathy Jordan and Australia's Elizabeth Smylie.

Women's tennis also will remember Pam for taking an active role in the governing of the women's game. For several years Pam served as an officer within the WTA, helping to shape the future of women's tennis.

In singles competition, however, Pam's career was riddled with disappointments. In 1987, at twenty-five, she was still the enduring quarterfinalist. Perhaps, as with Virginia Wade and Ann Jones, a major singles title awaited her late in her career.

I would need more than two hands on which to count the number of young women who broke into the top echelon of women's tennis in the 1980s and threatened, for a while, to become future superstars of the sport. Some rose quickly, shone brightly, and then faded, because of boredom, frustration, or injury. Others gained a place among the top twenty in the rankings and were incapable of rising further.

One of the brightest young stars was Canadian Carling Bassett, a baseline player who burst into prominence at fifteen, when she played in the nationally televised final of the 1983 WTA Championships and nearly beat Chris Evert. Carling became an instant celebrity not only because of her potential, but also because of her good looks, her bubbly personality, and her family. Ancestors of Carling's mother founded the Carling Brewery. Carling's father, the late John Bassett, was then the managing general partner of one of the United States Football League's teams, the Tampa Bay Bandits. "She lives in a wonderland," her father had said. "How would *you* like to be fifteen, pretty, have made a movie *[Spring Fever]*, and be a tennis champion?"

Canada's Carling Bassett Seguso was one of several stars in the 1980s who parlayed talent and good looks into a fortune in endorsements.

Although Pam Shriver became a contender in major championships in 1978, she was still seeking her first Grand Slam singles title ten years later.

When Carling's father died of cancer in May 1986, Carling was suddenly without her greatest inspiration. By the spring of 1987, her ambition was clearly waning. She had begun to find the tour tedious, frustrating, and cliquish. "Right now tennis is my priority, but there are so many things I want to do with my life," she said. "I want to act a little bit. I want to spend more time with my family." Carling said she did not want any more endorsements, because "that means I'll have to play tennis for the rest of my life."

A year later, Carling would put her career on hold. She was by then the wife of Robert Seguso, a doubles star for the United States Davis Cup team, and the mother of a baby boy.

Two young Americans who survived the tour's rigors were Zina Garrison and Lori McNeil. The two women, who had remarkably parallel careers, were born one month apart in 1963 and grew up playing against each other at Houston's MacGregor Park. Both developed their games under the guidance of John Wilkerson, the MacGregor Park coach; both have reached the semifinals of a Grand Slam tournament—Zina at Wimbledon in 1984, Lori at the U.S. Open in 1987—and as of 1987 both had won two professional tournaments.

The two women took divergent paths only after graduating from high school. While Zina immediately joined the tour, Lori first attended college at Oklahoma State University. At nineteen Lori left college because she feared she was not getting enough competition from intercollegiate matches. "I lost a bit of time on my tennis," she said. "But I also matured and learned some things abut Lori."

Zina and Lori were special for reasons other than their skills. They were the first black women to rank near the top of the game since Althea Gibson in the 1950s. Leslie Allen, who in 1981 became the first black woman after Althea to win a tour event, rose as high as nineteenth in the world. Zina and Lori finished 1987 ranked Number 9 and Number 11, respectively.

In September of 1986, at a tour stop in Tampa, Lori and Zina made history when they played each other in the first all-black women's final. Lori recalled the match as "emotional and difficult." Zina remembered it differently. "We were so relaxed it didn't bother either of us. We practiced that morning together, got in the car and went to the tournament." Lori won, 2–6, 7–5, 6–2.

Both Zina and Lori have won the all-black American Tennis Association's national championship, the same championship Althea had won four times before she was allowed to compete in tournaments sanctioned by what was then an all-white USLTA.

Zina and Lori, who never confronted the enormous racial barriers Althea Gibson faced, said they admired Althea for paving the way. "She was a great tennis player and must have been strong to come through what she did and still play really good tennis," Lori said.

Said Zina, "I think Lori and I are blessed that we came up in the time that we have. For Althea to do what she did—walking in the door of an all-white club—must have been really difficult."

Zina Garrison reached the Wimbledon semifinals in 1985 and established herself as a consistent member of the world's top ten.

Nevertheless, black players continued to face racism. Some have had trouble finding private housing while competing in junior tournaments. Leslie Allen once played a first-round match before a sparse crowd and had to listen to a man clap for every mistake she made. When Zina was a junior player, she was staying in a private home in New Jersey when a commotion awakened her. In the front yard, outside her window, some unhappy neighbors were burning a cross.

I admire Zina and Lori because, more than any other rising players today, they are fighting battles off the court and on, just as we fought for women in the 1960s and 1970s. The racism they face might have chipped away at their confidence, but they have persisted and are winning. Perhaps their struggle is also one reason why they do not allow their competitiveness to hurt their friendship.

Althea Gibson, who has followed Lori's and Zina's careers, fears Zina's serve may hold her back. At five feet four and a half, Zina is one of the shortest players on the tour, and her serve is not a potent weapon. "Now Lori

OLGA MOROZOVA
Soviet women's coach

"We are improving, but not as fast as we want to. All the girls I coach are from different cities, and it is difficult to have them all together because we still don't have a base for our national team. That's a big problem, especially during the wintertime. I always have to write a letter to somebody to get permission for my team to practice at a club.

"I think tennis is the most popular sport for participation in our country. There are hundreds of young girls playing in the USSR for sure. We don't have this big class difference. It's more equal. Anyone who has the talent can play. They're trying to introduce the sport to children at schools, but the problem is the facilities. So many people now want to play tennis and we're not able to say yes to everyone. There are perhaps 100 indoor courts around the country, which is nothing. We have a population of 270 million.

"Three years ago we had Wimbledon on TV for the first time, the semifinals and final. Now we have Wimbledon on TV for two weeks. One year we want to have the French Open, too. Everyone is watching tennis.

"I was very lucky when I was a girl because I lived next door to a club in Moscow, and tennis at that time wasn't very popular. I didn't play every day. I played three times a week at the club for maybe two years. At that time it was enough. My father was crazy about sports, especially soccer and ice hockey. When I started to play tennis he said, 'Fine, why not? If she's moving, that's good. If she's busy, that's very good.' And my mother was happy with this, too.

"If someone says anything about tennis in the Soviet Union, they always mention my name, always. There are still only two people who went to the final of Wimbledon, Alex Metreveli and I. But we hope, cross my fingers, that we will have another Wimbledon finalist soon.

"I am not a star in my society, just a normal person. But this year when my girls and I went through the customs in New York, I met a person who knew me from the time when I played tennis, and my girls had eyes this big. And once in Denver it was the same thing. We were getting our luggage and were standing and talking, and a man came up and said, 'Excuse me, are you Olga Morozova?' I said, 'Yes, I am.' He said, 'Welcome again. I really liked how you played tennis.' And my girls had a heart attack.

"I would like my players to do better than I did. But it's not so easy, because I was Number 4 in the world one year. Natasha Zvereva, our Number 1, is a very good girl. She is able to do everything, but it depends on which level. Now she is at the level of the best fifteen in the world, but we have to improve to go higher, to the best five.

"If Natasha would win Wimbledon, tennis would be even more popular in our country. It is just impossible for our people to realize that being Number 15 is great. They want to see only Number 1, like in America. They will criticize Number 2 in the world because he is Number 2 and not Number 1. That's how it is. I think it's part of our history. We come from a huge country."

[who is five feet seven] has improved her serve, and it looks as though she is about to be released," Althea said. "With a little more coaching and work, I hope she will become the second black woman to win Wimbledon. I hope that when the time comes I'll still be around. I would want to be there. If she reaches the final at Wimbledon, she is going to win it."

While women's tennis progressed toward a more rugged and physical plateau, a strong movement began running counter to the new athleticism. Off the courts women players were primping and posing as never before. The "feminization of women's tennis," as I call it, was endorsed by the WTA, which in 1985 began producing a calendar featuring tennis players wearing slinky gowns, bathing suits, heavy makeup, and jewelry.

I am not as opposed to the feminization of women's tennis as some might suspect. I think every beautiful woman has the right to promote her assets. I also think tennis's new pinup girls are not trying to apologize for their muscles as much as they are trying to sell themselves commercially. Although male sports stars like Jack Nicklaus and Michael Jordan are marketable on the basis of skill alone, some women tennis players still think they have to play the stereotypical role of glamour girl.

The agents who make the endorsement deals helped start the feminization of women's tennis by distributing photographs of their clients dressed not as tennis players but as fashion models. The agents learned quickly that a player did not need to be Number 1 to become rich.

Carling Bassett was one of the attractive stars who made enormous sums in endorsements—at least $500,000 a year from 1984 through 1986—without winning a major tour event. A promotional flyer released by Carling's agents showed her in strapless outfits and listed corporate affiliations as diverse as a leisure-wear supplier, an office-equipment corporation, and a bank-card system. The flyer also revealed Carling's height, weight, and dress size.

Another blonde, the five-foot-eleven Anne White, launched her endorsement career in unique fashion. The world's ninety-third-ranked player arrived for a first-round match at Wimbledon wearing a skintight white body suit—"this thing," as opponent Pam Shriver called it. After Anne and Pam split sets, Wimbledon officials postponed the match because of darkness; they also ordered Anne not to wear the body suit the next day. Playing in conventional attire, Anne lost the match, but she had already scored an important victory for the pocketbook. Her photograph appeared in newspapers and magazines around the world. In one afternoon, she had created a lasting image of a sleek and stylish woman athlete. Endorsement offers were sure to follow, and they did.

The unforeseen result of Anne's instant fame was the wondrous effect that it had on

Gabriela Sabatini was a product of the tennis boom that swept Buenos Aires after Argentina's Guillermo Vilas won the men's U.S. Open title in 1977.

her tennis. Her confidence soared along with her public profile. She began working harder, and within the year her ranking had risen from ninety-third to twentieth.

The tour's move toward glamour was clearly supported by Virginia Slims, which in 1983 returned as the major sponsor of the women's tour. Virginia Slims had always pictured glamorous, fashionably dressed women in advertisements for its product. It could not help but benefit from its association with women athletes who were not only successful but also trim and beautiful.

The new Virginia Slims tour was bigger than anything we had seen previously, and once again the name Virginia Slims became synonymous with women's tennis. Prize money rose steadily from $10.2 million in 1983 to $16.2 million in 1988. The richest tournament of all was the $1 million Virginia Slims Championships, a year-end event restricted to the tour's top sixteen performers. In 1984 it became the first tournament since the 1900s to feature women in a best-of-five-set final.

The Virginia Slims sponsorship was not immune from criticism, however. Antismoking groups in the United States picketed some Slims-sponsored tournaments, and although the vast majority of players felt Virginia Slims was a classy and generous sponsor, a few did express reservations about the product.

As long as the federal government does not prohibit cigarette companies from promoting sporting events, I believe Virginia Slims will remain a major sponsor of women's tennis for many years to come.

Most of the young players who held up physically and emotionally during the 1980s, including Helena Sukova, Zina Garrison, Lori McNeil, Gabriela Sabatini, and Steffi Graf—a sensational West German destined to dethrone Martina Navratilova—had a common denominator. They did not suffer serious injuries early in their careers, and they played a full-court game and thus played shorter points with more variety. Significantly, most of them hit one-handed backhands, which enabled them to hit both topspin and underspin from the backcourt and to volley proficiently at the net.

Increasingly, the successful players were European. Nearly every European nation had a star of its own: Rafaella Reggi of Italy, Catarina Lindqvist of Sweden, Arantxa Sanchez of Spain, sisters Manuela and Katerina Maleeva of Bulgaria, and Natalia Zvereva of the Soviet Union.

The rise of European women coincided with a rise in popularity of women's tennis in Europe. In the mid-1980s, for the first time since the days of Suzanne Lenglen, women's matches in the French championships drew as much interest as the men's. The women's Italian Open, disassociated from the men's championship in 1979, returned to Rome's Foro Italico in 1987 and was a huge success.

The inclusion of tennis as a medal sport in the 1988 Olympics was expected to further Europeanize women's tennis. ''The Olympics will open doors to a lot of countries,'' said Philippe Chatrier, president of the ITF. ''Their governments may have only limited money, and they will reserve it for Olympic sports. Tennis will benefit from that.''

It already had. Once the International Olympic Committee decided in 1981 to bring tennis back into the Olympics, the Soviet Union began putting more effort and money into the game. By 1987 the Soviets had a top-twenty player in Natalia ''Natasha'' Zvereva (their first since Olga Morozova) and two doubles stars in Svetlana Parkhomenko and Larisa Savchenko. Natasha, asked whether she would prefer to win Wimbledon or the Olympics someday, replied, ''The Olympics.''

The WTA, sensitive to the new demographics, changed its name to the Women's International Tennis Association (WITA) in 1986, the same year Merrett Stierheim, former Dade County (Florida) Manager, replaced Jerry Diamond as executive director. Stierheim increased the WITA's presence in Europe by hiring a public relations director fluent in five languages.

Why are the European nations forging ahead in tennis? From an American perspec-

Arantxa Sanchez, one of the smallest players in women's tennis at five feet five and 100 pounds, was Spain's leading woman player in 1986, 1987, and 1988.

tive, the tennis federations in Europe keep track of their talent more easily than we do because their countries are smaller than ours. (We have a population of 250 million, compared with Czechoslovakia's 15 million and West Germany's 20 million.) From a British perspective, children in Continental Europe have greater access to coaching and indoor tennis facilities than British children.

Furthermore, the European tennis federations are extremely well organized. The West German Federation, for example, charts the progress of its potential champions by computer, pays their traveling expenses, and provides them with superior coaching. Although Peter Graf receives credit for having coached his famous daughter, Steffi was also taught by West Germany's master coaches. "She always had the best of everything," said J. Howard Frazer, a member of the USTA's junior development committee.

Czechoslovakia funnels its top prospects into ten regional training centers and, ultimately, into a national center in Prague. Czechoslovak coaches, headed by former men's Wimbledon champion Jan Kodes, are among the best in the world. Those with the highest coaching certificates have studied physiology and psychology and have earned their master's degrees in the theory of sport. As in West Germany, the Czechoslovak Federation offers free coaching to players and underwrites travel expenses.

In a bittersweet 1988 French Open, Natalia Zvereva of the Soviet Union upset Martina Navratilova, then lost to Steffi Graf in the final.

In America, by comparison, the burden of producing champions has largely been left to individual families. Parents have had to pay for instruction, court time, and travel, which can exceed $20,000 a year, with no guarantee that their children were receiving the best possible coaching. Children whose families could not afford the enormous costs rarely had a chance to succeed in tennis, while those whose parents *could* afford the cost—sometimes just barely—risked becoming victims of undue pressure. Pat Sloane, the mother of American player Susan, has heard more than one angry parent say to a child, "We've come all this way on a trip we can't afford, and there you go and lose in the first round!"

In 1987 the USTA established a junior development committee, of which I am a member. We studied the decline of American tennis and recommended possible solutions. As a result the USTA in 1988 plans to spend $6.5 million on junior tennis to increase its chances of producing a new champion. The USTA aims to introduce more children to the game at the grade-school level, to provide regional training facilities for promising juniors, and to help finance members of a national junior team.

Until the emergence of Steffi Graf, Argentina's Gabriela "Gaby" Sabatini appeared the likeliest candidate to succeed Martina as the best player in women's tennis. In 1985, at fifteen, Gabriela became the youngest French Open semifinalist in history; at sixteen she was the youngest Wimbledon semifinalist since fifteen-year-old Charlotte "Lottie" Dod in 1878. She took a big circular windup on both her forehand and one-handed backhand, sweeping up the back of the ball, generating heavy topspin, and finishing with a triumphant follow-through.

Gabriela grew up in Buenos Aires, a city that had fallen madly in love with tennis about the time that Argentine Guillermo Vilas won the U.S. Open in 1977. By 1987 Buenos Aires and its surrounding area had 1,000 tennis clubs, 400 of which were affiliated with the Argentine Tennis Association. The city had also become an incubator for junior tennis players, producing an incredible 45,000 junior matches in a one-year period. Gaby, the daughter of a middle-level executive of General Motors, developed rapidly in this favorable tennis environment and soon became one of the best junior players in the world.

At thirteen Gaby left home and moved to Key Biscayne, Florida, to train with Patricio Apey, a former Chilean Davis Cup player who had become a coach and tournament promoter. Soon Gaby was winning major eighteen-and-under tournaments. At fourteen she had a long line of endorsement opportunities and a world ranking.

As tennis observers crossed their fingers, Gaby weathered the early years without incident. By age seventeen she had developed into a strong young woman, at five feet nine and 140 pounds. She had also become a goddess in Argentina, where people approached her on the street and kissed her hand. A poll revealed that she was second in popularity only to the president.

In 1987 Gaby hired a new coach, former Spanish Davis Cup player Angel Gimenez, and soon showed signs of dramatic improvement. She developed more stamina and confidence, and began to attack the net more. Despite her improvement, however, Gaby was no longer regarded as the future Number 1 in women's tennis. That honor had been seized by her teenage rival—Steffi Graf.

Between 1984 and 1986 Steffi developed from a skinny little girl with an excellent forehand into a tall, sinewy athlete with one of the best strokes ever seen in women's tennis. Relying heavily on her lethal forehand, she won eight tournaments in 1986, beat Martina and Chris for the first time, earned $612,118 in prize money, rose to Number 3 in the world, and showed she was ready to challenge for the major titles. At the U.S. Open she held three match points against Martina before losing in the semifinals, 6–1, 6–7, 7–6. The score of the third-set tiebreaker was 10–8. A year later Steffi won her first Grand Slam tournament, the French Open, and became the top-ranked woman in the world.

Germany was destined to produce a champion like Steffi and might have done so sooner if the world wars had not decimated its thriving tennis scene. After World War I, Germany was not invited back into the ILTF for ten years. By the 1930s Germany had renewed its tennis tradition and had female stars in Cecile "Cilly" Aussem and Hilde Krahwinkel Sperling and a men's champion in Gottfried von Cramm. That renaissance was dashed by World War II, which left Germany defeated and in ruins. The first Germans with no recollection of the war era were children born in the 1960s, and a series of fine German players came from that generation, joining the tour in the late 1970s and early 1980s. Bettina Bunge, Sylvia Hanika, and Claudia Kohde-Kilsch came first and were followed by Germany's most successful pair of all, the young male player Boris Becker and Steffi Graf.

Steffi grew up in the village of Brühl, near Heidelberg. Her father, Peter, gave her a sawed-off racket when she was not yet four years old and created a makeshift court inside the house by fastening a string between two chairs. Peter and Steffi batted the ball back and forth, at the cost of a broken lamp now and then. Peter, sensing his child had talent, offered rewards for further excellence: a breadstick for ten successive hits, ice cream and hot strawberries for twenty-five. Peter frequently slammed the ball away from Steffi on the twenty-fourth exchange, "because you can't have ice cream every time." When Steffi did well in later years, Peter gave her new clothes for her precious Barbie dolls.

At age five and a half, Steffi played in the seven-and-under division of the annual "Bambino Tournament" in Munich. Conny Konzack, a West German free-lance journalist specializing in tennis, said that even then "you could see this girl would be something in tennis."

Steffi's mother, Heidi, drove her to tournaments, and her father, a car dealer, spent more and more time coaching her. When Steffi was ten Peter took a job as a teaching professional at the tennis center in Brühl, where he coached Steffi for two hours a day.

Steffi won the national German eighteen-and-under championship at thirteen and was acclaimed as a prodigy throughout her country. The sportswriters nicknamed her "Grafin" (*Gräfin* means duchess) and praised her for her "German attitude," embodying toughness, ambition, and a streak of stubbornness. Steffi also gained a reputation as the girl who never smiled. Some thought her father pushed her too hard. Her mother once said to her, "Steffi, I would love to see one picture of you in the papers in which you are smiling." Steffi replied, "What do you want me to do, Mother, smile or win?"

As for her father's influence, Steffi said confidently in an interview: "You can push a good player to become better, but it is not possible to push a great player to do anything. When I'm on the court, I don't play for my father. I'm responsible for myself."

Tennis had not seen such single-minded dedication in a champion since Tracy Austin. Journalist Konzack reported that at seventeen Steffi said, "I know most girls my age think of boys, boys, boys. I think of tennis, tennis, tennis."

"Some girls like tennis but they don't enjoy practicing it every day," said Paul Slozil, a former Davis Cup player for Czechoslovakia, who became Steffi's coach and practice partner in 1986. "She does. She loves tennis. In practice she runs for every ball. If the first ball is a short one she goes for it. I say yikes, why is she running for it now? It comes from her father. He always told her to go for every ball as early as possible."

Other than tennis, Steffi at eighteen had few interests. She enjoyed reading, cooking, and playing with her dogs. When at home, she did her own laundry and sometimes prepared the family's meals.

Steffi kept her distance from players off the court and often intimidated them on the court with an air of supreme confidence. Like Maureen Connolly in the 1950s, she walked briskly to the serving or receiving position between points, dictating the tempo of her matches and often rushing her opponents.

Steffi was more obsessed with perfection than with reaching the top. "My dream is to be as perfect a tennis player as I can be," she said. "It is for myself; it is not for being Number 1 or anything."

Peter Graf eventually quit his job and focused his life on Steffi's career. He traveled with her full-time, oversaw her endorsement commitments, and scouted her opponents. He also became known for coaching her from the stands, in defiance of the rules. Keenly aware of the risks posed by too much competition too soon, Peter from the beginning limited Steffi's schedule to fifteen or fewer tournaments a year. During prolonged breaks Steffi would return to Brühl, where she worked to improve her game, particularly her backhand and serve. Players who sniped that Steffi was protecting her ranking by not playing more should have known better. Women's tennis could not afford to lose another star.

The heart of Steffi's game was her forehand, a product of quickness, timing, and

West Germany's Steffi Graf, with her ruthlessly efficient ground strokes and her ability to overwhelm even her keenest rivals, evoked memories of Little Mo.

Steffi Graf has just beaten Martina Navratilova to win her first Grand Slam title, the 1987 French Open. She would win the first three legs of the Grand Slam in 1988.

strength. Steffi was so fast that she could hit the forehand from any position on the court, even while standing in the backhand corner. She took a circular windup and then unleashed herself into the ball, hitting it flat, without topspin, and striking it at its highest point. Without spin to slow it down, the ball streaked over the net like a bullet—faster than the shots of some men—and landed deep in her opponent's court. "It is a special stroke," Slozil said. "You must have very good footwork, and your timing must be excellent. It is not so easy to learn something like this. This is the future game of tennis: to go for it and not play the ball 100 times over the net."

Indeed, the stroke came to symbolize Steffi's fearlessness. "I always take the risk," she said, "no matter what stage of the match."

Without question, Steffi and her generation are better as a group than the women of my day. But many former players will tell you that today's young players are not as interesting to watch as the champions of the past. Olga Morozova of the Soviet Union, a touring professional in the 1970s and now the coach of the Soviet girls' team, said, "Sometimes we miss the part shown by players like Billie Jean and Maria Bueno. They were not only giving strength to the sport, they were giving music also. They were giving art to the tennis. Now it's a more powerful game. It is more of a hitting system—hit, hit, hit—and less thinking."

I agree. Style and artistry are being driven out of women's tennis, because the players hit too hard. Women are stronger and taller than in previous generations, and they use much more powerful rackets. If I had faced Steffi's forehand while in my prime, I doubt that I could have played with my usual finesse. I would not have had enough time to prepare my creative shots. My main concern would have been simply to get my racket on the ball.

Steffi began staking her claim to Number 1 in the spring of 1987 at the Lipton International Players Championships, a hard-court tournament played in Key Biscayne. Steffi crushed Martina Navratilova, 6–3, 6–2, in the semifinals and whipped Chris Evert, 6–1, 6–2, in the final. Each match took less than an hour. Steffi then won the French Open, beating Martina in a grueling three-set final to become the youngest champion in that Open's history. Toward the end of the year she won the $1 million Virginia Slims Championships at New York's Madison Square Garden. In Federation Cup play, Steffi and teammate Claudia Kohde-Kilsch led West Germany to its first title ever, beating Chris Evert and Pam Shriver in the decisive doubles match.

Steffi, who won eleven of thirteen tournaments in 1987 and compiled a 75–2 match record, finished the year ranked first in the WITA's computer ratings and in a poll of her peers. Yet her two defeats left a gaping hole in her record: they came against Martina at Wimbledon and in the U.S. Open, the two most prestigious tournaments in the world.

Martina struggled in 1987 as she came to grips with Steffi's new and different methods. She also stewed over the latest turning point in her life; she had at last turned thirty. She did not win a tournament all year until Wimbledon. Trying to find her old magic, she changed rackets, abandoning her faithful Yonex for the Dunlop model used by Steffi.

"I was getting doubtful as to whether I could still win," Martina said. "Those doubts hit you very quickly. All those things you've won don't seem to mean anything; all you can remember are the losses and you think, 'Maybe my time is up.' "

With encouragement from her friends, Martina regained her confidence in time for Wimbledon, where she was the five-time defending champion. Martina was still tense; her topspin backhand was not so much in evidence as in her years of total dominance. Nonetheless, she played superbly in beating Chris Evert in the semifinal and appeared ready to make history. "She wants to be remembered as the greatest player ever, and I don't think she's too far from that," Maria Bueno said. "If she wins the final I think she will have accomplished what she's aiming for."

Martina went on to break one of the oldest records in the game and to tie another. She beat Steffi and in so doing eclipsed Suzanne Lenglen's record of five successive Wimbledon titles and equaled Helen Wills's record of eight total championships.

Was she the best player of all time? It was possible, even likely; but Martina chose not to make that claim. "I've always wanted to be one of the greatest, or *the* greatest," Martina said after the victory. "But the closer I get to the goal, the more I realize it doesn't matter. There have been so many great players from different eras. There's no telling what Helen Wills would do today, or what I would have done fifty years ago."

After Martina had won her historic eighth championship, Steffi congratulated her and said, "How many more do you want?"

Martina smiled. "Nine is my lucky number."

Two months after the 1987 Wimbledon, during the U.S. Open, Steffi suffered from a fever and influenza. She suffered from familiarity as well; by then her opponents had determined how to play against her. They attacked the net repeatedly, forcing Steffi to pass them with her weaker backhand, and they did not allow her to rush them into starting a point before they were ready. Although Pam Shriver challenged Steffi in the quarterfinals, she could not win enough of the big points to win the match. In the semifinals Lori McNeil came closer but lost in three sets. That

Martina Navratilova accepts congratulations from Steffi Graf in 1987 after winning her eighth Wimbledon singles title and tying the forty-nine-year-old record held by Helen Wills.

match, Steffi said later, "took almost everything out of me." Against Martina in the final, she played one good set, losing it, 7–6, and then folded—"I didn't have any strength anymore," she said—and lost the second set, 6–1. Martina also won the women's doubles and mixed doubles titles. Her triple crown was the first in a Grand Slam tournament since my triple crown at Wimbledon fourteen years earlier.

Nevertheless, Steffi had arrived. Some analysts estimated her 1987 earnings from prizes and endorsements at more than $4 million.

In 1988 Steffi was overpowering. Wielding an improved serve, backhand, and net game, she won the first three major tournaments of the year—the Australian, French, and Wimbledon—to come within one leg of winning the first traditional Grand Slam since Margaret Court's in 1970. Steffi beat Chris Evert, 6–1, 7–6, in the final of the Australian Open, which was played on asphalt instead of grass for the first time. At Paris she crushed Soviet Natalia Zvereva, 6–0, 6–0, in the first shutout in a singles final ever at the French championships.

At Wimbledon the West German was only slightly less dominating. She demolished her first six opponents, conceding only seventeen games, and then took on six-time defending champion Martina Navratilova, who had struggled to win her quarterfinal and semifinal matches. Martina led, 7–5, 2–0, and appeared on her way to an unprecedented ninth Wimbledon singles title when Steffi lifted her game to new heights. In a breathtaking show of youth, speed, and power, Steffi blasted winner after winner to take twelve of the last thirteen games from the fading champion, who suddenly looked slow, uncertain, and every bit her thirty-one years. Steffi won, 5–7, 6–2, 6–1, to become, at nineteen years and eighteen days, the youngest women's Wimbledon champion since Maureen Connolly.

A sad yet gracious Martina applauded her conqueror during the awards ceremony. "This is definitely the end of a chapter," Martina later said. "The torch has been passed."

As I think about women's tennis when it began more than 100 years ago and women's tennis today, I know we have come a long way. The male players who occasionally criticize our game—reminding us that they can still beat us and that we normally play only two out of three sets—only show their ignorance. In recent years we have upstaged the men at numerous Grand Slam tournaments with our shorter, more dramatic matches. I also think women's tennis will continue to improve. The "brave new athlete" is here to stay, and she will get stronger, taller, and faster as the years go by.

Will a good woman be able to beat a good man ten years from now? Probably not. The men keep getting faster and stronger, too. But I predict the gap between the best men and the best women will continue to close, as more and more women have the chance to test themselves in tennis, as more of them grow up believing that they should try to fulfill their potential as athletes, and as more of them have mothers and fathers who encourage them to run, kick, and throw when they are small.

In one sense women's tennis—like all women's sports—is still in its infancy. We have yet to see an entire generation of women who have grown up receiving the same amount of encouragement to compete in sports as their male counterparts. Statistics suggest that if a girl is not introduced to sports by the time she is nine years old, chances are good that she will never be active in athletics. I look forward to the day when all young girls learn that sports are a great way to have fun.

The byword for the future of women's tennis is *opportunity.* We need to ensure that women receive even more opportunities than they have now, beginning at the grass-roots level. We need to do for young tennis players what the Little League system has done for baseball players: We should make it easy for children to become part of an organized program. We need to direct them to the courts and arrange round robins and team matches for them. Coeducational programs are ideal; they are fun for children, and they almost guarantee that the very best girls will still have adequate competition—from the boys.

We need more opportunities at the professional level as well. Although the tour offers at least one tournament every week of the year, players who consistently lose in the first and second rounds do not get as much competition as they should. I would like to see women's tennis adopt a two-tier format with a primary series of lucrative, sixteen-woman draws for the top players and a second-level series consisting of dozens of smaller events with smaller amounts of prize money for players still on the way up. Under such a system the lesser players would play more matches and would spend their time learning how to win instead of learning how to lose. Ultimately, women's tennis would generate a larger core of players at the top.

Women's tennis today is bigger, better, and more popular than it has ever been, and I will never forget the people who brought us here. From the earliest days of lawn tennis and garden parties, when women refused to stay on the sidelines despite the heavy, long dresses and corsets that hindered their mobility, our game has been distinguished by one milestone after another.

Before the turn of the century Charlotte Dod spoke out bravely when she said, "Ladies should learn to run and run their hardest, too, not merely stride.'' In the 1900s May Sutton shortened her hemlines, pushed up her sleeves, and hit the cover off the ball. In the 1920s the incomparable Suzanne Lenglen, our first superstar, brought ballet, fashion, and thousands of new fans to tennis and, after a stunning amateur career, became the first woman tennis player to tour professionally. In the 1920s and 1930s Helen Wills set a new standard for consistency, and her successor, Alice Marble, showed that women could play explosively as well as beautifully.

During the 1940s Pauline Betz played with abandon, diving for shots whenever necessary, and Margaret Osborne duPont and Louise Brough earned a reputation for playing ''like men'' because of their excellence at the net. In 1950, Althea Gibson broke the color barrier at Forest Hills and several years later became the first black to win the United States and Wimbledon championships. In 1953 Maureen Connolly became the first woman to win a Grand Slam.

Maria Bueno made our sport bigger as she enchanted spectators worldwide with her grace and brilliant shotmaking in the 1960s, and Margaret Court, the first woman to train with weights, made it better. Then in 1970 a group of women stood up to financial inequities spawned by the open era and formed the first professional tour for women only. When I beat a noisy male chauvinist before a television audience in the millions in 1973, women tennis players became household names, and when Chris Evert came along, combining lace and ribbons with perfection, a generation of young girls took up the game. In the 1980s Martina Navratilova charted an untraveled path toward greatness and created new standards for training, fitness, and excellence. Tracy Austin and Andrea Jaeger helped clear a minefield for the children who followed them by revealing the dangers that professional tennis poses to young bodies and souls. And in 1988 Steffi Graf appeared ready to raise our game to yet another plateau.

Each one of these women, through her own unique qualities and skills, added something special to the game. Each brought us a step closer to our full potential as athletes and as entertainers. We should not assume, however, that the last hurdle has been cleared. Women's tennis can, and should be, even bigger and better than it is today. When I think about women's tennis in the future, I know we still have a long way to go.

Sources

The following sources were used as important references in the production of *We Have Come a Long Way*:

BOOKS AND OTHER PUBLISHED WORKS

Cleather, Norah Gordon, *Wimbledon Story,* Sporting Handbooks Ltd., London, 1947.

Clerici, Gianni, *The Ultimate Tennis Book,* Follett Publishing Company, Chicago, 1975.

Connolly, Maureen, *Forehand Drive,* MacGibbon & Kee, London, 1957.

Court, Margaret, with George McGann, *Court on Court,* Dodd, Mead & Co., New York, 1975.

Current Biography Yearbook, H. W. Wilson Co., New York, 1951, 1957, 1965, 1973, 1977.

Danzig, Allison, and Schwed, Peter, *The Fireside Book of Tennis,* Simon and Schuster, New York, 1972.

Davidson, Owen, and Jones, C. M., *Great Women Tennis Players,* Pelham Books, London, 1971.

Engelmann, Larry, *The Goddess and the American Girl,* Oxford University Press, New York, 1988.

Frayne, Trent, *Famous Women Tennis Players,* Dodd, Mead & Co., New York, 1979.

Gibson, Althea, *I Always Wanted to Be Somebody,* Harper & Brothers, New York, 1958.

Hart, Doris, *Tennis with Hart,* J. B. Lippincott Co., New York, 1955.

Hart, Stan, *Once a Champion, Legendary Tennis Stars Revisited,* Dodd, Mead & Company, Inc., New York, 1985.

Herrett, Elizabeth Louise, *A Thesis in Physical Education,* University of Pennsylvania, Philadelphia, 1977.

Jacobs, Helen Hull, *Beyond the Game,* J. B. Lippincott Co., Philadelphia, 1936.

Lichtenstein, Grace, *A Long Way Baby,* William Morrow and Company, Inc., New York, 1974.

Little, Alan, *Dorothea Chambers* (1985), *Lottie Dod* (1983), *May Sutton* (1984), and *Maud Watson* (1983), the Wimbledon Lawn Tennis Museum, London.

Little, Alan, *Suzanne Lenglen,* the Wimbledon Lawn Tennis Museum, London, 1988.

Little, Alan, and Tingay, Lance, *Wimbledon Ladies, A Centenary Record,* Wimbledon Lawn Tennis Museum, London, 1984.

Marble, Alice, *The Road to Wimbledon,* Charles Scribner's Sons, New York, 1946.

Marchadier, Jarard, *Sixty Years of Tennis,* La Manufacture, Lyon, France, 1987.

Navratilova, Martina, with George Vecsey, *Martina,* Alfred A. Knopf, New York, 1985.

Olliff, John, *The Romance of Wimbledon,* Hutchinson & Co. Ltd., London, 1949.

Schickel, Richard, *The World of Tennis,* Random House and The Ridge Press, Toronto and New York, 1975.

Shannon, Bill, the *USTA Official Encyclopedia of Tennis,* Harper & Row, New York, 1981.

Tingay, Lance, *100 Years of Wimbledon,* Guinness Superlatives, London, 1977.

Tingay, Lance, *Tennis—A Pictorial History,* William Collins, London, 1977.

Tinling, Ted, *Love and Faults,* Crown Publishers, Inc., New York, 1979.

Tinling, Ted, *Sixty Years in Tennis,* Sidgwick & Jackson, Ltd., Great Britain, 1983.

Wade, Virginia, with Rafferty, Jean, *Ladies of the Court,* Atheneum, New York, 1984.

Wills, Helen, *Fifteen-Thirty,* Scribner's, London, 1937.

Wind, Herbert Warren, *Game, Set, and Match,* E. P. Dutton, New York, 1979.

World of Tennis manual, International Tennis Federation, Willow Books, London, 1987.

PERIODICALS

Pastime, The American Cricketer, American Lawn Tennis, Lawn Tennis (American), *Lawn Tennis* (British), *Ladies' Home Journal, Collier's, Literary Digest, Saturday Evening Post, Life, World Tennis, Tennis, Sports Illustrated, Time, Newsweek, The New Yorker.*

NEWSPAPERS

The New York Times, The Times of London, *The Philadelphia Inquirer,* the *Los Angeles Times,* the London *Daily Telegraph,* the London *Evening News, The Boston Globe, USA TODAY, The Cincinnati Enquirer, The Philadelphia Evening Bulletin.*

CREDITS

Chapter 1

The sources of quotations were: The quote about Lady Margot on page 2, paragraph 5, from *The Royal and Ancient Game of Tennis,* by Lord Aberdare, page 21. The All England Club Committee's quotes on page 5, paragraph 5, from *Wimbledon Ladies, A Centenary Record,* by Little and Tingay, page 3. The observer's quote about Maud Watson on page 7, paragraph 3, from *Pastime,* July 23, 1884. *Pastime*'s quote on page 8, paragraph 2, from issue of May 27, 1885. The Charlotte Dod quotes on page 9, paragraph 2; page 9, paragraph 7; and page 11, paragraph 2, from the *Westminster Gazette,* "An Interview with Miss Dod," July 20, 1893; page 11, paragraph 1, *World Sports,* "Great All Rounders—First Lady of Wimbledon," by Denzil Batchelor, October 1949; page 11, paragraph 7, *Lawn Tennis and Badminton,* an interview with Arnold Herschell, 1951; page 11, paragraph 8, *Lottie Dod,* by Little, page 13. Quote about Charlotte Dod on page 11, paragraph 1, from *Ladies of the Court,* by Wade, page 23. Blanche Bingley Hillyard quotes on page 9, paragraph 5, from *Lawn Tennis,* by H. W. W. Wilberforce, with a "Ladies' Chapter," by Blanche Hillyard, George Bell & Sons, London, 1891, page 50; page 10, paragraph 3, *Lawn Tennis for Ladies,* by Dorothea Lambert Chambers, Methuen, London, 1910, page 114. *Outing* magazine quote on page 9, paragraph 5, from May 1901 edition. Charlotte Cooper Sterry quote on page 9, paragraph 6, from *Wimbledon Ladies, A Centenary Record,* page 9. Grace Roosevelt Clark quote on page 12, paragraph 3, from the *Sunday Courier,* Poughkeepsie, New York, 1940. Ellen

Sources

Hansell Allderdice quotes on page 14, paragraph 3, and page 15, paragraph 1, from *Fifty Years of Lawn Tennis in the United States,* the United Lawn Tennis Association, New York, 1931, page 40. Helena Hellwig quote on page 14, paragraph 6, from *Official Lawn Tennis Bulletin,* February 7, 1895. Lyle Mahan quote on page 16, paragraph 2, *Lawn Tennis,* July 10, 1901. Elisabeth Moore quote on page 16, paragraph 3, from *Lawn Tennis,* February–March 1902, page 116. Hazel Hotchkiss Wightman quotes on page 17, paragraph 2, from *American Heritage,* August 1975; page 21, paragraph 1, *The Boston Globe,* December 6, 1974. Dorothea Lambert Chambers quotes on page 18, paragraph 1; page 19, paragraph 5; and page 19, paragraph 8, from the *Bradford Observer,* June 29, 1931. Quote about Dorothea Chambers on page 19, paragraph 1, from *The Queen,* July 4, 1903.

Chapter 2

The sources of quotations were: Elizabeth Ryan quotes on page 24, paragraph 4, from "Lenglen, Wills, Ryan, Marble," by Bob Considine, *The Fireside Book of Tennis,* page 145. Suzanne Lenglen quotes on page 24, paragraph 6; page 41, paragraph 2, from "Why I Became a Professional," an article by Suzanne Lenglen in her North American tour program, 1926; page 26, paragraph 2, *Wimbledon Story,* by Cleather, page 59; page 26, paragraph 7, and page 30, paragraph 6, "The Temperamental Jeanne d'Arc of the Tennis Courts," *Literary Digest,* August 27, 1921; page 31, paragraph 4, the London *Sunday Express,* June 27, 1926; page 39, paragraph 6, the London *Evening News,* July 6, 1926; page 39, paragraph 8, the London *Evening News,* July 3 and 6, 1926. Mary K. Browne quotes on page 26, paragraph 6, and page 26, paragraph 7, from "Fit to Win," by Mary K. Browne, *Collier's,* October 16, 1926; page 26, paragraph 8 to page 27, paragraph 1, "What I Learned from Suzanne," by Mary K. Browne, *Collier's,* May 7, 1927; page 40, paragraph 4, to page 41, paragraph 1, *Saturday Evening Post,* April 30, 1927. Charles Lenglen quote on page 27, paragraph 3, the London *Evening News,* June 22, 1926. Molla Bjurstedt Mallory quotes on page 29, paragraph 4, from *Literary Digest,* August 28, 1915; page 31, paragraph 4, the London *Sunday Express,* June 27, 1926. A. Wallis Myers quote on page 30, paragraph 3, from *American Lawn Tennis,* November 15, 1921. Albert de Joannis quote on page 31, paragraph 2, from *American Lawn Tennis,* December 15, 1921. *Lawn Tennis and Badminton* quote on page 40, paragraph 3, from August 14, 1926, issue. Helen Wills quotes on page 31, paragraph 6, from *Fifteen-Thirty,* by Wills, page 18; page 32, paragraph 5, *Collier's,* September 18, 1926; page 36, paragraph 3, *Fifteen-Thirty,* page 84; page 41, paragraph 6, *Saturday Evening Post,* April 4, 1931; page 45, paragraph 6, *American Lawn Tennis,* September 5, 1933; page 49, paragraph 2, *The Boston Globe,* July 2, 1938. Hazel Hotchkiss Wightman quotes on page 33, paragraph 5, from "The Story of Hazel Hotchkiss Wightman," by Herbert Warren Wind, *The Fireside Book of Tennis,* page 55; page 49, paragraph 3, *The Boston Globe,* July 2, 1938. Helen Wills's exchange with linesman at Cannes on page 37, paragraphs 4–5, and Wills's comments after the match, page 38, paragraph 3, *The New York Times,* February 17, 1926. George Lott quote on page 44, paragraph 3, "The Greatest in Women's Tennis," by George Lott, *The Fireside Book of Tennis,* page 343. Alice Marble quotes on page 50, paragraph 5, from *The Road to Wimbledon,* by Marble, page 38. Clark Gable quote and Alice's response on page 52, paragraph 5, *Tennis USA,* September 1985.

Chapter 3

The sources of quotations were: Doris Hart quotes on page 55, paragraph 3 to page 5, paragraph 1, from *Tennis with Hart,* by Hart, page 52. Allison Danzig quote, page 56, paragraph 2, *The Fireside Book of Tennis,* page 326. Pauline Betz quotes on page 57, paragraph 1, *Time,* September 2, 1946. Quotes about Pauline on page 61, paragraph 2, from *Time,* September 2, 1946; page 61, paragraph 3, "The Rebuttal to Lott's Ranking of Women," by Peter Wilson, *The Fireside Book of Tennis,* page 346. *The Times* of London quotes on page 60, paragraph 9, June 15, 1946; page 68, paragraph 2, July 4, 1949; page 72, paragraph 5, June 26, 1949. *The New York Times* quotes on page 61, paragraph 2, September 9, 1946; page 68, paragraph 2, July 4, 1949. Ted Tinling quotes on page 71, paragraph 7, from *Sixty Years in Tennis,* by Tinling, page 121; page 72, paragraph 2 and page 72, paragraph 4, the London *Daily Express,* June 27, 1949. Gussy Moran's quotes on page 72, paragraph 5, from *World Tennis,* May 1957; page 72, paragraph 9, *The Cincinnati Enquirer* (article by the Associated Press), May 21, 1958.

Chapter 4

The sources of quotations were: Althea Gibson quotes on page 74, paragraph 7, *I Always Wanted to Be Somebody,* by Gibson, page 29; page 77, paragraph 6, *I Always Wanted to Be Somebody,* pages 72–73; page 95, paragraph 6, *I Always Wanted to Be Somebody,* page 86; page 96, paragraph 2, *The New York Times,* July 5, 1957. *Sports Illustrated* quotes on page 96, paragraph 6, July 15, 1957. Alice Marble's quote on page 76, paragraph 8, from *American Lawn Tennis,* July 1, 1950. Maureen Connolly quotes on page 82, paragraph 5, from *Forehand Drive,* by Connolly, page 3; page 82, paragraph 6, *Current Biography,* 1951; page 83, paragraph 6, *Forehand Drive,* page 172; page 84, paragraph 5, *Forehand Drive,* page 25; page 85, paragraph 3, *Forehand Drive,* page 49–50; page 86, paragraph 1, *Current Biography,* 1951; page 88, paragraph 9, *World Tennis,* April 1955. Lance Tingay quote on page 83, paragraph 5, from the July 5, 1954, issue of the London *Daily Telegraph.* Quotes from Teach Tennant and Helen Wills on page 84, paragraph 5, from *American Lawn Tennis,* November 1948. *The New York Times* quotes on page 85, paragraph 7, September 6, 1951; page 96, paragraph 7, September 9, 1957. The Ted Tinling quote on page 86, paragraph 4, from *Sixty Years in Tennis,* by Tinling, page 145. The Sarah Palfrey quote (page 92, paragraph 4) and Shirley Fry's cable (page 92, paragraph 9) from *Sports Illustrated,* September 3, 1956.

Sources

The *Time* quote on page 94, paragraph 5, from edition of August 26, 1957. The Gardnar Mulloy quote on page 95, paragraph 1, from the London *Daily Sketch,* June 24, 1957. The *World Tennis* quote on page 95, paragraph 4, February 1957.

Chapter 5
The sources of quotations were: The David Gray quote on page 102, paragraph 4, from *The Guardian,* July 6, 1964. The Darlene Hard quote on page 103, paragraph 4, from *Time,* July 13, 1959. The Angela Mortimer quote on page 104, paragraph 4, from *My Waiting Game,* by Angela Mortimer, Frederick Muller Ltd., London, 1962, page 166. The Karen Susman quote on page 105, paragraph 2, *Sports Illustrated,* August 27, 1962. Ann Jones quotes on page 107, paragraph 6, from *A Game to Love,* page 27; page 118, paragraph 4, *A Game to Love,* page 127. The Frank Butler quote on page 111, paragraph 6, from the July 5, 1964, issue of *News of the World.*

Chapter 6
The sources of quotations were: The Julius Heldman quote on page 121, paragraph 5, from *Sports Illustrated,* June 22, 1964. The Rex Bellamy quote on page 122, paragraph 4, from *The Times* of London, July 4, 1970. The Margaret Court quotes on page 123, paragraph 3, *World Tennis,* July 1973; page 144, paragraph 5, *Sports Illustrated,* May 21, 1973. The Jack Kramer quote on page 124, paragraph 8, from *World Tennis,* November 1970, page 14. The Evonne Goolagong quote on page 132, paragraph 9, from *Evonne! On the Move,* by Goolagong, page 32. The Walter Bingham quote on page 134, paragraph 5, from *Sports Illustrated,* July 12, 1971. The Cliff Turner quote (page 138, paragraph 6) and *The Charlotte Observer* quote (page 138, paragraph 13) from Harry Lloyd's column, "The Upset Sensation," *The Charlotte Observer,* September 22, 1970. The Herbert Warren Wind quote on page 140, paragraph 2, from *The New Yorker,* October 2, 1971. The Chris Evert quote on page 140, paragraph 3, from "The Young Champion," by Vincent Hanna, with Julie Heldman, *World Tennis,* November 1971. The columnist's quote on page 143, paragraph 6, from *The Cincinnati Enquirer,* by Tom Callahan, May 13, 1973. The Rosie Casals quote on page 143, paragraph 7, from *Sports Illustrated,* May 21, 1973.

Chapter 7
The sources of quotations were: The Bud Collins quote on page 148, paragraph 8, from *Sports Illustrated,* December 20–27, 1976. The Chris Evert quotes on page 148, paragraph 9, from *World Tennis,* January 1978, page 33; page 149, paragraph 2 ("No point . . .), *A Long Way Baby,* page 86; page 149, paragraph 2 ("Too long a . . .), "Match of the Year," by Peter Ross Range, *The New York Times Magazine,* June 23, 1974; page 160, paragraph 3, *The Cincinnati Enquirer,* article by the Associated Press, July 8, 1978. The Martina Navratilova quotes on page 152, paragraph 7, from *Martina,* by Navratilova, page 74; page 152, paragraph 8, *Martina,* page 76; page 152, paragraph 10, *A Long Way Baby,* by Lichtenstein, page 80; page 159, paragraph 3, *The Cincinnati Enquirer,* article by the Associated Press, March 30, 1976; page 160, paragraph 4, *Inside Women's Tennis,* July 2, 1978; page 161, paragraph 3, *Sports Illustrated,* July 17, 1978. The Virginia Wade quotes on page 158, paragraph 2, from *Famous Women Tennis Players,* by Frayne, page 142; page 158, paragraphs 3 and 4, *Game, Set, and Match,* by Wind, page 179. The Andrea Jaeger quotes on page 164, paragraph 6, from the *Chicago Tribune,* August 8, 1980; page 164, paragraph 7, *The Cincinnati Enquirer,* September 6, 1980.

Chapter 8
The sources of quotations were: The Charles Lenglen quote on page 172, paragraph 1, from the London *Evening News,* June 21, 1926. The Martina Navratilova quotes on page 173, paragraph 6, from *Newsweek,* September 6, 1982; page 173, paragraph 8, *The New York Times,* September 8, 1982. The Ted Tinling quote on page 173, paragraph 7, from *Sports Illustrated,* May 24, 1982. The Chris Evert quotes on page 176, paragraph 3, from *Time,* July 15, 1985. The Jerry Diamond quote on page 179, paragraphs 4 to 6, from "Jaeger's Burnout Symptomatic of Tennis's Troubles," by Cindy Starr, *The Cincinnati Enquirer,* August 15, 1984. The John Bassett quote on page 181, paragraph 4, from *USA TODAY,* April 27, 1983. The Conny Konzack quotes on page 188, paragraph 2, and page 188, paragraph 6, from *The Cincinnati Enquirer,* April 26, 1987. The Steffi Graf quotes on page 188, paragraph 5, *Time,* June 29, 1987.

Index

(Page numbers in **boldface** refer to color plates. Page numbers in *italics* refer to captions of black and white illustrations throughout text.)

Index

Index

Index

Index